THE BELT AND ROAD CITY

THE BELT AND ROAD CITY

Geopolitics, Urbanization, and China's
Search for a New International Order

SIMON CURTIS
AND IAN KLAUS

Yale

UNIVERSITY PRESS

New Haven and London

Maps by Roger Walker.

Yale University Press books may be purchased in quantity
for educational, business, or promotional use. For
information, please e-mail sales.press@yale.edu (U.S. office)
or sales@yaleup.co.uk (U.K. office).

Set in Janson type by IDS Infotech, Ltd.
Printed in the United States of America.

Library of Congress Control Number: 2023942814
ISBN 978-0-300-26690-0 (hardcover : alk. paper)

A catalogue record for this book is available from
the British Library.

This paper meets the requirements of ANSI/NISO Z39.48-1992
(Permanence of Paper).

10 9 8 7 6 5 4 3 2 1

For the little gardeners and city builders

Alice and Finn
Louisa and Remy

Contents

Introduction

WHEN CHINA ANNOUNCED ITS Belt and Road Initiative (BRI) in 2013, it signaled its intent to follow in the footsteps of other Great Powers that had, throughout history, sought to shape cities, and the connections between them, well beyond their own borders. With the BRI, an immensely ambitious strategy to connect the Eurasian landmass and surrounding maritime routes, China seeks to harness the power of infrastructure and urbanism to build a new kind of international order—one constructed not simply through military might or imperial command, but also by laying the material foundations for the projection of Chinese power and Chinese domestic political and economic models.

Not since the Marshall Plan, implemented after World War II under the leadership of the United States, have we seen a program of infrastructure investment by a Great Power on the scale of the BRI. There are parallels between the two initiatives, both of which were designed to exercise geopolitical influence in moments when international order was in flux. The BRI now touches over 140 states, which represent more than two-thirds of the world's population. Its eventual price tag has been estimated to be anywhere up to $8 trillion.[1] Its timeframe for completion is mid-century, and it may help to generate a world very different from that of today. It has been at the heart of Chinese grand strategy for a decade—and it is, at its core, a recognition of the ways in which influence over urbanization can also influence international order. The BRI comprises six major urban developmental corridors, each linked by road, rail, energy, and digital infrastructures, as well as a Maritime Silk Road linked by a series of port cities. It is intended as an engine of economic

I

development, a way to shift the nature of global urban hierarchies, a way to introduce into the world a new form of urban life—one linked to the growing power of the Chinese state and its preferences, and, ultimately, to the foundation of a new type of international order.

Despite their intimate interconnection, as demonstrated by the nascent BRI, cities and urban forms are often considered topics, and areas of expertise, apart from that of diplomacy, foreign policy, and geopolitics. This theoretical divergence is, however, a historical fallacy. City building and shaping have historically accompanied the extension of power, and the expansion and deepening of the international system. When Alexander of Macedon struck out to the east to conquer half the ancient world, he left behind a string of new cities in his wake, indelible material forms that helped to perpetuate ancient Greek culture for centuries to come. The Roman Empire left urban and infrastructural legacies across vast swaths of the ancient world. Much later, Britain connected a globe-spanning empire by rail and sea, reshaping cities around the world and leaving new ones behind. And in the late twentieth century, the United States was instrumental in building and maintaining a global economy that generated, and was in turn underpinned by, a new form of Global City: a novel urban form that was connected to others around the world in networks of communication and transport that harnessed new digital technologies and facilitated the movement of talent and capital.

There is, then, a historical pattern to be found here. Although it is often overlooked, the nature and history of international order, and the ability to project enduring forms of power, run through cities and their connecting multi-layered infrastructural forms. The materiality of the urban landscape and its infrastructures is an indispensable carrier, and repository, of power. It allows empires and powerful states to project and instantiate their own values and preferences about how to order society and civilization, and to realize them by redesigning spaces in order to control and corral flows of people, goods, ideas, energy, and germs. Without the material exoskeleton of cities and their connective sinews, no durable modern complex society would be possible. The same holds true for international societies and international orders.

Because the costs involved in founding or reshaping cities, and in building or retrofitting the major infrastructure systems that connect them, are so great, these projects create deep path dependencies that tend to lock in particular ways of life for generations. The metaphorical train of the future arrives on tracks laid now. Cities and infrastructure connections, nodes and networks, are instruments and icons of power in the present that project their influence into the future, even after the driving forces behind their development have retreated into the past. This means that the power to design and shape cities and urban spaces is of world historical significance.

This is why the BRI, despite its novelty, is so significant today. It is a rare historical moment when the rise of a Great Power coincides with a wave of infrastructure building and city shaping. China's strategic initiative is being implemented squarely in the middle of one of the most intensive periods of urbanization in human history. Between 2015 and 2050, roughly four billion people will be added to the global urban population. This growth, which will occur almost entirely in middle- and low-income countries, will have consequences for economic opportunities, geopolitics, and climate change.[2] Ultimately, then, the success of China's strategic vision will turn on the durability of, among other things, the urban spaces it tries to shape.

Consider the earth's surface. Unless trends are altered, the increase in urban land cover from 2000 to 2030 will actually exceed all previous such growth in human history.[3] The myth of pastoral history may be just that, a myth, but today's urban growth, in terms of scale, is undoubtedly one of the twenty-first century's defining megatrends. Yet this urban growth, both in terms of population and urban spaces, is not evenly distributed. More than 90 percent of population growth in the coming decades will occur in Africa and Asia, with much of it in locations where the BRI seeks to extend its reach. This is a moment that brings together geopolitical power, economic relations, and ideological visions with urban construction, expansion, renovation, and innovation. It is through its influence over such urban and infrastructural forms that China is quite literally building the foundations for an alternative political and economic order.

The nature of this order, and the infrastructures that underpin it, are at the heart of this book. We journey through some of the many cities and infrastructural forms that are being shaped as a result of the BRI, or are being enrolled in the broader BRI narrative. We explore how they are being molded by China's rising power and ambition to project its own visions of international order, and its own norms and values, beyond its borders, along diverse landscapes of steppe, desert, tropics, coast, and sea, and from the depths of the oceans into outer space. We will track some of these developments and attempt to unravel some of their implications.

Not the least of those implications is the apparent need for the West to respond to these developments. New York, Tokyo, London, and other Global Cities that were transformed during American hegemony continue to thrive in many ways. But the United States and the rest of the West need to adapt their own approaches to national and international connectivity in order to respond to the challenges posed by China's rise, and the threat it poses to their own position in the world.

There are signs that these challenges are beginning to be recognized. President Joe Biden began his term in 2021 by designating the relationship of the United States with China going forward as one of deep strategic and systemic competition. In doing so, he was the third successive US president to try to refocus US grand strategy on China's ascent, following on from President Obama's "pivot to Asia," and President Trump's more hardline approach to the Chinese Communist Party and use of tariffs. The 2017 National Security Strategy defined the Indo-Pacific as the new key arena of Great Power contestation.[4] The 2022 National Security Strategy has only intensified this focus on China as a systemic and strategic competitor, with infrastructure increasingly seen to be at the heart of this competition. The document asserts that, "in the competition with the People's Republic of China, as in other arenas, it is clear that the next ten years will be the decisive decade. We stand now at the inflection point, where the choices we make and the priorities we pursue today will set us on a course that determines our competitive position long into the future."[5]

In September 2021, in his first speech to the UN General Assembly in New York, Biden had already affirmed this geographic focus. He spoke from within the General Assembly building, which sits in the shadow of the Secretariat tower, itself the symbolic centerpiece of the post–World War II international order, housed at the core of perhaps the preeminent Global City of the contemporary era. The complex—a self-contained legal island sitting along Manhattan's East Side—was designed after World War II by a team of international architects, including Oscar Niemeyer and Le Corbusier. The land was financed by the Rockefeller family, and sections of the design ultimately were guided by Wallace Harrison, a Massachusetts-born architect who did much to promote, if not deliver, the vision of New York as the capital of the Cold War world.[6]

But what does strategic and systemic competition mean in the twenty-first century? At the 2021 G7 summit in Cornwall, England,

President Biden offered an answer, with which China would undoubtedly concur, when he threw US weight behind the G7's Build Back Better World infrastructure plan for the global South:

> The United States is committed to using our resources and our international platform to support these voices, listen to them, partner with them to find ways to respond that advance human dignity around the world. For example, there is an enormous need for infrastructure in developing countries, but infrastructure that is low-quality or that feeds corruption or exacerbates environmental degradation may only end up contributing to greater challenges for countries over time. Done the right way, however, with transparent, sustainable investment in projects that respond to the country's needs and engage their local workers to maintain high labor and environmental standards, infrastructure can be a strong foundation that allows societies in low- and middle-income countries to grow and to prosper. That's the idea behind the Build Back Better World.[7]

Successive speeches and strategic documents have begun to give the post-COVID-19 desire to "build back better" some shape. Indeed, in the past year the program has itself been rebranded, in the wake of travails by Biden's domestic legislative program of the same name, as the Partnership for Global Investment and Infrastructure (PGII), which brings together US, EU, and UK infrastructure investment programs into a $600 billion fund, to be distributed over the next five years.[8] Most of the details of this program are yet to emerge. China, with its BRI now almost a decade in the making, has clearly gained the initiative across much of the world, a lead with implications that the West is only just now waking up to.

As the West struggles to even begin to articulate a geopolitical and urban response to the BRI, China, harnessing its growing power, is sensing its moment. Reading the 2008 financial crisis, the political turmoil unleashed by the 2016 US election, and the growing fault lines in the European Union as a moment of geopolitical opportunity, China has begun to build the long-term foundations for an alternative form of international society in which it hopes its own political culture, state-led economy, and urban and infrastructural developmental models can recraft the nature of international order. The BRI is at the very heart of this ambitious undertaking. It offers a slowly evolving set of transnational material conduits on which this new order can gradually solidify over the coming decades—tying a vast Afro-Eurasian space together, linking it via new patterns of urbanization, but in ways in which China comes to sit at the center of a new economic and political configuration. This new pattern recalls, albeit imperfectly, the shadowy outlines of past centuries before the rise of the West, when China claimed centrality, and other states were considered part of its tributary empire.

The size and scope of the BRI also means that this could never be a simple imposition of China's vision onto a vast swath of the world. As China's relative power grows, as it engages more and more with the world, so too its own domestic model of leadership, its values, its relations with others, its understanding of its own place in international society, will all inevitably be transformed. Many questions will need to be answered. Can China realize a new vision that can challenge the Westphalian paradigm that has characterized international society for four centuries? Can it undergird that vision with durable cities and infrastructures? Can it offer sustainable urban solutions for the great global challenges of the twenty-first century: climate change, economic crisis, inequality, global governance, and international security, and the cascading and compounding risks that bring these challenges together? Will the Belt and Road City find forms that inscribe these solutions in space in ways that reshape and retool life for billions in the twenty-first century—giving expression in physical form, perhaps, to the new Chinese thinking about generating an "ecological civilization" from the ruins of the carbon-extraction-based industrial model? Or will China realize the worst fears of its critics: the carbon-intensive construction and export of a dystopian techno-authoritarian control society, materialized in cities throughout large tracts of the world?

China is challenging the West, then, by explicitly linking infrastructure building and urbanization to a new and evolving type of international order, one in which it offers investment and support to other states to enroll in its BRI, while also subtly shaping their economies and societies via the construction of these urban spaces.

By contrast, the West has, for some time, been living off of decaying legacy infrastructures, while relying on private finance to augment them in highly specific ways. This approach has linked valued fragments of urban space together unevenly, in ways that prioritize the global economy over national integration. As President Biden intimated, it is increasingly clear that this model, and these decaying infrastructures, cannot meet the needs of the twenty-first century, and, in particular, the vast transformation required to meet the challenge of the climate emergency, which will require sustainable and resilient models of urban life. The economic and social model that has come to dominate many of the world's developed societies is now running up against its limits, as well as those of the earth's systems. Breakdown in the earth's ecosystems from human-driven warming, protracted financial crises, rampant inequality in and between cities and states, and now the COVID-19 pandemic: all of these crises point to a pressing need to find new and better social and economic paradigms, and to the centrality of infrastructure in their deployment. Build Back Better is a slogan that captures this need—but the West will need to articulate how it will do so, and quickly. Although China's competing paradigm has yet to fully find its form, it is gaining momentum, especially in its ability to influence nations in the global South.

Moreover, in responding to both the COVID-19 pandemic and the challenge of climate change, the interventionist state has had something of a comeback. The massive state-led economic and social interventions during the pandemic—an event that seems to have had the qualities of a catalyst, acting on longer-term trends by accelerating some, while slowing others—may lead to a post-pandemic world beyond the neoliberal order that has seemed so moribund and rudderless for over a decade now. The pressing need to retool our societies to meet the environmental targets identified in the Paris Agreement would also, it seems, require a central role for the state in pushing markets to move faster. Here China's use of the resources of the state to catalyze change is a distinct challenge to the reliance of liberal models on market forces to do this job. Around the world, a consensus is building around the notion of "green modernization" in its various slogans, guises, and contexts: Green New Deal, Build Back Better, Sustainable Development, Green Growth, Climate Resilient Development, Ecological Civilization. All will require massive mobilization of society's economic and intellectual resources. While the findings of the Sixth Assessment Report of the Intergovernmental Panel on Climate Change (IPCC) perhaps come closest to a scientific consensus on what is needed, there is as yet no clear political consensus on how to achieve this task. But the political will, regulatory power, and financial tools and resources of the interventionist state would now seem to be indispensable to such an undertaking.

As China offers to the world one path forward, the need to articulate an alternative becomes ever more pressing. Liberal democratic countries are signaling that they must find a response. And although China's one-party, authoritarian system of governance may not be attractive to many people around the world, policymakers in democratic states take this for granted at their own risk. The heartlands of Western liberal democracy have not been immune to aspects of the democratic backsliding seen in the rise of right-wing governments around the world, and of populist nationalism and the authoritarian style in politics. This makes it even more pressing to articulate a better urban future, one that not only challenges some of the less-appealing aspects of the emerging Chinese model but can also move us beyond the inequalities, injustices, and environmentally ruinous models of urbanism baked into the urban and infrastructural forms of the past four decades. The Global City, and the international order of which it is a key component, will need to evolve if it is to survive.

From Global City to Belt and Road City

When we write of Global Cities, we use the term to describe a historically specific urban form that emerged in the late twentieth century in many places around the world in the context of a unique set of geopolitical and geoeconomic conditions. As an analytical concept, the Global City has been with us for some decades now—used by many urbanists as a marker to signal the set of urban transformations linked to the restructuring of the world economy in the 1970s, and the retooling of the Bretton Woods system that had characterized the post–World War II economic order.[9] During that period, stretching across the past four decades, the embrace of what has come to be known as a neoliberal mode of capitalist regulation had the (perhaps not fully anticipated) effect of revolutionizing those cities that were linked to these new flows of capital and resources.[10]

Urbanists flocked to the question of why the world's cities were being transformed, but it wasn't until a later generation of international relations scholars engaged with the question that this urban phenomenon became understood as linked to the nature of the international system and a unique geopolitical context.[11] In particular, it was the power of the United States—a liberal hegemon able to shape the international environment to conform to its own ideological and material preferences—

that had set cities around the world on a new developmental path. Such Global Cities are open, cosmopolitan, and dynamic; vast in size, sometimes spreading across national borders to form transnational urban regions, linked together in globe-spanning technological networks and sucking in resources from the accelerating global economy; and relatively unconcerned about international security (at least until September 11, 2001, and the attack on New York's World Trade Center, a preeminent symbol of this new world). Such cities could have emerged only in such a liberal international order, one undergirded by US security and shaped, in the last analysis, by US power, especially in its post–Cold War unipolar moment.

And so, in the last decades of the twentieth century, and for most of the first decade of the twenty-first century, Global Cities were supercharged by their openness to the relatively benign liberal-world-trading order. Growing in power and prestige, many began to challenge their own host states on issues of interest and international governance. They also began to take a more active role in international politics themselves, in the halls of the United Nations and its system of institutions, as well as in the many hundreds of Global City networks that had formed. Sometimes this diplomatic activity has approached the level of a parallel global governance system, in which cities could intervene directly in world politics independently of the states in which they were housed.[12]

But the multiple intersecting crises we outlined above—climate breakdown, financial instability, inequality, and polarization—mean that this world of Global Cities is under threat. The potential waning of the historical moment of US hegemony and unipolarity inevitably brings with it consequences for a world in which Global Cities have played a key role in defining the shape of globalization over the past four decades. The rise of China, its search for a place in the framework of international order, the new infrastructures that it is in the process of building, and the urban spaces that it is in the process of shaping, may well eventually generate an alternative order—offering the distinct prospect of a fracturing of international order into rival systems. And the pressing need to respond to the climate emergency, which will entail the wholesale reinvention of infrastructural and urban paradigms in the transition to sustainable forms of economic and social life, may further strengthen China's appeal if it can get this response right, and if the West cannot respond quickly or effectively enough with its own infrastructural and urban paradigm.

Our focus on the Belt and Road City emerges naturally from a longer endeavor to understand the relationship between cities, Great Powers, and international order. With multiple hats as researchers, authors, policymakers, and commentators, we have over the past decade sought to enhance understanding of the nature of and significance of Global Cities—those astonishing, planet-shaping urban artifacts of late modernity; the product of a distinctive form of US-led liberal international order. As the wheels of history grind on once more, turning to the Belt and Road City is a natural extension of this larger project to understand how states shape urban form, and how urban form, in turn, gives durability to states' ambitions and power across geographical distances and through the centuries. We continue, in light of the rise of China, to pursue this project to understand the connections between Great Power competition, infrastructural geopolitics, urban life, and international order, as well as the ways in which these elements are increasingly intertwined with the flows and structures of the material world.

We stress the ways in which these different elements cannot be considered as separate; instead they are intrinsically connected and deeply co-constituted. The very sinews of international order are formed by urban infrastructures and technical systems, for example, while the very materiality of those infrastructures and technical systems are, in turn, shaped by the social configurations and ideological preferences of the Great Powers that help to enable, finance, design, and build them. We might think of these configurations as huge assemblages of entwined material and ideational components, combining elements at the smallest scales of urban life to the very grandest scales of international order. China's efforts to imagine and materialize the BRI, its recrafting of existing urban forms or generation of new ones, its own emerging model of state-capitalist political economy, as well as its still-forming visions for future international order, are all part of such a multi-scalar, fluid, coalescing assemblage of political order that introduces novelty into the world. As China seeks to pursue long-term strategies designed to weaken the US grip on international order, all of these components become relevant to understanding its capacities, ambitions, and prospects.

This book is also an invitation to further study and debate. We are very much aware that the BRI is only a decade into what has been designated as a half-century project, and that the changes that are being wrought in urban spaces along its routes are only beginning to take shape. The BRI is a vast undertaking, and changes to cities and urban areas, particularly with regard to the built environment, infrastructure, and even economies, often take decades. Waiting for the effects of contemporary geopolitics to fully exhibit themselves in cities would allow for the advantages offered by the historical method: the potential for greater objectivity, balance, and the study of a wide array of sources, both primary and secondary. But it would also put off discussion by a number of contemporary audiences: political scientists, journalists, policymakers and diplomats, and urban residents. Even with the benefit of historical distance, sweeping studies of the world's cities are difficult to produce. The complexity of the cities we love, their secrets and nuances, defy generalization. Yet such studies transport us—as scholars and travelers—from cities we know to those we do not. The benefit of such travel, of introduction, reintroduction, and comparison, in other words, comes with its own limitations, as does any effort at contemporary history.

In this book we seek to explore cities of immense size and complexity on multiple continents, to do so by analyzing changes that continue to take place while we write, and, critically, to relate these changes to the wider tectonic shifts in the geopolitical environment that are shaping them. Governments and international organizations have produced a vast array of data on our contemporary urban world, and we make wide use of those resources. The historical lessons of geopolitics and urbanization are well developed by scholars, too, and surround most urban dwellers every day. That said, we seek here to be neither all-encompassing nor authoritative, but instead to contribute to a now-forming conversation about what twenty-first-century globalization will mean for the spaces in which most of us work, eat, drink, sleep, love, and live.

When we write of the Belt and Road City, then, we write not of a roster of specific cities, but of a movement toward a historically new form of city, and of a new connection forming between urban form and process and the rise of new Great Power, China, with its historically specific features, and its ambitions to reshape political order. Like the concept of the Global City, the Belt and Road City functions as a heuristic device that can help us to understand the entry into the world of both a distinctive new form of urban life, and a distinctive vision of geopolitical order, both of which are in the process of becoming. As a concept it links together observable urban transformations in existing and new cities across Afro-Eurasia driven and shaped by the rise of Chinese geopolitical power, but also negotiated, adapted, and transformed by other forms of agency—not least the states with which China negotiates, trades, and bargains. It captures the emergence of new political, social, economic, and technological tendencies as they take form in buildings, marketplaces, city layouts, urban technologies, changing urban hierarchies, transnational corridors, large technical systems—and in the incessant reshaping of these and other elements of the urban world. But all of these elements are molded by ideological visions and social contexts. China's current political system and social order, as well as its strategy for geopolitical power, will guide the BRI in profound ways, and will continue to be expressed by the infrastructural projects and urban morphologies in which they find form, both within China and beyond its territorial borders.

So although the Belt and Road City is, for us, primarily a conceptual tool to help us to cut through the noise and confusion of a rapidly changing planetary urban landscape, it is a concept that has its roots in the changes being wrought in real cities. We might say that the different cities influenced by the BRI are, in this sense, forming around an ideal typical Belt and Road City, an abstract diagram, or virtual attractor, signifying the tendencies toward which real cities are moving.[13] In just the way that there is no one Global City, but many cities around the world that have been influenced by the neoliberal paradigm that generates Global City tendencies and features, so too there are, and will be, many cities shaped by the BRI and Chinese infrastructural geopolitics. And just as Global Cities have responded, in the similar yet multiple forms they have taken, both to systemic logics of global capitalism and power and to local histories, agencies, and contexts (this is especially the case in the global South), so too will Belt and Road Cities be influenced by both.[14]

As we will see, some of the core features of the Belt and Road City that seem to be emerging include:

- a focus on logistics and trade, tied in to emerging urban corridors
- the generation of new urban "gateways" that link these corridors
- a sense of the city's connectivity to infrastructure, logistics, and movement, with the Belt and Road City always existing, spatially, as part of new regional concepts and corridors
- the layering of new forms and structures onto existing ones, which often requires that existing urban populations are moved—as in the case of Boten and Vientiane, Laos, and the urban spaces in between, where people had to be moved, and even then remained a presence in the city (exercises in utopian urban terra nova—long a way to project and deploy power utilized by strongmen and dreamers alike—are not the BRI norm)

- urban spaces shaped via explicit bilateral joint agreements, with provision for forming governance structures that give companies or corporations a role in governmental policies and responsibilities
- the use of architects and designers, as well as wider acknowledgments of the need to develop housing as well as basic urban service delivery, although these experts are not deployed in an integrated urban-systems approach
- cities that evidence the labor needed to drive global infrastructure but not the talent—the Belt and Road City is not a battle for the global creative class
- the emergence of downtowns, central business districts, and other significantly developed areas that have been sites for the construction of discrete new buildings that are explicitly linked to the rhetoric and narrative of the BRI, and so intentionally link the urban and the global rhetorically, and tie those in with the idea of an emerging international society shaped by Chinese leadership

This is by no means an exhaustive list; nor is it universally applicable to all the cities that the BRI will touch. In trying to answer the question of what the Belt and Road City is, can, or will be, we have come to think of it as both a provocation and a call to further research. These are cities yet to fully find their form, and the BRI itself is barely a decade old. The BRI has also run into problems and resistance—local and global—and is beginning to generate alternative initiatives from other powerful actors, such as the United States, European Union, and Japan. In other words, the BRI may fail. Its cities may not find a durable form, and this moment and its potentialities may be swept away by other historical tides. And yet, as the French urbanist Henri Lefebvre once argued in relation to an earlier capitalist transformation of the urban world, successful societies must produce their own historically distinctive spaces, in their own image.[15] As China seeks to reshape both its own society and the wider international society of which it is a part, the success or failure of its ambitions will depend on this ability to produce a distinctive form of space, and a distinctive form of urban life, both for its own people, and for the many people living in the territories and cities that the BRI touches. The Chinese Dream of a revised international order will endure only if the forms of urban life it seeks to shape and build can be made to endure.

A Moment of Transformation?

For years, the world's leading scientists, as well as economists, anthropologists, and other experts, have gathered as part of the Intergovernmental Panel on Climate Change. IPCC scientists have, as part of this work, identified as key to addressing climate change four systems—energy; land and ecosystems; industry; and urban and infrastructure. In 2022 they added a fifth, societal choices, to include consumption and lifestyle habits. Owing to the global nature of their assessments—stretching across all regions, and capturing issues from health to biodiversity—the reports offer something of a snapshot of both the challenges facing contemporary international society, and how the radical global action needed to limit warming might develop. Indeed, these systems offer one way to think about a globalized world, with sectors such as shipping cutting across multiple systems like urban infrastructure and energy—and with the impact of major projects and local habits being felt across regions and, in some cases, the world.

Crucially, the scientists of the IPCC have come to recognize that all of the systems, and many of the activities that encompass them—land-development patterns, for example, or the state of ecosystems—have significant impacts on cities. And, turning that around, that what happens in cities and urban areas will affect the climate future, and with it, the economic and social well-being of billions. In other words, global processes—many of which are captured within the wider BRI strategy and particular projects—have urban impacts; and cities will shape those processes, and the international order that informs them. It is for this reason that the actors and/or stakeholders captured in these scientific reports are especially broad: national policymakers, international leaders, nongovernmental organizations, local officials, local communities, and the private sector. But while the IPCC operates at the cutting edge of peer-reviewed science when describing emissions and their impacts, the attention to geopolitics is underdeveloped—and intentionally so.

What is missing from these kinds of reports, and what seemingly cannot be addressed by those working in such multilateral settings for political reasons, is that one of the key factors driving transformation is geopolitical strategic competition. Different Great Powers, each with distinct value systems, visions, interests, and economic and technological models, will be crucial in driving systemic transformation. And the result may well be rival socio-technical and geopolitical systems, and a potential fracturing of international order, as such competition configures systems of energy, land, ecosystems, industry, and urban infrastructure in very different ways. As has long been recognized in international relations and historical scholarship, international order is shaped by the states that successfully wield their power in the ebb and flow of history's immense tides.[16]

In seeking to understand the potential for international transformation arising from the nexus between Great Power states, infrastructure development, and urban change, then, we have had to look outside the mainstream of international relations scholarship, because it has mostly failed to capture, or even see, the dynamics we seek to analyze. The literatures and sources that inform some of our arguments here draw from a variety of disciplines, including sociology, philosophy, political geography, history, science and technology studies, and design theory.[17]

Material infrastructure is like the dark matter of international theory: it is a largely invisible mass in most mainstream accounts of the international system, an essential component of successive international orders.[18] And when we include material infrastructure in our analyses, a new picture emerges that more fully embraces the entangled nature of the age of the Anthropocene in which we now live: one where material infrastructures are designed and shaped by a plethora of agents, where the disposition of infrastructure space determines the organization and circulation of objects; and where multiple actors vie to shape global flows of energy, matter, and ideas.[19]

A few short decades have transformed the planet in ways that much international theory fails to register. At some point early in the twenty-first century, the world passed a tipping point—it became a majority urban world, where more people, for the first time in history, lived in cities than outside of them. It is estimated by the United Nations that this figure will rise to nearly 70 percent by midcentury—resulting in an urban population of almost seven billion. Between 1990 and 2000 alone there was a 30 percent increase in the size of urban settlements in the developed world and a 50 percent increase in the developing world. In less than a generation, cities have boomed on every continent, taking us far beyond the predominantly rural world of the recent past—a world in which, we should remember, most of our political institutions were shaped.[20]

Today, a satellite image of the night sky reveals the glow of coastal megacities and inland urban corridors of unprecedented size and scope. Maps of Global City networks, megacity regions, and urban corridors, too, show new functional economic geographies and connectivities that bring into question traditional state-centric notions of global politics. Alongside and through these urban patterns run other, huge, materially integrated physical structures that enable mass-scale society: transport systems, supply chains, air travel networks, submarine internet cables, broadband networks, data centers, satellites, and research labs.[21] Tracing such maps of transport networks, logistics systems, and energy pipelines tells its own story of how new forms of international order are emerging, as energy and matter are corralled to supply human societies.[22] Overlaying these systems, too, are planetary-scaled technologies of computation, a new megastructure comprising smart grids, cloud-computing platforms, and sensor nets.[23] Such immense infrastructure projects that connect disparate parts of the globe in new ways need to be urgently brought into the conversations about the nature of international order and its transformation.

If we also begin to view such systems as components of particular hegemonic orders, we can see that they play a crucial role in allowing particular forms of political life—particular iterations of international society—to unfold across time and space.[24] Our approach attempts to show how the BRI is an attempt by China to articulate and activate a novel diagram of international order; how that order is being constructed from both the creation of new ideational and material components and capacities, while also reorienting elements of previous forms of order; and how it will generate new forms of transnational governance and agentic capacities at new and larger scales.[25] Ideational and material components are always entangled: as we will see, multiple narratives, histories, and theoretical positions inform how the BRI is being materialized via infrastructures and other urban forms.

At the same time, any assemblage as large and open-ended as the BRI, which enrolls the cooperation of many other state and non-state actors, will inevitably escape the control of its progenitors and designers: it will inevitably have multiple fractal edges by which its internal consistency and form can be influenced from outside. The emerging nonlinear relationship between the BRI components (such as highways, railways, ports, central business districts, submarine data cables, investment banks, and stock exchanges), the Chinese state, the natural world, and the productive forces of society will be central to the politics of the twenty-first century. But the BRI, or the massive complex object-in-formation that it denotes, is also a highly unstable object. As an eruption of a new idea and vision into the world, it will always be subject to challenge, as the top-down visions and narratives are confronted by the inherent nonlinear movements of open systems. The eventual form of the BRI, then, may look very different than contemporary Chinese politicians and policy-makers are imagining—and even then it will remain open to continual transformation.

One distinctive feature of our approach is that we emphasize the gradual accretion of order from the connection of components at multiple scales. In one sense, the layout of the book can offer the reader a journey not just across the multiple connections that are forming from the BRI, but also upward, through the different scales of its assembly. We can begin with the infrastructural fragments linking urban spaces together in new ways: roads, ports, pipelines, railways, buildings, squares, gardens, cables, data centers. We then might move to the urban layout, the organizational diagram of the city, the emergent whole of the city. The next scale comprises systems of cities, whether these be systems within the national territory, or, as is increasingly the case, transnational systems of cities, and the ways in which the BRI is redrawing and influencing established urban hierarchies. Cities, and the infrastructural connections between, might also be considered large technical systems that spread across and integrate vast tracts of transnational space, carrying with them the imprints of the societies that design and implement them.[26] In the case of the BRI, the formation of huge integrated transnational urban corridors are central to this restructuring. At yet another scale, we consider the importance of the power struggles that occur at the level of the international institutions that are financing, shaping, securing, and designing such systems. We then consider the largest scale, that of international order, and the ways in which Great Powers shape, challenge, and reshape it. The accumulation of all of these infrastructural and urban fragments is as much a part of the construction and maintenance of political order as is the balance of military power, or the formation of the durable norms and institutions of international society.[27]

This is a historically rare moment of immense urbanization and infrastructure investment and construction, occurring alongside the rise of a Great Power that is reshaping the nature of international order. As the forms of the BRI become locked in, they have the potential to shape the future of a great part of humanity. In particular, given its scope and global footprint, the urbanization of the BRI represents an opportunity to reset destructive and environmentally unsustainable patterns of urban living—an opportunity that if not taken will have irreversible repercussions. Belt and Road Cities could, in theory, offer a more balanced and equitable form of urbanism than did the destructive excesses of the Global Cities of the past four decades of unbridled market liberalism. But they may also augur a future of growing integration between authoritarian regimes and the new surveillance technologies wending their way through the evolving urban fabric.

As we will show, the BRI and the evolving Belt and Road City are also eliciting a geopolitical response, as powerful Western states, in particular the United States and the European Union, seek to counter China's head start in infrastructure construction in the global South. It may well be that we are moving into an era of huge, continent-spanning infrastructure megaprojects, in which states are key agents, and cities are important actors. On present trajectories there is a distinct possibility that the BRI is ushering in an age of fractured international order, in which rival forms of infrastructural and technological systems form the basis for diverging worlds. These trends and ongoing questions make the conjuncture of infrastructure, urbanization, and a rising and restless Great Power a central analytical site for understanding geopolitics today.

CHAPTER ONE

Ties of Silk and Steel

I N SEPTEMBER 2013, WHEN the Chinese president announced the Belt and Road Initiative in a speech delivered in Astana, the capital of Kazakhstan, he deliberately linked the future of China to an ancient past. The lands of Kazakhstan had been an important link along the Silk Roads, which had tied together the peoples of Afro-Eurasia through commerce, culture, and exchange for over a thousand years before the balance of world power tipped toward the West.

Standing at the lectern at Nazarbayev University in Astana, President Xi Jinping evoked the sense of a romantic past of exploration, trade, and cultural discovery: "Shaanxi, my home province, is right at the starting point of the ancient Silk Road. Today, as I stand here and look back at that episode of history, I [can] almost hear the camel bells echoing in the mountains, and see the wisp of smoke rising from the desert."[1]

Xi spoke of centuries of connection and shared history between the peoples of China and Kazakhstan, and the pivotal role of the Kazakh peoples in facilitating exchange between the East and the West. They had witnessed, and contributed to, the streams of envoys, pilgrims, caravans, merchants, scholars, and artisans that made the Silk Roads such an important element of world history.

In the context of this longer story, Astana, one of a series of newly turbo-charged cities across Eurasia and home to approximately one million residents, has had a relatively brief history. Established in the mid-nineteenth century along the Ishim River, Astana was transformed by urban development after World War II and, more recently, by transnational architectural influences. Aldar, a UAE-based developer, in partnership with London-based Foster + Partners, constructed two of the iconic buildings of the Central Asian capital's emerging urban landscape: the Palace of Peace and Reconciliation, a 203-foot pyramid; and the Khan Shatyr Entertainment Center, a futuristic, translucent tent. These architectural wonders both herald a new future and echo features of the nomadic empires that shaped the history of the Eurasian steppes.[2]

But Xi's remarks were not fundamentally about the history of urbanization or Astana's architecture. They were about geopolitics. He sought in his speech to reawaken memories of a long and glorious lineage of trade, cooperation, and connection among the peoples of this enormous region, in service of a grand strategy underpinned by the Belt and Road Initiative.

The BRI currently spans more than 140 countries, and while clear figures are difficult to come by, over $1 trillion has been slated for foreign investment over the next decade, and up to $8 trillion may eventually be spent on the almost half-century plan.[3] Part of the difficulty in pinning down a total is the nature of the endeavor: the BRI is not a fixed and clearly bounded project, but rather a loose, open-ended vision of a possible future thirty years hence. The name, too, does not translate comfortably into English; the overland "belt" and maritime "road" are, in actuality, six major economic corridors across Eurasia, and a series of maritime routes.[4] Together these are intended to form the material backbone of "an interconnected system of transport, energy and digital infrastructure [that will] gradually develop into industrial clusters, free trade zones and then an economic corridor spanning construction, logistics, energy, manufacturing, agriculture, and tourism, culminating in the birth of a large Eurasian common market."[5] Those corridors and routes pass through at least fifty cities with populations of more than a million.

Xi's appeal to history in Astana, and the dozens of other sites he would visit to tout the BRI, was not arbitrary or nostalgic. His strategy was to shift the geographic focus from the West and to offer a historical tableau on which to imagine a different future, one in which China would recapture the prestige, power, and leadership of bygone days. The ancient Silk Roads are for many in the West a mythical world, belonging to unnumbered centuries and crossing little-known countries and lands, whose relevance to the modern world has faded like the map in Jorge Luis Borges's empire past. But for China, which is growing in power and influence in a world that has been dominated for centuries by structures and systems constructed by Western powers, the memory of the Silk Roads offers an alternative vision of international order—one in which the West is pushed back to the fringes of the map. With the shifting of economic activity and potential eastward in recent decades, this narrative also chimes in a timely way with the return of marginalized and forgotten peoples to the center of world history.

The Silk Roads imaginary, with its emphasis on trade, culture, and intellectual ferment, also ties China's recent rise to a narrative of relatively peaceful coexistence shaped by trade and cultural exchange, while downplaying the sometimes violent history of the region. It is a period of history in which China hopes to be recalled as a benefactor, a provider of international public goods, a hegemonic power at the center of its own universe—even as today China flexes its growing power in ways that alarm some of its neighbors.

Xi's instrumentalization of history isn't only an act of imagination, of course. The Silk Roads were the meshwork generated by the meeting of ancient empires. Some spread east from the Mediterranean Sea: the conquests and city-building projects of Alexander the Great of Macedon (336–323 BCE), for example, and, later, the legacies of the Roman Empire's expansion into Asia. Others spread westward, beginning with Han dynasty China (206 BCE–220 CE) and continuing with the empires and kingdoms of the Middle East, Central Asia, and the Indian subcontinent—some of which came to include maritime trade routes that tied in Africa, or overland paths that connected to nomadic peoples of the steppe grasslands.[6] Until their decline at the end of the fifteenth century, these networks crisscrossed desert and mountain, plain and steppe, weaving together many different peoples and cultures in ways that sensibilities shaped by modern political structures might not recognize. This was a world long predating the bounded territorial state units that have come to dominate our contemporary political geography; it was a world of "composite cultures" very different from the bounded nations of today.[7]

Networks need nodes, and the Silk Roads passed through and met in Silk Road cities. Some are now forgotten, erased by the ceaseless ebb and flow of sands, waters, and history. Some endured through the centuries. Yet others are coming to the fore again. There is a temptation, a habit, to look to the ancient past through pastoral lenses, but the history of cities is nearly as long as that of settled agriculture. The farm and the city emerged together.[8]

The world's first cities were born in the heartlands of Eurasia, along the Fertile Crescent of ancient Mesopotamia, beside the alluvial plains of the Tigris and Euphrates. And as early kingdoms rose and fell, and great empires expanded, urban life spread across Eurasia, and would be linked by the tendrils of the Silk Roads. Cities like Kashgar, Kabul, Merv, Venice, Damascus, Baghdad, Isfahan, Constantinople, Samarkand, Karakoram, and Xi'an, and many hundreds of others, emerged across the centuries, drawing the region together in an increasingly sophisticated and interconnected urban world. In the words of Peter Frankopan, such cities were "dotted across the spine of Asia . . . strung like pearls, linking the Pacific to the Mediterranean."[9]

Such cities were born of empire, or, in some cases, generated empires. They were connected across vast distances by roads and maritime routes. And they were critical in generating and maintaining ways of life across the Eurasian space. Then, as now, urbanism generated and sustained economic activity.[10] Cities and their networks spurred economic dynamism, while competition between urban centers catalyzed great architectural achievements like monuments, libraries, conservatories, gardens, and places of worship, as well as advances in science, mathematics, medicine, and philosophy. There is a special quality inherent to cities and urban life that has long generated intellectual ferment and progress.[11] These are the kinds of historical achievements that may animate the thinking of those who envision a new Eurasian golden age, with China at its core.

For over a millennium, these urban, cosmopolitan worlds tied together an expansive network of trade and culture that shaped life across Asia, the Middle East, Africa, and much of Europe. Like empires, cities rise and fall, and the cities of the Silk Road were no different. These urban worlds were gradually displaced by explosive developments in the West: European voyages of discovery in the late fifteenth century, both to the Americas and around the Cape of Africa, that injected silver into the European economy and opened a European trade route to India and beyond; the trans-Atlantic slave trade and its evolution into an industry that fueled and reshaped economies on at least four continents; and the governance experiments of European princely states, with their associated philosophical and material transformations. As these overlapping structural shifts occurred, the influence of the Silk Road world began to fade.

Cities and International Order

The reemergence of China as a regional and global power is the preeminent geopolitical story of the late twentieth and early twenty-first centuries. Gone are the faded Silk Road empires, replaced by modern powers and nation-states with regional and global ambitions. But like the Silk Road world, this new world has its important urban nodes. And as China rises, internal migration is playing a crucial role in its economic and social development. Looking forward, migration to, from, and between cities will continue to shape China's political stability, social resilience, and economic innovation and strength.

But these internal developments are only part of the story of China as a global power. China has realized the importance of cities and infrastructure for constructing alternative forms of international order. Although the selective use of Silk Road history by China is a carefully crafted narrative, designed to legitimate an emerging form of Chinese-led international society, the BRI is also a vastly ambitious attempt to *materialize* that narrative, to turn ideas and stories into structures made of concrete, wood, and steel. As the French sociologist Bruno Latour has argued, any ordering narrative that is to endure across time and space must take material form.[12] The philosopher of urban form Henri Lefebvre once claimed, too, that any successful society must produce its own distinctive form of space, one reflected primarily in cities and urbanism.[13] The processes are extraordinarily complicated to be sure, but the core idea is simple: the production of space—rooms, squares, buildings, bridges, the shape of entire cities and regions—necessitates, asserts, and maintains influence and power. Cities and urbanization are the predominant platforms and processes through which human societies produce space. Throughout history, cities and urban forms have reflected the dominant social values, and political and economic structures, of their time.[14] For example, those first cities on the banks of the Tigris and Euphrates, such as Ur and Uruk, built central temple and citadel complexes to reflect the separation of the emerging ruling class of king and priesthood. Since the advent of modern capitalism, cities have been shaped and reshaped by the abstract forces of the market because they sit on commodified parcels of land.[15] Over the past forty years, we have seen the emergence of a new type of city—the Global City—that draws its form and power from a historically specific combination of globalized finance capital and US geopolitical hegemony.[16] And now, with the rise of China, we may be seeing the emergence of yet another distinctive configuration of urban form and Great Power politics, as the newly assertive power influences the development of urban spaces across Eurasia and beyond.

There is, then, a deep connection between Great Powers, geopolitical order, and urban form in different historical periods. Great Powers and hegemons have long sought to influence the shape and scale of cities far beyond their borders. The urban ruins of the Roman Empire stretch to northern England, North Africa, and the Middle East. Indeed, for Edward Gibbon, a preeminent historian of ancient Rome, the city and the empire were natural partners and collaborators.[17] The infrastructure and drainage projects of the British Empire continue to inform the shape of New Delhi and Mumbai. It was not merely in an exercise of theory that the Bolshevik revolutionaries hotly discussed urban theory and design in the 1920s and 1930s. The magistrales, metro stops, and massive housing projects of the Soviet Union continue to provide transportation and housing in the former Eastern Bloc. In the immediate post–World War II period, even US diplomats and development experts sought to use urban planning to expand the commercial reach of the United States and project US values. Buckminster Fuller, Walter Gropius, and Charles and Ray Eames all designed physical spaces explicitly in dialogue with Cold War tensions.[18]

This connection between geopolitical order and urban space is often overlooked. After all, in both theory and practice, they make something of an odd couple. Scholars of international relations have rarely considered the role of cities and infrastructures in sustaining different historical configurations of world order. Most conversations about Great Power politics ignore city dynamics, dismissing references to urbanization or city-focused efforts as naively post-Westphalian. Urbanists, meanwhile, have focused on urban dynamics such as planning, public space, and service delivery, proceeding with little sense for geopolitical trends at the state level.

This is partly a function of an academic division of labor. But it is also the product of a specific historical configuration of cities and states. The Westphalian arrangement—a political system in which the territorial state internalizes the city and constrains its activities within its own territorial shell—is relatively unusual in the long run of history, being limited to the past few hundred years. During this period, the city has been seen as internal to the territorial state, not relevant to understanding the international context, and due to a state-centric worldview, this state-city relationship has been taken for granted, as something natural and unchanging.[19]

At least in their development of urban spaces along BRI corridors, Chinese policymakers do not seem limited by the same blinders; they are intentionally generating new patterns of urban life across Eurasia. The transnational scope of the BRI and its connection to a pre-Westphalian era brings to mind the incredible historical diversity of international systems. Although the nation-state continues to prove extraordinarily resilient, Chinese policymakers will be aware of a much longer historical record, one which shows a far greater diversity of relations between geopolitical units: with cities, city-leagues, empires, and nomadic peoples all offering alternative arrangements to the modern territorial state at different times.[20] An awareness of this diverse history of arrangements for international order is important, because it may well be that future Chinese-led or other forms of international order will also not resemble the Westphalian model.

When President Xi looked back into a past before the rise of the West, he would also have seen a world before the rise of the modern territorial state system: a world whose contours and structures were very different from today's. The modern state system was a product of a set of political ideas generated in Europe in the early modern period, ideas first given legal expression in the peace treaties that followed the Thirty Years' War (1618–1648), then exported around the world through various mechanisms of imperialism and emulation. But for vast stretches of historical time, before these centuries, the modern territorial sovereign state was not a political form, nor were cities necessarily subordinate to larger political entities. Indeed, the mingling of political entities and territorial forms such as city-states, city-leagues, empires, and kingdoms has been far more common. Additionally, the many varied international societies of the past exhibit a wealth of normative arrangements and governance structures: consider ancient Persian empires, the ancient Greek city-state system, the Roman Empire, the Islamic caliphate, medieval European Christendom, and various Chinese dynastic and tributary systems.[21] The form of international order we have today, whose basic building block is the territorial nation-state, is very unusual across the broad expanse of world historical configuration.

Consequently, although we take for granted many of the normative ideas that underpin the current US-led, liberal version of the Westphalian order, it is possible that they may be relatively fleeting. The international institutions that have lent order and stability to the post–World War II era were always a reflection of the underlying power of the West, and eventually, the hegemony of the United States.[22] There are distinct signs that that era is starting to wane, that its zenith has passed. The United States has recently vacillated on its commitment to global leadership, and there is no guarantee that President Biden's return to multilateralism will survive the turbulence of US domestic politics in the future.[23] These portents have not gone unnoticed in China, whose policymakers see in these events the beginning of the end of US hegemony and China's own opportunity to fill the breach. Whether these tectonic shifts lead to a new Cold War, as some have argued, or a return to multipolar regional hegemonies, as others have asserted, is as of yet unclear, but either future international order would look very different than the one in place today.[24]

Crucially for our discussion, a core mechanism by which successful international norms are extended and made durable is through urbanization and infrastructure construction, both within aspiring hegemonic powers such as China, and beyond their own territorial space. The core geopolitical vision behind the BRI includes not simply infrastructure construction, but also an attempt to construct multiple conduits for disseminating a new form of international society. This means that right now is one of those rare historical moments when we can see new forms of international order being assembled before our very eyes.

Shaping Cities

Any new political order that replaces current structures and arrangements will generate its own distinctive form of the state-city relationship. The sheer scale and reach of China's global project recalls how infrastructure has historically combined with the great animating ideas and institutions of the past. Rome's empire was connected by its road networks. Maritime empires, such as the Portuguese or British, relied on systems of coastal port cities. Britain joined together the disparate territories of its empire through great railway construction projects. China once unified its internal domains with vast networks of canals, and fortified its border with the Great Wall. In the late nineteenth century, the world was transformed by telegraphs, railways, steamships, and unprecedented urbanization; it was an age of technologically induced globalization stabilized by the imperial power of Great Britain. US military power could only have been projected during the Cold War, and beyond, via a global system of military bases underpinned by a radically different take on geographic space than that of previous empires.[25] And the oil- and gas-focused global energy economy of the post–World War II era has a radically different material layout than the previous coal-fueled economy had.[26]

Infrastructures allow forms of international society to colonize geographic space, to endure across time, and to project forms of social power. Once in place they extend agency into the future and are hard to reshape. Infrastructural projects of the scale of the BRI require massive mobilization and investment, laying down path dependencies that will shape the development of international systems for decades, if not centuries, to come.[27] In this sense, infrastructure is both geographic and temporal in its reach. The shaping of cities takes time—decades, sometimes centuries—so it is still early to be scrutinizing the cities along the BRI. But it is all the more important to do so now, because it is in these early moments that cities are most open to being shaped in ways that will later lock in particular forms of urban life. It is today, at the beginning of their transformation, that we can discern in these cities the outlines of a future that is beginning to coalesce.

The materiality of infrastructure and urban form is, then, entangled with the historically specific social ideas, norms, discourses, technologies, and design principles that generate them. That sounds terribly abstract, but it is really rather simple: the streets we walk or bike down, the benches we sit on, and the offices we may work in, result from ideas that rise and fall at given historical moments, ideas adopted and utilized both from the top down, and bottom up, as it were. The systems through which ideas become material, however, are by no means simple. Technologies and technical systems, including cities and their connecting infrastructural tissue, are never politically neutral: they are shaped by political, societal, and economic norms. They are complex, and their politics are woven through their design and evolution.

A particularly well-known and notorious illustration of this entanglement of worldview and infrastructural design is found in the morphology of New York City in the 1960s and 1970s, when the now-vilified Robert Moses imprinted his own political priorities, and social and racial prejudices, into his plans for the city. He designed many of the parks, roads, and bridges of New York between the 1920s and 1970s, and it has often been suggested that he designed the extremely low-hanging overpasses on Long Island specifically to make it impossible for twelve-foot-tall buses to use the parkways—and so to exclude the poorer classes in New York from using the parkways for leisure and commuting. Despite this reprehensible outcome, Moses's approaches were admired and adopted abroad.[28] Langdon Winner, in his influential discussion of the politics of infrastructure and technical artifacts, uses this example to illustrate the power of infrastructure design to shape society, and the way in which technological systems are designed to instantiate particular political dispositions.[29] This ability of design to shape what Keller Easterling calls "infrastructure space" is a significant form of power.[30]

Easterling calls this entanglement of ideas and materiality the *disposition* of a particular infrastructural form. The concept of disposition builds on much work in the sociology of technology, and is used to explain how infrastructures instantiate in space particular visions, narratives, and ideologies, opening up future paths that are advantageous for certain groups and actors. Infrastructure space is, for Easterling, a medium of information. Encoded within it are the rules that govern the space of possibilities of everyday action, shaping all the many everyday choices made by urban dwellers. Infrastructure space is politically active: it always has a disposition.

This concept of disposition is, for us, essential to exploring the underappreciated relation between Great Powers, geopolitics, and cities. Urban form becomes a way in which states project their values and power across space and time, shaping possibilities for millions of people. The BRI has the potential to do just that: it is shaping, and will continue to shape, the life chances of millions, if not billions, of people across Eurasia and Africa—and possibly further still, as it hardens into the exoskeleton of a potentially new form of international society. The infrastructures and forms of order generated by the BRI are beginning to reveal their own disposition, facilitating certain political, social, and economic outcomes, and, just as importantly, closing down others.

China's current commitment to an uneasy and possibly unstable fusion of state capitalism and single-party rule would give such an international order a very different character to that of existing liberal-inflected patterns. The BRI's evolving disposition, for example, will be drawn, in part, from the distinctive character of the Chinese model of political economy as it influences various technological and material forms, including, but in no way limited to, smart surveillance cities, high-speed rail connectivity, electric and smart vehicles, social-capital rating systems, and even massive, industrial-scale urban gardens. We can begin to discern its components and even its emerging form by considering the character of city layouts, architectural designs, urban plans, infrastructure systems, roads, railways, air-transit hubs, ports, power infrastructure, digital communications networks, parks, and other material elements; the evolution of urban linkages and shifting urban hierarchies; and how these express the dominant design principles and political and social theories that shape them. All of this together will become what we call the Belt and Road City—a distinctive new urban form.

As much as Chinese grand strategies are shaping the Belt and Road City, they do so in conversation with an array of other forces. The Silk Roads were never exclusively Chinese, and China has no monopoly over their history. Not all of the peoples or states across this vast region welcome China's selective appropriation of the past, nor do they welcome the amalgam of past and present that may be forged by the BRI. And the Chinese state is but one actor struggling to impose itself within a complex field of forces. It too is in flux, subject to its own competing ideas about identity, ideology, and historical destiny.[31]

The disposition of the Belt and Road City is subject to the competing voices of not only those within the Chinese state and establishment, but also those on the outside, including scholars, business leaders, architects, planners, technologists, labor leaders, and many others. As we now know, even Shenzhen—the Chinese city that famously exploded in population from 30,000 in 1980 to over ten million today—has been the product of an intense dance involving powers from above and those pre-existing from below.[32] The Belt and Road City's disposition is also tied to China's geopolitical strategy, economic models, and domestic political system, as well as the local interests of the many states with which it will interact. A project of this scale is perhaps ultimately beyond the ability of any one state, no matter how large, to control its ultimate form. It will also be shaped and driven by planetary-scale systems with logics at least partially outside the state system, such as capitalism. And we should not forget interactions with the non-human agencies of the natural world, including those that produce climate change and pandemics.[33]

Twilight of the Global City

We find a foil for our concept of a Belt and Road City in the very different historical circumstances and disposition of the Global City, a much-discussed concept among academics and theorists, and a familiar urban model—even if unknown as a concept—to residents of New York, Los Angeles, London, Paris, Tokyo, Seoul, Shanghai, Sydney, Dubai, and beyond.

The term Global City has become synonymous with the great transformation of many of the world's cities over the past four decades of liberal globalization, as economic restructuring and technological transformation have empowered and connected economic hubs. In this sense, the term, now ubiquitous in public discussions about leading cities, is designed to pick out and identify a historically specific form of city: one linked to the freeing of global finance capital, made possible by the restructuring of the Bretton Woods system in the 1970s; one that has been empowered to use its natural attributes to foster agglomeration economies that can attract power and wealth from deregulated global flows; one to which large segments of populations have been compelled to move, either because they must find work as migrant labor across borders, or because they have been displaced; but also one that, via the concentration of key firms, has become the locus of core decision-making about investment and production in the global economy, particularly as the nation-state stepped back from that role.[34] The Global City also represents a critical shift in urban scale and connectivity, toward the linking together of the transnational, national, and local in globe-spanning networks and border-bursting megacity regions. This transformation of connectivity and scale has also partially lifted some of the most globally connected cities out of their national contexts, opening up tensions, in multiple ways, between increasingly assertive urban constituencies and nation-states. Global Cities, and their mayors, often to the frustration of national governments, are now international players.[35]

In practice and concept, the Global City is both economic and political. It is a product of a particular configuration of the global economy, and a particular configuration of the international system, during the high-water mark of US hegemony. The morphology of Global Cities such as London, New York, Tokyo, Chicago, Dubai, and many others, has tended to reflect all of the contradictory forces of deregulated economic growth and rocketing levels of inequality that global capitalism has entailed, even accounting for local histories and contexts.

The economic underpinnings of Global Cities—most importantly the free movement of capital and talent—have favored certain forms of connectivity. In particular, such cities offer an arrangement of objects and infrastructures that increasingly segregates and differentiates access to various spaces. As these cities' infrastructure has become ever more privatized and fragmented, both in its provision and its usage, so have they become increasingly "splintered."[36] The "integrated ideal" of a modern nation-state based on equal access and opportunity has become fractured. Consider the emergence of a selectively sited and maintained transnational infrastructure such as the Dubai International Airport, or Terminal 2 at Mumbai's Chhatrapati Shivaji Maharaj International Airport—which was built in the middle of one of the city's famous informal districts, yet is open to only a relatively select population of travelers. Or how in both the global North and global South, elites have begun to inhabit private work and living spaces, and transport networks, high above the everyday street life. With their towering new skyscrapers, or in the case of São Paulo, private helicopter fleets that soar over the crime and congestion of the streets below, polarized Global Cities are beginning to display some familiar features of dystopian science fiction—including increasingly apparent moves to secure privileged spaces through surveillance and militarized forms of policing and private security.[37]

Exclusions and expulsions are built into the very fabric of these contemporary forms of urbanism. And part of the reason for this situation is that the nation-state, which following World War II made a commitment to support the welfare of all of its citizens, has, over the past four decades, handed off its responsibilities to private actors.[38] In other words, the ideology of a market-based society converged with infrastructural and other material forms, leading to a distinctive kind of space—one with its own historically unique disposition.[39] This form of city—indeed this form of political, social, economic, and metabolic order—now faces multiple converging crises that strike at its very foundations.

The era of governance crafted predominantly by Western states in the wake of World War II, as well as the model of capitalism that shaped the post–Cold War era of globalization, face existential challenges. The escalating climate-change crisis is set to reshape the patterns of modern urban life that were set in the twentieth century at the height of Western liberalism. Though the wording is carefully calculated and the science complex, the world's leading climate scientists have been clear: even with a significant reduction of emissions, global warming will exceed 1.5°C in the next twenty years; and without immediate and deep reductions in greenhouse gas emissions, the world will exceed the 2.0°C threshold in the next thirty years.[40] Even more alarming, 3.0°C by century's end is highly possible. Writing for an urban audience, IPCC scientists concluded:

> There is no historical precedent for the scale of sociocultural, economic, and technological change needed to limit warming to 1.5°C, but routes forward are emerging. In some cities and regions an incremental approach to adaptation will not suffice, especially in the face of higher overshoot pathways. Transformational adaptation seeks deep and long-term systemic changes that can accelerate the implementation and localisation of sustainable

development to enable the transition to a 1.5°C world. It implies
significant changes in the structure or function of an entire system
that go beyond adjusting existing practices.[41]

Along with this need to retool infrastructures and urban spaces to
cope with the coming ravages of a warmer world, two other crises have
also helped to reconfigure the relationship between state and market in
recent years: the 2008 financial crisis, which damaged the credibility of
the neoliberal model of the past four decades, and the 2019 COVID-19
pandemic, which has required massive state interventions to stabilize societies around the world.

In retrospect, 2008 and 2019 may come to be seen as markers of the
end of a historically specific configuration of capitalism and geopolitics
on which the Global City as an urban form has rested. The Global City
has been defined by US hegemony and a neoliberal market orthodoxy
based on principles of minimal regulation, privatization, and the relatively unfettered movement of capital and goods. Both the financial crisis
and the global pandemic required states to intervene massively in the
economy. In the case of the pandemic, too, governments were forced to
engage in spending practices normally seen only in wartime, and the notion that an economy can be separated from its broader environmental
and material underpinnings was exposed as an illusion. For these reasons,
the COVID-19 pandemic may someday be seen as the first crisis of the
age of the Anthropocene.[42]

Amid these crises, the Global City is under pressure from constituencies within the West, in particular from the populist Right and progressive
Left. But it is also being challenged in the international arena. China, along
with many other states in the region, has rejected many of the core principles of the Western-led liberal order, including much of its normative content defining the relationship between the state, markets, and individuals.
As a potential challenger or successor to this period of neoliberal globalization, the Belt and Road City will look and feel very different. China, via the
BRI, seeks to reshape the tumultuous forces of global urbanization in its
own image—an image that is, itself, in flux—both within and outside of its
own territorial borders. It is doing so, in part, by supporting the development of Chinese expertise in new forms of technological knowledge, via
new funding models and the founding of new institutions.

In order to understand the new forces shaping the BRI and global
urbanization, we need to look to the origins of China's current rise, its

increasing assertiveness in the last decade, and the geostrategic and economic drivers that have pushed China to develop the BRI and back it so
strongly.

The Rise of China

China's meteoric rise over the past four decades in many ways represents
a return to a more historically typical center of political and economic
power. European preeminence and that of the Atlantic-centered world,
including the United States, while centuries in the making, does not represent any natural historic order. Within China, its diminishment on the
global stage over the past two hundred years is seen as a result of Western
and Japanese imperialism, and in particular a series of unequal treaties
that followed imperial invasions and incursions into China's sovereignty
from the mid-nineteenth century onward.[43] China's "century of humiliation" began with its defeat by the British in the First Opium War (1839–
1842). The terms of the Treaty of Nanking forced China to give up Hong
Kong and opened up five more treaty ports: Guangzhou, Xiamen, Fu-
zhou, Ningbo, and Shanghai. So began a run of military defeats that cul-
minated with Japanese occupation in the twentieth century, and the start
of a long period of economic stagnation that began to be reversed only
after World War II, under the Chinese Communist Party (CCP).[44]

Since the death of Mao Zedong in 1976, China's orientation has increasingly turned outward, regionally and globally. China embarked on a
new direction in economic policy in 1978 under the leadership of Deng
Xiaoping, and up to now, China's economic growth, industrial development, and levels of urbanization have been turbocharged. This "Reform
Period" focused on gradually opening up China to world markets and institutions, and shoring up the legitimacy of the CCP with high levels of
economic growth and modernization, all while carefully trying to defend
a distinctive non-Western modernity with Chinese "characteristics."

Early efforts under Deng Xiaoping focused on normalizing diplomatic
relations with the United States, and following a developmental model
similar to that undertaken by the successful "East Asian Tigers"—Hong
Kong, Singapore, South Korea, and Taiwan. In 1978, China began to experiment with a number of special economic zones (SEZs) in urban regions along the southeastern coast, such as Guangdong province, and later
implemented them around Shanghai and the Yangtze Delta. China carefully opened up to the world market, adopting a number of Western-style

economic strategies, while never fully embracing liberal market practices: it kept tight control of many national industries, for example, and resisted floating its currency.

During the final decades of the twentieth century, and into the twenty-first, China benefited from the relative stability of Western-led globalization. It accepted Western institutions and practices, while carefully yet ambitiously urbanizing, industrializing, modernizing, and reforming its economy and society. There was some decentralizing of the state, some empowerment of local government, and China joined existing international organizations: the International Monetary Fund (IMF) and World Bank in 1986, and the World Trade Organization (WTO) in 2001. Levels of foreign direct investment in China skyrocketed, exports boomed, growth accelerated (leading to an annual growth rate of 10 percent between 1978 and 1992), while tens of millions of people moved from rural areas into cities. Indeed, cities played a key role in China's economic miracle, providing platforms for experimentation, keeping labor costs low, and transforming areas like Guangdong into the new manufacturing workshops of the world. As the increasingly post-industrial Global Cities were embracing finance capital and services, the older manufacturing jobs that characterized earlier urban life in many of these cities were reappearing half a world away.

Despite these successes, China has been haunted, since the military defeats and occupations of the nineteenth and twentieth centuries, by a fear that it will fail to modernize, to seize the geopolitical moment and ride the waves of technological innovation. Modern Chinese history has been characterized by this sense of being left behind, of being a great civilization brought low and humiliated as a result of a failure to keep up with foreign competitors. The inability of the Qing dynasty (1644–1912) to compete with the rising power of Western nation-states, and then a modernizing Japan, continues to resonate. There is today a strong sense in Chinese policy circles that another such moment of epochal flux and opportunity is under way—and that this time, if China can react in the right way, it could reverse the historical disaster of its removal from the center of the international system. President Xi's foreign-policy pronouncements have referred to "Great Changes Unseen in a Century"—that is, a perceived decline in US power, both internationally and from domestic decay within, as well as a perceived wider fragmentation of the Western powers, including, for example, Britain's exit from the European Union. A sense is building that this is the moment for China to grasp its geopolitical opportunities, after long decades of quietly biding its time and developing its economic strength.

While Western policymakers hoped such domestic reforms and multilateral engagement would lead China to democratize internally and be a responsible actor on the global stage, this approach was never meant to be, and indeed could not be, permanent, and in the past decade China's policy of careful growth within the established international order has shifted. The more assertive foreign-policy initiatives under Xi, including the vastly ambitious nature of the BRI, appear to mark a shift in China's orientation. And to some extent they clearly do—because they end long decades of foreign policy carefully designed to maximize the opportunities offered by globalization in the post–Cold War period, under the relatively stable security environment offered by US hegemony. Yet as Rush Doshi has outlined in a recent influential analysis that utilizes decades' worth of Chinese-language sources, there are many lines of continuity in China's grand strategic positioning and thinking over the past four decades.[45] Rather than the maverick innovator he sometimes appears to be, Xi reflects this continuity. His strategic approach is the outcome of a long-standing party consensus that has remained consistent over time and is designed to adapt to shifting international conditions and relative power distributions.[46]

Indeed, although Xi has sought to associate much of the shift in Chinese policy in recent years with his own personal leadership and philosophy— part of an emerging personality cult codified in *Xi Jinping Thought* and not seen at the top of the CCP since Mao—in fact much of China's move into Eurasia is a response to ideas and debates that predate his leadership. This is the case with two ideas that have come to be associated with the BRI: "peripheral diplomacy" and the "Chinese Dream" of a "community of common destiny for mankind." Strategic steps toward peripheral diplomacy, which refers to China's relations with its neighbors in the region, were initiated in the closing years of the Hu Jintao period, while the notion of the Chinese Dream has recurred throughout Chinese history, albeit in various forms.[47] Once again, the 2008 global financial crisis proved a pivotal historical moment. It was, in fact, the tumultuous effects of this 2008 crisis that led to the BRI, and the path to a new peripheral diplomacy. Reliance on US and Western global markets, the stability of US-led globalization, and even long-term US international leadership were all brought into question. This opened the door for China's leaders to consider possibilities for China to reclaim international leadership and strengthen its position in world markets. Over the past decade, these ideas have been operationalized with policy and material backing on a grand scale.

Chinese thinkers began to see China's near neighbors in new ways: not through the old lens of fear of strategic encirclement, but as foundational sites for a major new program of infrastructure-led regional economic development, one that would also profitably soak up the huge reserves of capital that China had been building over the past decades.[48] This was the intellectual context in which Xi took power in 2012, and the BRI was the eventual result of these ideas.

The BRI, then, effectively signals the end of decades of careful Chinese foreign policy that sought to take advantage of Western-led globalization without seeking to revise or disrupt the political and economic order that sustained it. A deliberate strategy, the BRI is designed to reposition China at the heart of regional and international order, to redirect the flows of the global economy, and to realize an integrated "Eurasia," with China as its driving force and core—in a role that allows it to reclaim its longtime historical dominance.

The BRI as Grand Strategy

Like other Great Powers before it, and the United States today, China has needed to look beyond its borders for the material necessary to run a modern economy. And here the BRI offers China access to the energy and mineral resources of Central Asia, Africa, the Middle East, and Russia. The maritime component of the BRI seeks to herald the beginning of an expanded maritime commercial system—while having the added strategic benefit of securing Chinese influence over key strategic choke points such as the Strait of Malacca and facilitating the development of a blue-water navy that can project Chinese power globally. A notable element of the BRI so far has been the construction of strategically important ports, such as Hambantota in Sri Lanka and Gwadar City in Pakistan. The BRI is also seen as a way to promote peaceful coexistence and security in a troubled region. Eventually the BRI may end up drawing China into becoming a security provider across the whole arc of political instability connecting these regions.

But perhaps equally importantly, the BRI is a way out of a structural problem that other Great Powers have faced under capitalist modernity. As China has swiftly transitioned into a more fully capitalist state, it has begun to experience the fundamental tension between a political system built on state territoriality and a transnational economic system that seeks constantly to transcend borders and limits.[49]

Seen in this light, the BRI can be viewed as China's way of putting in place mechanisms and institutions to succeed the United States as an economic hegemon for the twenty-first century.[50] It is important to see the BRI, and the ultimate goal of a Chinese-led unified Eurasian market, in this perspective of historical capitalism: as just the latest and largest iteration of the conflict between nation-state territoriality and transnational capitalism that has been playing out across the modern period. Even now Eurasian trade is worth double that of transatlantic trade. What would its potential be if it were to be unified by a fully connected infrastructure, without trade barriers or security concerns?

In the Reform Period, China built up a huge capital and foreign-exchange surplus through its manufacturing and exports. It also accumulated productive overcapacity in various industry sectors. These have become a drag on Chinese growth and domestic political stability, with falling profits, rising debt, unemployment, and bankruptcies. China, many have argued, finds itself on the brink of a classic "middle-income trap"—it is no longer very cheap in terms of wage levels for labor-intensive commodity production, but its workers are not yet able to compete in the higher value-added sectors because their productivity remains too low.

The promise of the BRI is to forge a new path through the world economic system for China and Chinese economic actors, which, for historical reasons, today find themselves in a subordinate position within global value chains. Dependency theorists, who are held in high regard in Chinese Marxist scholarship, have argued that existing structures lock in the most valuable positions within the economic system.[51] And China has found itself, in recent years, needing to break out of its position as a developing country. A slowdown in its economic growth, a tailing off of new technology transfers from more advanced economies, worries over property bubbles, environmental degradation, and the potential political unrest that may result from any of these developments, all make rising up the global value chain an important next step for China.

The *Made in China 2025* strategic plan, adopted by the CCP in 2013, envisages China moving away from its position as "workshop of the world" and low-cost manufacturing hub, and instead becoming a high-tech, high-value economy. The idea is to capture lucrative revenue streams in areas such as biotechnology, pharmaceuticals, artificial intelligence, robotics, automated vehicles, lithium-battery production, aerospace, and shipping—with an emphasis on green and sustainable production.[52]

The BRI is crucial to this goal because it would enable partner countries along the BRI to move into the low-cost manufacturing markets that China would vacate. So, for example, Pakistan and countries across Southeast Asia might provide the components and inputs needed for higher-value-added activities that would now be undertaken by Chinese firms. The development of the China-Pakistan Economic Corridor (CPEC), a core element of the BRI, is testament to this approach.

China is not unique historically in looking beyond its borders as a strategy for economic and social development. Empires, nations, and even city-states have long sought "spatial fixes" to overcome blockages to internal development.[53] Such spatial fixes have taken different forms historically, from the creative destruction of waves of historical urbanization, to various forms of imperialism. The BRI—with its huge transnational scope, its vast investments and engineering projects, its infrastructural forms and urbanizations (both within China and beyond its borders)—can be seen as just such a spatial fix for China.[54]

This approach, with its focus on both networks (corridors) and nodes (cities), reflects several ideas about developmental economics, including the importance of regional integration, economic corridors, special economic zones, and urban gateways. The anticipated growth in urban population in Asia and Africa will require both the extensive retrofitting of existing urban infrastructure and buildings, as well as the construction of new versions. Regional integration, linking zones and territories, will take urban form, connecting cities across Eurasia economically, administratively, politically, and materially, as urban land cover continues to enwrap the earth's land surface.

Economic corridors, special economic zones, and special administrative zones have a long history. Carved-out administrative territories like Hong Kong or Shanghai have offered empires like Britain's the ability to experiment with policy and adapt bureaucratic codes and law. They continue to be used around the world today, and have become critical components of Chinese thinking about economic development.

Economic corridors develop networks between economic agents, connecting urban nodes across a defined geographical space. In the case of the BRI, the larger goal is to create transnational territories, with unimpeded trade flows and excellent connectivity, that can plug into wider global networks of production and trade. The corridors are intended to act as conduits for the massive levels of investment linked to the BRI, shaping and directing the simultaneous and mutually reinforcing dynamics of infrastructure construction, urbanization, and economic development. Transport infrastructure, such as roads, railways, ports, power grids, and digital networks, will generate new forms of BRI urbanism, which in turn will stimulate the natural agglomeration economies of urban areas.[55]

China's use of the economic corridor to underpin the BRI, then, is fully in line with contemporary theories of economic development. China has made an $18 billion investment in fifty economic and trade cooperation zones related to the corridors and zones along the BRI.[56] The six major corridors of the BRI, which will structure cross-border connectivity across Eurasia, are the New Eurasian Land Bridge Economic Corridor; China-Mongolia-Russia Economic Corridor; China–Indochina Peninsula Economic Corridor; China–Central Asia–West Asia Economic Corridor; Bangladesh-China-India-Myanmar Economic Corridor; and the China-Pakistan Economic Corridor.

The New Eurasian Land Bridge Economic Corridor is envisaged as linking China and Europe across the entire Eurasian landmass, bringing together cities as diverse as Xian, Urumqi, Khorgos, Almaty, Astana, Moscow, Warsaw, Berlin, Rotterdam, and London with new rail links that will, for example, span the nine thousand or so miles from Shenzhen to Rotterdam. The China-Mongolia-Russia Economic Corridor will tie together cities such as Beijing, Ulaanbaatar, Novosibirsk, Omsk, Yekaterinburg, and Saint Petersburg. Both of these routes will clearly require Russia's cooperation. Russia's invasion of Ukraine in 2022, and the subsequent deterioration of EU-Russian relations, have complicated the construction of this hoped-for Eurasian land bridge.

China's influence has grown in recent years in the former Soviet republics of Central Asia. There new investments in infrastructure underpin the China–Central Asia–West Asia Economic Corridor, which involves Kazakhstan, Kyrgyzstan, Tajikistan, Turkmenistan, and Uzbekistan, an Iran that is increasingly moving into the Chinese orbit, and at the endpoint, a resurgent Turkey experimenting with its own neo-Ottoman revival. This corridor is intended to generate the material and urban foundations for an arc of authoritarianism across the center of Eurasia, linking some cities reminiscent of the majestic old Silk Roads with others that blend the ancient with the new: Kashgar, Samarkand, Tashkent, Tehran, Ankara, Istanbul.[57]

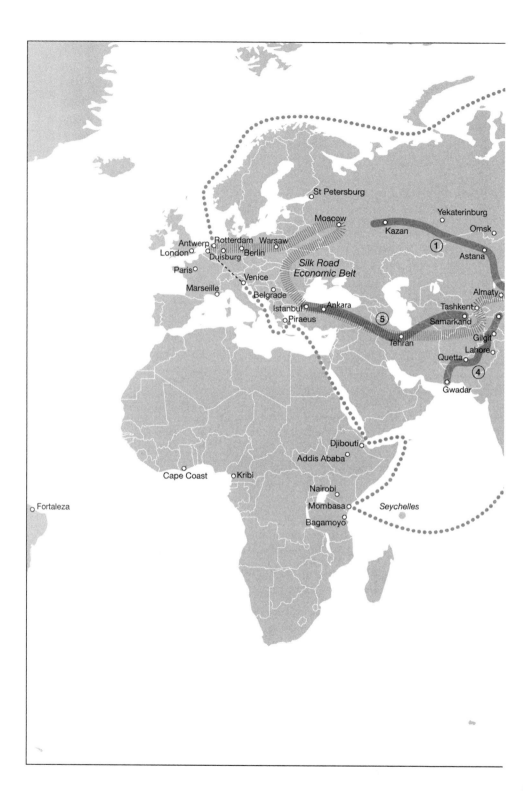

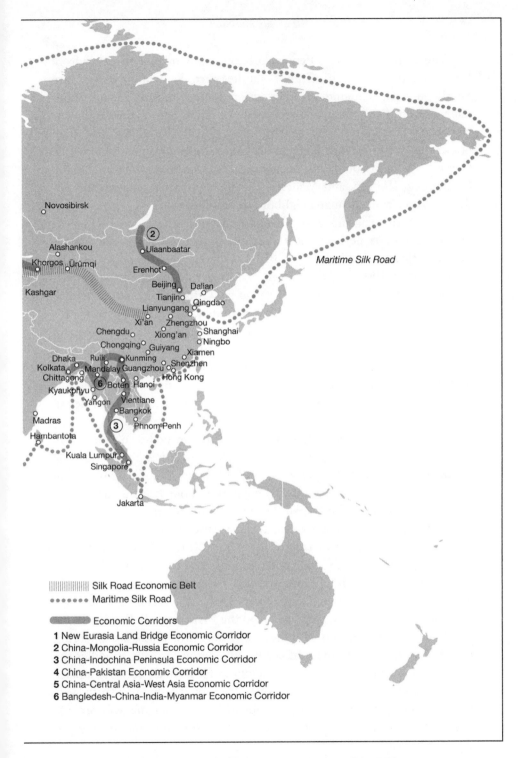

Economic Corridors and Maritime Routes of the BRI

The China–Indochina Peninsula Economic Corridor stretches from Kunming, the capital of China's southeastern Yunnan province, into Southeast Asia, stringing together urban centers such as Hanoi, Vientiane, Phnom Penh, Bangkok, and Kuala Lumpur, terminating in the entrepôt of Singapore. Also snaking down from Kunming, but then branching west, is the Bangladesh-China-India-Myanmar Economic Corridor, which would link such cities as Mandalay, Yangon, Dhaka, Chittagong, Kolkata, and Madras—although India has shown little enthusiasm so far for its huge neighbor China's ambitions.

Finally, the flagship example—and the one where the BRI's economic strategy is perhaps most fully developed so far—is the China-Pakistan Economic Corridor (CPEC). One of the backbones of BRI connectivity, CPEC has also played a leading role in enhancing China's position in global value chains. Of course, CPEC is the only corridor of the six that includes just one other country, which may account for its greater development and coherence than the other corridors. All told, along the CPEC there are eighteen cities with populations over 100,000, and twelve with over one million inhabitants. And while most of Pakistan's population, among the youngest in the world, does not yet live in cities, the country is urbanizing at one of the fastest rates in South Asia.[58]

CPEC offers an example of the role of urban nodes in this vision, too, with the developing port city of Gwadar, which has been funded by Chinese loans, and developed with Chinese labor. Gwadar City sits on the Arabian Sea near the Gulf of Oman and about two hundred miles west of Karachi near the Iranian border. Its construction, driven by the CPEC vision, offers coastal access to East Africa and beyond, and indicates the importance of a string of ports both within China and stretching across Afro-Eurasia and potentially beyond, such as Dalian in northeast China, or the Chinese-funded redevelopments of Piraeus in greater Athens, Greece, or Colombo in Sri Lanka. Taken together they form the basis for what China has called the Maritime Silk Road.

As with the sea, so too with the land. Many urban hubs are emerging rapidly. Khorgos, a city that physically and administratively straddles the border of China and Kazakhstan, is about as far from an ocean as a place can be. Its expansion, like that of the village of Irkeshtam, also in Xinjiang province, and the city of Erenhot in Inner Mongolia, will provide new trade, transit, and customs gateways for Chinese economic and political influence.

The corridors of the BRI include a range of city types. Captured in the earlier lists are coastal cities that over the next eighty years will suffer from sea-level rise; mountain cities that will experience increases in both drought and rainfall; and inland and seaside cities that will deal with more heat waves. There are cities that are expanding outward, like those in Ethiopia, and those extending upward, like Astana. There are ancient cities and newfangled ones; and those that rely on formal or informal economies. Differences like these, particularly as they apply to corridors, grant some leverage or influence to local authorities engaging with BRI-related officials, and taken as a whole, serve as a reminder of the grand ambitions of the project.

For China, corridorization offers a way to restructure its relations with countries across the region, even though the development of the corridors will also be shaped by local dynamics, cultures, and agencies. The corridors, as they develop, will generate new forms of boundaries, new inclusions and exclusions, and new transnational dynamics. States will need to consider that being outside of the BRI could involve significant costs in the longer term. Indeed, the transnational corridor is key to China's strategy of securing its own future by allowing it to reassemble regional political economies without overtly undermining Westphalian sovereignty.

In a further boon to China, the BRI also generates its own export demand, as Chinese loans to other states allow them to fund infrastructure development projects that then involve Chinese firms and Chinese expertise—in constructing high-speed rail systems, roads, ports, digital infrastructure, and energy systems. These projects also help to absorb surplus Chinese raw materials, such as concrete and steel. At the same time, massive infrastructure investment has helped to address the historical imbalance between the prosperous eastern coastal regions of China and the western provinces that had grown even wider in the post-Mao Reform Period, by both providing new forms of connectivity and urban and economic development within China, and developing access to the oil and gas reserves that will help to fuel them.[59] These western regions now provide a hinge into the newly developing lands at the center of Eurasia—which represent a growing, and potentially immense, market—as well as a model for urban-led development.

Markets, however, are shaped by norms, culture, legal orders, and institutions, and China is emerging into a global economic system where the rules and institutions were set up by other states in a context of Chinese weakness. Just as nineteenth-century Germany arose in a world already parceled up into European empires, so China is reemerging into a world where other states have shaped the world economy to their advantage.[60]

Some have argued that China seeks ultimately to supplant existing powers by reshaping the mechanisms and institutions of the global economy, shifting itself from a peripheral player to one at the core of global economic value. In this sense, the BRI offers the first stirrings of a world beyond those Bretton Woods institutions that have given leading Western states structural power in the world economy since the late 1940s.[61] Alongside the infrastructure construction projects, the BRI incorporates new institutions and mechanisms with which to finance them, such as the Asian Infrastructure Investment Bank (AIIB), which now operates alongside the work of the new $40 billion Silk Road Fund, and that of the big domestic Chinese Policy Banks, such as the Export-Import Bank of China and the China Development Bank. This approach also fits with China's goal, in the wake of the 2008 financial crisis, to break its dependency on the United States, including by easing away from its use of US debt instruments to invest its capital surplus.

The BRI has also catalyzed attempts to develop new ideas about financial markets, currency, standards, legal systems, digital technologies, economic models, and forms of urbanism. Alongside the investment programs and material infrastructure construction have come measures to improve the operations of financial markets and credit, banking, and insurance systems, both within China and across the BRI. Shanghai, once and still a Global City, is well placed to become a pivotal hub for financial services and commercial strategy development within the BRI via the Shanghai Free Trade Zone. Outside of China, Astana in Kazakhstan— a gateway city linking the two halves of an emerging Eurasian assemblage—is also developing into a crucial hub for financial and legal services. China needs to reassure BRI partners about the legal status of their investments, and Astana has become a place where this reassurance can happen. A new legal platform for the BRI features Astana as an arena for the arbitration of contract disputes, one that relies on British legal practices and norms, and, for now, British-trained judges and barristers.

But the BRI's economic and financial dimensions are only parts of a larger domestic and geopolitical vision. Just as the American Dream was couched in universal ideals, the Chinese Dream envisions a new international order, one in which China is the guiding force in an evolving "community of common destiny." Yet whereas any realization of the American Dream was measured in generations, Xi's version of the Chinese Dream takes as its time horizon three decades, or roughly one generation. The BRI's completion has been slated for 2049, to coincide with the hundredth anniversary of the Chinese Communist Party's victory over the Nationalists in the Chinese Civil War. The world that the mature BRI might bequeath may look very different by the midpoint of this century.

Some have seen the emerging vision of China in international society as something of a reversion to the past, a twenty-first-century version of *tianxia*, or "all under heaven," where China sits as a political and moral orderer at the center of a series of expanding concentric circles, with various dependent communities owing it loyalty and allegiance. This worldview harkens back to China's more majestic dynasties, and incorporates various Confucian values such as sincerity, honesty, amity, obligation, and deference to power. Some have been quick to see this as a neo-tributary or neo-colonial vision of international order.[62] China's policymakers do not necessarily see these connotations as negative. Indeed, an emerging Chinese School of International Relations scholarship has come to the fore in recent years, attempting to articulate new understandings of the international that draw on indigenous philosophy, history, and practice. As we will argue later, many of these ideas complement the types of material foundations being forged by the BRI. The interplay of these non-Western concepts and ideas about international society and the unfurling transnational material infrastructure shaped by China will be critical for the unfolding nature of international politics in the twenty-first century, constituting the *disposition of infrastructural space* of the BRI.

The immense ambition driving the Belt and Road Initiative puts it in the category of a grand strategy aimed at hegemonic transition. But whereas in the past this type of transition was accompanied by war among the Great Powers, today, in a world of nuclear weapons, the BRI might offer the material footings for peacefully building an alternative system of economic and political leadership. The rise of China already points to a rebalancing of the international system and a profound shift in the balance of power. Indeed, China's new outward orientation and engagement very deliberately coincide with a moment when the United States and other leading Western states seem to be losing confidence in globalism, turning inward, and building both metaphorical and real walls.

How can China (and, by extension, the United States, as its main competitor for shaping international order) avoid the "Thucydides trap" that has characterized such radical shifts in the balance of power in the past, whereby international orders have been unraveled and reconstituted by hegemonic war?[63] How might China deal with the interests of rival powers who fear its rise, while reordering an international system whose structures and institutions have been set in an earlier, Western-centered era? The BRI seems to offer Chinese policymakers a potential long-term solution to these problems, one that also neatly addresses, in the short to medium term, domestic concerns about an economic slowdown.

CHAPTER TWO

Infrastructure
Materializing the Chinese Dream

J UST A MONTH AFTER President Xi made his 2013 Astana speech announcing the BRI's ambitions to reinvigorate the ancient land
routes of the Silk Roads, he made a counterpart speech in Jakarta,
Indonesia, where he announced the Maritime Silk Road. Jakarta is
a sprawling metropolitan region of more than thirty million residents,
and Indonesia has experienced an expansion of urban land cover in the
early twenty-first century second only to that of China—with urbanization rates in Indonesia expected to hit more than 70 percent by 2029.
Jakarta, too, has some of the worst traffic for a capital city, leading the
government of Indonesia to start searching for not just new transport
options, but also a new capital. By early 2020, construction of the BRI-
backed Jakarta-Bandung High-Speed Rail Project had only worsened the
traffic, clogging key transportation arteries around the capital.

Xi gave his speech to the Indonesian Parliament. It was ostensibly an
occasion to announce a comprehensive strategic partnership between the
two countries that included several infrastructure projects related to
dams and bridges, as well as, significantly, the establishment of the AIIB.
But Xi's speech has also come to mark the inauguration of the Belt and
Road Initiative's maritime element, which is designed to employ maritime routes and gateway port cities to invigorate the land corridors
stretching across the Eurasian heartland.

Standing in front of a huge map of the Indonesian archipelago, islands picked out in gold and resting in an onyx sea, Xi spoke of the bonds of friendship between the two peoples that had long faced each other across vast oceans. The waters, Xi explained, had acted not as barriers, but as mediums of connectivity, on which ships laden with goods, and carrying merchants and explorers, had created and fostered ties of exchange and friendship.

Just as Xi, when speaking in Astana, had drawn on the romantic legacy of the overland trade routes that crisscrossed the Eurasian mountains, deserts, and steppes, so in Jakarta he called back to another idealized element of Chinese history: the voyages of the Ming dynasty navigator Admiral Zheng He, who first visited the Indonesian archipelago in the fifteenth century and so helped Southeast Asia become an important Chinese trading hub along the maritime Silk Roads.

Zheng He, a Yunnanese Muslim eunuch, explorer, and diplomat, traversed the South China Sea and the Indian Ocean on behalf of the Yongle emperor. Although his mission was short-lived, abandoned after the Yongle emperor's reign ended in 1424, Zheng He's majestic flotilla of more than two hundred treasure ships, which carried around twenty-five thousand men, plied routes to Vietnam, the Philippines, Indonesia, Sri Lanka and the southern coast of India, the Arabian Gulf, and the eastern coast of Africa. With these voyages, Zheng He showed the peoples of these regions the power of Chinese civilization and the supremacy of Chinese technology and knowledge, while clearly signaling to them the assumption of Chinese centrality, and an expectation of tribute and fealty.

The Chinese were masters of shipbuilding and navigation, and their ships dwarfed any others the world had ever seen. Some Chinese vessels were over four hundred feet long.[1] But the Ming dynasty Chinese did not embark on a European-style age of conquest. Nor did they build great global maritime trading networks. Instead, it seems that the stately voyages of Admiral Zheng He's armada were less about trade, and more designed to demonstrate to other peoples and lands the intrinsic superiority and centrality of Chinese civilization, with the seas seen as a way to connect others to, and expand, the Central and East Asian tributary system. Envoys from these newly connected lands went to Beijing to give tribute, and received gifts and wisdom in return. The fleet was accompanied by troops to demonstrate the might of the Middle Kingdom, but not to extend it by conquest, or to colonize other peoples.[2]

Admiral He's voyages, and the maritime links they created, were an attempt to transform foreign regions, peoples, and cultures through displays of power, knowledge, and technological superiority. Today, over half a millennia later, echoes of this earlier time of Chinese centrality, connectivity, and patronage take on a new resonance.

The Many Lives of Infrastructure

Great Powers seek influence and leverage, and have, throughout history, developed material conduits through which to build such influence and to project power. Building infrastructure, both at home and in foreign lands, generates such conduits, tying together different spaces via filaments of stone, concrete, iron, steel, or fiber-optic cable. Although seemingly mundane and prosaic, without these sinews of connectivity no Great Power could reach across either geographic space or time, two measures never far from strategic consideration. Roads, railways, bridges, canals, ports, power grids, pipelines, dams, cables, satellite constellations, and cellular networks: these are the ways in which power is made manifest, social and economic systems are built, and the everyday lives of billions are shaped.

To be sure, every grand strategy has its dramatic displays: militaries on parade or in training; generals astride on frontiers; diplomatic brinkmanship. Its games are played by heads of state, ministers, diplomats, military leaders, and often profiteers and adventurers. Its terms are set by military capacity and the maneuverings of states, or the dominant norms, values, or competing interests governing diplomacy in the halls of international organizations. But the hard material of infrastructure, and connectivity—the ability to move on, within, and through that infrastructure—are just as crucial in allowing forms of international society to endure. They are, to steal a metaphor from the natural sciences, the dark matter that binds international systems together, an unnoticed and largely unlooked-for mass holding different international orders in place.

There is a long-standing historical relationship between the rise of Great Powers and major spates of infrastructure building. These are the moments of world-making that shape pathways of the future for populations across vast regions; generate the cities and habitats in which people live, including the way they travel between places; and redefine social interactions, shaping the way people think and act.[3] It may not have the cache, or visibility, of military strategy or high diplomacy, but infrastructure is the exoskeleton of power. Rome had its roads, the British Empire its railways, and both founded new cities beyond their own borders, then connected them to their imperial system. Later, in the ruins of post–World

War II Europe, the United States injected vast sums into the Marshall
Plan, a program of infrastructure investment designed, among other
things, to moderate the domestic politics of European states and keep
them from falling into the orbit of the Soviet Union. The BRI is frequently likened to the Marshall Plan in its scale and scope: infrastructure
as geopolitics.[4]

The shapes and forms that infrastructure takes are vital to understanding the circulation and distribution of resources; how the movement
of people, ideas, goods, materials, energy, and microbes are controlled;
who is included and excluded from wealth and prosperity; and how
human society interacts with the systems of the natural world. And those
forms have been heavily shaped by the polities most powerful during their
development. As China projects beyond its borders its own growing
power and its own value systems, while explicitly recognizing the need to
maintain a stable and peaceful international system, it has fastened on the
construction of new infrastructural conduits of connectivity as a means to
simultaneously serve these two—to some, seemingly contradictory—ends.

Infrastructure investment offers China's neighbors a path to economic development. Asia alone will have an estimated investment gap of
$1.7 trillion per year over the next decade, and states desperately require
infrastructure upgrades.[5] China has accumulated a vast mountain of reserves in recent decades, and loans for infrastructure development have
put this money to productive use, both across Afro-Eurasia where the infrastructure is being built, and in China, as funds are reinvested in those
Chinese enterprises supplying expertise.

China sees fostering this economic interdependence as "win-win"
in its wider effort to gain political influence, and eventually, reshape
the international order. Critics have pointed to the risks of Chinese "debt
diplomacy." But this is only part of the story. A more profound consideration is that infrastructure development is inseparable from the nature of
political order itself. The BRI's ambition is not just a series of hundreds
of disconnected projects, although China's bilateral and ad hoc approach
to most BRI deals sometimes give this impression. Instead, the vision is
an overarching one in which states become gradually tied into a symbiotic set of relationships, with China at the core of an emerging and consolidating transnational system. Infrastructure projects do not simply
provide building blocks for development or financial influence, but also
deeply entwine the site of construction with the social norms and values
of the society that shapes it. Such was the influence of the car, with its

close ties to the American cultural ideas of individual freedom and commerce, on twentieth-century urban development. But in this case, the infrastructure is tied to a Chinese state with a particular contemporary political orientation and drive to reclaim its central Great Power status in the region and the world.[6] In other words, the primary way that China is trying to make its Chinese Dream come true is through infrastructure development.

These connections between the Great Powers' future-oriented political projects and dreams and their materialization via infrastructure construction should alert us to the deep entanglement between the world of thought and the material world. When paired with finance or power, dreams, strategic visions, and ideologies mold concrete, bend steel, and redraw the contours of the natural world, corralling its energies and processes. Even aborted dreams, such as those of the early Soviet utopian "constructivists," have left deep and enduring legacies, imprints in urban and natural landscapes that remain long after the dreams themselves have faded away. New powers, actors, and agencies have to contend with such legacies of the past, and the vast works that human ingenuity, knowledge, and labor have left behind. Looking forward, this means that building such a material legacy now will allow today's human societies and cultures to project their influence forward in time—creating path dependencies that will shape the world of future populations.

Infrastructure is not inert matter. Roads, pipelines, power plants, all of the shapes and forms of cities and regions, contain within them the essence of politics and power. They selectively connect and disconnect; they distribute resources and opportunities; they warp and bend space and time in ways that draw together some people and places, while leaving others in darkness, or outside of history. They have the power to make nations, to shape the character of international systems and entire historical eras. Infrastructures are never neutral, never purely technocratic, never just the product of scientists and engineers. Infrastructures are socially shaped; they bear the stamp of the society and the context in which they were forged; they bear the traces of the politics that made them, the power struggles that are retained in their foundations.[7] And those origins go on to bend the future in certain directions, opening up and materializing some pathways, drawing new connections and new fields of possibility, while closing down others.

Infrastructure, then, is at heart a technology of governance. It matters who is producing it, how, and with what ends in mind. It matters what forms it takes, because those forms are shaped not just by the demands of connectivity, or economic logics, or the demands of physics, but also by the political and social systems of the contexts in which they are generated. Although this role of infrastructure in generating international political outcomes has been largely overlooked in the past, it has begun to be recognized, not least by the regime in China, as an arena where struggles over social power are played out.

If infrastructure is a strategic terrain of power and governance, it also offers a way to analyze and understand the fault lines within societies.[8] Much recent work on understanding the political significance of infrastructure has been driven by the ways in which infrastructures in the developed world—which have long been relied on to keep society in place, but have remained invisible because they functioned largely unproblematically—have begun to wear down. Moments of failure have become windows into the subterranean filaments that hold worlds together: consider the power-grid failure and blackout of 2003 that affected the Northeastern Corridor of the United States.[9] This failure contrasts starkly with the ambitious Tennessee Valley Authority projects of the New Deal era, which were at the time showcased to dignitaries from around the world. Western states have been living off the decaying Keynesian infrastructural legacies of the post–World War II period for a very long time now, and the creaks in the system are making audible those states' decline in power.

But infrastructure stretches beyond the material—dreams made manifest are also still dreams of a people and of individuals. Infrastructure is a technology of governance that shapes and corrals people, enabling or restricting their movements and possibilities. It becomes woven through their very consciousness, internalized, taken for granted as the horizon of possibility. This link between subjectivity and the way material objects are designed and laid out was explored by the French theorist Michel Foucault, who investigated the history of how different forms of social order are shaped both by historically specific dominant ideas and by the material components that give them durability and instantiate them in space and practice.[10] In this way, material or technological objects are assembled within an existing discursive formation that helps to organize their orientation. So, for example, architectural technologies such as buildings, or populations of buildings (comprising neighborhoods, cities, and city-regions), might be read as a form of text, one that describes how that society, or, in our case, international society, has ordered, sustained, and reproduced itself. The shape of our cities, the ways that they are connected to each other and how they interface with the natural world: these features of urban life tell the story of how different human societies down the ages have organized themselves, which principles and regimes of knowledge they have sustained themselves by, and the various metabolic relationships with the environment that have powered their survival.

The dominant infrastructures and urban spaces of the past 150 years were created in an era of Western-led capitalism, a period in which two successive hegemonic liberal powers, the United Kingdom and then the United States, underwrote the international order and helped to shape it in their own image. This was also the era of carbon power, when the automobile reigned, and infrastructures and urban forms reflected this dominant metabolic and technological reality. Even the world-spanning Global City networks that emerged in the late twentieth century—that is, the tangled skeins of digital connections via submarine internet cables and satellites that connect valued urban spaces worldwide in real-time networks—were shaped by a historically particular interplay between technological innovation, urbanization, and political and economic liberalism, as the sociologist Manuel Castells outlined in his study of a historically unique "network society." The BRI, and the cities it molds and connects, will necessarily take on a very different form, not least because all of the varieties of political and economic liberalism that have characterized Western forms of modernity are explicitly rejected by those in power in China.

BRI infrastructural forms will instead express the different governing logics and developmental approaches emerging from the Chinese context, and from Chinese interactions with other states and institutions. As these logics and values begin to take material form, they will solidify particular futures. The vast labor and store of materials needed to construct infrastructure on this scale will cause new path dependencies to emerge from this moment. BRI infrastructures, once in place, will last many decades, if not centuries, leaving a powerful legacy that will be expensive and difficult to overturn. Yet as it engages with the governments, lands, and communities that the BRI touches, China too will be changed. Influence has never flowed in only one direction nor been entirely predictable, and China cannot hope to control the results of a process that involves more than 140 states and billions of people.

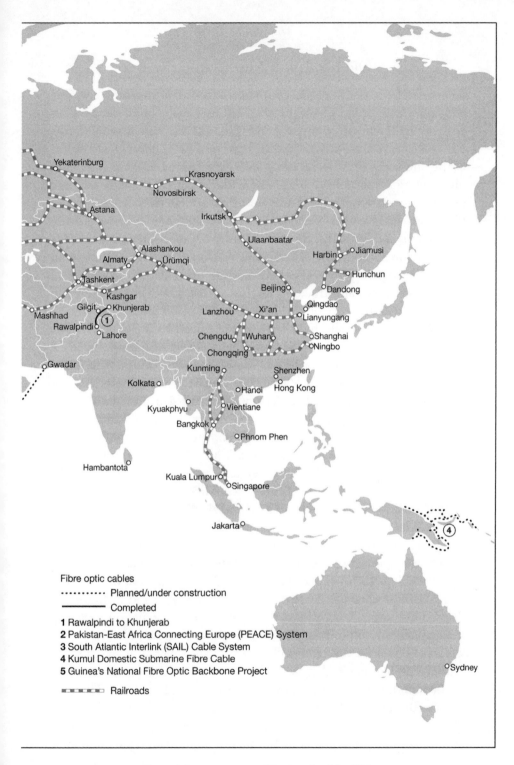

Fibre optic cables

·············· Planned/under construction

————— Completed

1 Rawalpindi to Khunjerab
2 Pakistan-East Africa Connecting Europe (PEACE) System
3 South Atlantic Interlink (SAIL) Cable System
4 Kumul Domestic Submarine Fibre Cable
5 Guinea's National Fibre Optic Backbone Project

▪▪▪▪▪▪ Railroads

Digital Connectivity and Railroads of the BRI

Old Roads and New Connections

There can be no new world. Quite apart from the dreams, ideologies, and legacies of empires past, the great Chinese geopolitical project does not confuse the world or any of its parts for a tabula rasa or vacant lands. The BRI is certainly an attempt to forge new paths through the variegated landscapes of Afro-Eurasia. Newly constructed railways, highways, pipelines, and cables have been sent snaking out from China to forge new relationships with both near and distant countries, or to connect them to the new center of economic gravity offered by Chinese growth, investment, and financing. But the BRI is also a reorientation of existing infrastructures into a new system, and many of the component parts of the BRI have been proposed or originated in other states. It connects to, and redirects, the infrastructural legacies of the past, which continue to exert a shaping influence on the present and its possibilities.

The BRI is also not simply a set of disconnected and diffuse projects, but, as we shall see, more of an overarching concept, almost a brand, in which older infrastructural legacies—Soviet railways, British Empire cities, and Sri Lankan ports—are being amalgamated and repackaged as part of China's bid for regional leadership, and enfolded into the Chinese dream. Consider Pakistan, home to empires past, today a modern nation-state, with contested territories aplenty—and an entire territory being reshaped by BRI infrastructure projects. The China-Pakistan Economic Corridor is one of the BRI's new keystone projects, with vast potential consequences for regional politics and economics. CPEC passes through or touches no small number of consequential cities: Peshawar, Islamabad, Lahore, Quetta, Multan, Hyderabad, Karachi, Gwadar, and, within China, cities such as Ürümqi and Kashgar. It seeks to generate a deepening economic symbiosis between China and Pakistan, linking China with territories stretching all the way to the Gulf of Oman via a skein of highways, natural gas pipelines, fiber-optic cables, power plants, and hydroelectric dams. This means developing new infrastructure and renovating existing infrastructure in some of the world's most politically restless lands.

In some senses, this effort follows a familiar playbook, with roads and railways at its center. A new highway crossing Xinjiang province in northwestern China to link up with the well-worn Karakoram Highway will cut through the Kunlun Mountains, crossing the Khunjerab Pass at almost 3,100 miles above sea level, in the borderlands between Kashgar (a once prosperous oasis city of the ancient Silk Roads) and Pakistan. It will also pass through the disputed territory of Kashmir, in the Gilgit Baltistan region, and on across Pakistan, to eventually join the seaports of Karachi and Gwadar. Gwadar Port City, which is being developed by China Overseas Ports Holding Company, is part of a maritime strategy to generate an alternative shipping route to those traversing the Strait of Malacca, which have long been carefully watched by the US Navy. China has also developed new rail and sea freight connectivity between Yunnan province and Karachi. These new routes now join together western China, Central Asia, and northern Pakistan into an emerging spatial and economic entity that is central to both China and Pakistan's development strategies. China's influence is reshaping Pakistan from the inside out.

At the same time, the new infrastructures of the BRI extend north-ward via the vast New Eurasian Land Bridge Economic Corridor. As part of this corridor, new rail links for freight are being created that are designed to open up new markets by traversing the vast landmass and endless steppe of Eurasia in new ways. Via a combination of new railways and existing networks, many a legacy of the faded Soviet Empire, a 7,500-mile route between Yiwu, in China's Zhejiang province, and the ports of southeastern England at the far side of Europe, has now been made viable. In less than three weeks, freight trains can now cross some of the world's most remote terrain, speeding across the deserts of north-western China, pushing through Astana (where President Xi first laid out his vision for the BRI in 2013), traversing Russia and the Ural Moun-tains, on through Belarus, Poland, Germany, and France, then diving be-neath the English Channel and up into the gentle flatlands of the southeastern coast of Britain, ending in East London's Eurohub freight terminal at Barking Station. This freshly upgraded Eurasian land route can shave half the time from the equivalent maritime shipping route.

On their long journey, these high-speed freight trains will pass through the new urban gateway of Khorgos, which straddles the border between Kazakhstan and China. A "gateway city," Khorgos is designed to streamline both the technical and political elements of cross-border trade. It is the world's largest "dry port," and the point at which cargo containers are switched from the Western standard railway gauge used in China to the wider-gauge system used throughout the former Soviet sphere. (Those trains continuing past those old Soviet areas, into Europe, are switched back to standard gauge in Belarus.) These infra-structural relics of a bygone age of Soviet power are yet another example of path dependencies and lingering power dynamics, even as they are now given bit parts in the newer infrastructural projects and ambitions of a rising twenty-first-century power.[11]

The freight trains passing through Khorgos are by no means bound exclusively for Europe; other destinations beckon from its gateway. Kazakhstan provided a crucial way station for the Silk Roads in ages past, and is now sometimes referred to as the "buckle" on the Belt and Road because of its pivot-point location. One other path from Khorgos leads to the Iranian metropolis of Tehran, the largest city in western Asia with sixteen million people. Tracking across the old Soviet rail networks for part of its journey, this route turns south, tracing the memory of the historic Silk Roads as it passes through the faded glory of Tashkent, Samarkand, and Bukhara, in Uzbekistan and Turkmenistan, on its way to the Iranian capital.

China aims to capture new markets and pull states such as Iran further into the orbit of its geopolitical power. But there is an additional motivation for these new connections. Central Asia, the Middle East, and the Persian Gulf are rich in oil and gas, access to which is a vital strategic aim of the BRI for resource-poor China. Despite its longer-term ambitions in sustainable energy and green technology, in the near term China's billion plus citizens are hungry for energy, and new infrastructural linkages to these regions can feed this need. Complementing the new road and rail links, urban gateways and ports that cut new routes across Central Asia and the Indian Ocean are capturing and relaying natural gas to China. The Central Asia–China Pipeline again builds out from an existing Soviet-era network, but via repurposed infrastructures and new conduits, China can now tap into the 265 million cubic feet of natural gas reserves from Turkmenistan's fields. Russia, which also has a deal to supply 1.3 trillion cubic feet a year of natural gas to China, watches on as the Chinese modernize and upgrade infrastructures that were once meant to undergird a glorious Soviet future, and are now reoriented toward the Chinese Dream.

Urban Corridors

At the heart of the BRI vision is a connected and integrated Eurasia. Reorganizing a space that spans an immense swath of countries and habitats begins with transportation. New highways and roads, high-speed railways, maritime ports, and urban gateways will lay down the material pathways needed to warp this space into new forms, and be the basis of a developmental strategy built around the concept of the economic corridor.[12] The guiding principle is that new pathways and forms of connectivity attract economic activity along their routes, including urban and industrial agglomeration. It is this property of economic clustering that the corridor seeks to catalyze. The grand goal is to generate a new system of cross-border production, a series of functional transnational territories that are increasingly urbanized and deeply interconnected, and that, by smoothing out barriers to movement and commerce, can also interface with wider global networks of production and trade, and so draw in further investment.

In addition to the economic land corridors designed to connect China with Europe via the Eurasian heartlands, the BRI, as currently imagined, will be complemented by the "Maritime Silk Road" linking China to the Indian Ocean via the South China Sea and opening access to the African continent, and via the Suez Canal, Europe. At the same time, a new "Digital Silk Road" will be constructed via a series of submarine cables, data centers, and Smart Cities, offering the material foundations for an alternative internet. This infrastructure will form the material basis for a selective reshaping and re-engineering of Eurasia's spatial composition via new forms of connectivity, and, inevitably, exclusion. In particular, China sees the new economic corridors as a way to reposition itself in global value chains—and so shift the world economic system in its favor.

In emergent new spaces, such as the China-Pakistan Economic Corridor, China sees itself moving from the low-cost, low-value, segments of the world economy, and being replaced in that realm by Pakistan and other recipients of BRI development in East Africa, Southeast Asia, and Eastern Europe. China needs to lift itself out of its "middle-income trap," and the corridors pass through reservoirs of cheap labor, where China could relocate some of its more basic economic activities. China could then position itself at the end of production cycles for higher-value products.[13]

Transportation infrastructures are a necessary part of this process, because they bootstrap and accelerate the development of cities along the economic corridors. By enhancing the economic growth, division of labor, and specialization that naturally accompany urban life, they increase urban agglomeration.[14] Belt and Road Cities as diverse as Khorgos, Gwadar, Ulaanbaatar, Vientiane, Astana, or Ruili have already became key nodal points along these new networks. They have begun to shift the global urban hierarchy in interesting ways—as new switching points and conduits that redirect flows of global communication, trade, information, and people. In a sense, they are rewiring the world.[15]

A 2019 analysis by the World Bank has shown that Belt and Road transport corridors have significant potential to improve trade and foreign investment for participating countries, though further policy reforms will be needed to optimize this potential while mitigating risks.[16] One of the core features of the theory of "corridor urbanism" is that it relies on forms of standardization.[17] The spaces within the corridors become formatted to particular technological or measurement standards—whether these are for IT systems and databases, or freight containers. Standardization helps to draw new borders around a "technological zone," borders that generate efficiencies within the zone, and costs for being outside of it.[18] For example, as technology and transport upgrades are realized in the low-income countries that are part of the BRI corridors, travel times will be cut and trade and investment will be increased, giving those countries an economic edge and potentially lifting tens of millions of people that live there out of poverty. China, as the standard-setter, will also win big: by increasing its social power and generating revenue streams directed toward its own industries and state coffers, China will cement its vision as a regional leader, a development benefactor for the global South.

Some BRI projects have failed, and others will likely fail. Some questions have emerged concerning construction quality, debt sustainability, economic viability, or recipient countries' political stability. Some of the free-flowing largesse of early BRI projects may well involve debts that will never be repaid, and more careful and smaller-scale investment may be the model going forward. Many projects have been downgraded or downsized, while some have been junked entirely. There have also been cases of pushback from some of the societies that have received BRI funding and expertise. The flagship project of Gwadar Port City, for example, provoked resistance from the so-called Baloch Liberation Army, which targeted Chinese nationals in a 2019 attack on the Pearl Continental Hotel in Gwadar, claiming that the new relationships with Chinese firms were extractive. Similarly, the Greek Union of Dockworkers has been heavily opposed to the leasing of Piraeus Port to the Chinese.[19]

Although the transnational corridors sketched by the BRI seem to offer the semblance of a master plan, the reality is far more piecemeal, stochastic, and ad hoc. Nowhere does the Chinese government offer a definitive list of BRI projects, and many pieces of the mosaic are arrived at by bilateral agreements, which are often opaque. Indeed, many BRI infrastructure investments are actually older projects that have been re-branded under the BRI moniker.[20] The shape and features of those previous, and still ongoing, projects complicate a pure integrity of vision.

But coherence may be neither a goal nor a virtue at this stage, for the BRI is a vision of a future in which all roads lead to China. As much a clever branding exercise as a carefully laid plan, the BRI project is about crafting a narrative of a future international order that will offer a powerful alternative to the Western-dominated world of the past few centuries (and one that, as we will see, China has linked to a particular idealized version of its own history). The elements are being laid one piece at a time, to coalesce at some point in the next decades into a very different geopolitical and geoeconomic landscape. Its aim is to capture the narrative that leads to the future—to persuade others that China's vision for international order is one they want to be part of, and to begin to make it concrete, one project at a time, across steppe, desert, and jungle. Although at this point these projects may be disconnected across the Eurasian space, they will, in the minds of the BRI strategists, together serve a new, grand vision, one that will rewire existing arrangements from the bottom up. As the late sociologist Bruno Latour has argued, this is always how societies are assembled.[21] International societies are no different.

Highways and Railways

If it is difficult to find a definitive list of BRI projects, or even a boundary for the BRI's spatial limits, perhaps some of the least visible yet most efficacious projects are the BRI's new highways, or upgrades and expansions of existing road networks.

New road networks are branching out across the Eurasian supercontinent, improving connectivity and economic efficiency, cutting new paths across steppes or flowing through new tunnels freshly bored through mountain ranges, such as in the upgrade to the Karakoram highway expansion linking Kashgar in Xinjiang province to Islamabad in central Pakistan. That iconic road forms the basis for new routes into Pakistan that will coalesce along the CPEC linking western China to Pakistan's heartlands, which are also now enhanced in their connectivity via a range of other road-building projects. Modern highways are also forming new or enhanced connections throughout Central

Asia. The northerly Mongolian capital Ulaanbaatar, once a waystation on medieval caravan routes to Beijing, and later known for its Soviet-style mass housing, has had its routes to both China and Russia upgraded. In Russia itself, the Siberian city of Novosibirsk, in days gone by an important stop and settlement on the Trans-Siberian railway, is now linked by a new highway to Urumqi, the second-largest city in Xinjiang province, at four million people; then Khorgos; and in turn the mountainous Almaty, Kazakhstan's largest and most culturally cosmopolitan city, with a population of two million. New road-building projects now crisscross Mongolia, Russia, Kazakhstan, Kyrgyzstan, Uzbekistan, and beyond.

A new 1,200-mile highway from Kunming, the capital of China's southwestern Yunnan province, which is famed for its stone forests and otherworldly landscapes, does much the same for Southeast Asia, barrelling down through the verdant tropics on the way to Bangkok. The China–Indochina Peninsula Economic Corridor, through which it passes, touches cities such as Hanoi, Vientiane, Phnom Penh, and Kuala Lumpur, before ending in Singapore. Similar road- and bridge-building initiatives are linking countries in locales as diverse as East Africa and Eastern Europe—forging new connections with billions of dollars of Chinese loans, labor, and construction expertise.

Perhaps the most visible and high-profile projects of the BRI are the spate of new railways that have been constructed. China has world-leading expertise in high-speed railway construction, partly gained through technology transfers from past partnerships with Japanese, French, and German companies.[22] New rail connectivity has become a central component of the BRI, with trains branching out from China to connect cities as far-flung as London, Tehran, and Singapore.

China has been keen to push the narrative of new connections from Chinese cities to European cities, evoking the idea that Chinese technology and innovation are conquering vast geographic areas, and redrawing the direction of travel from eastward to westward in our romantic imaginaries. The multiple BRI rail-building projects have recently been subsumed under the brand of the China Railways Express, with regular connections now linking around sixty Chinese cities to approximately fifty European cities.[23] Flagship railway projects branch out in all directions: across the Central Asia steppe via Russia and into Europe, forming the backbone of the Eurasian Land Bridge; through Uzbekistan, Kyrgyzstan, and Kazakhstan, connecting Russia's traditional backyard with new configurations of influence; within Pakistan to bolster its central status to the BRI; through Southeast Asia (under construction or planned); south from Yunnan province through Laos, Thailand, and Malaysia to Singapore; westward to Myanmar; eastward to Vietnam and Cambodia; and through East Africa in ways that both make new connections and alter long-standing regional dynamics. New railways are also extending all the way to commercial waterways, tying in the new or reconfigured ports, such as Gwadar City, Hambantota, and Piraeus.

New freight-train services now race across Eurasia and through continental Europe as far as London, shaving weeks off the journey and making these services economically viable for some mid- to high-value goods such as electronics and computers (although the extent to which China subsidizes these routes is not known). In 2018, container freight from the newly constructed dry-dock/super-rail hub of Khorgos to the German port city of Hamburg could make the trip in sixteen days. A decade earlier, the same journey took over a month.[24] The China-Europe Freight Train (CEFT) now operates over eighty routes that connect almost a hundred Chinese cities to two hundred European cities, as well as many others across Central Asia and Southeast Asia. Its growing network of large and more peripheral cities are beginning to give it a durability and resilience, as demonstrated by its ability to adapt to the 2022 conflict in Ukraine, where it has continued to move freight, and by its development of alternative routes into Europe via Azerbaijan, Georgia, and Turkey—which have brought new benefits to cities such as Tbilisi and Istanbul.[25]

Even with the new freight routes, however, railways will not be as efficient as large-scale container shipping. In 2016, rail carried only 1 percent of trade by volume from China to Europe; the vast majority instead traveled by sea in huge container ships that can each carry hundreds of times more cargo than a freight train. Many of the freight trains making the trip from China to Europe, too, return with empty containers. The built-in economic limits of rail freight suggest that China's motivations in building this skein of connectivity westward through the Eurasian heartlands are more political than economic.

The sheer scope of these and other infrastructure projects carries risks for China, including the danger that Russia will place obstacles in the way of its grand vision. The BRI, as currently imagined, will pass through Russia's traditional sphere of influence in Central Asia, and will link to the old Soviet infrastructures in this region. Russia, then, is in a pivotal position to either facilitate or scupper the connectivity plans behind the BRI. Although Russia's relative weakness has made it a reasonably compliant partner so far, its invasion of Ukraine may complicate China's broader vision of connectivity across Eurasia.

In addition, linking into Eastern European rail networks has embroiled China in the politics of Eastern Europe and generated tensions with the European Union, as it appears to seek to prize the loyalties of some European regimes away from the organization. A high-speed railway line from Belgrade to Budapest has helped to cement a Hungarian and Serbian partnership with China, which China hopes might eventually form the basis—a so-called dragon's head—of another BRI corridor pushing out from the Port of Piraeus in Greece. China's diplomatic initiative in Eastern Europe, the 17+1 grouping, an annual meeting of seventeen Eastern European states (twelve in the European Union) and China, has raised concerns for many in the European Union, because they fear the possibility of a wedge being driven by China into the very heart of the union. In 2016 and 2017, the five non-EU members of the group—Albania, Montenegro, Serbia, North Macedonia, and Bosnia and Herzegovina—received around half of China's infrastructure investment directed toward the group, primarily because China's investment does not have to play by the EU rulebook.[26] Recently the future viability of the initiative has come under question—with Lithuania pulling out, effectively making it a 16+1 group, and with calls for the EU states to maintain a united front. The tactic of dividing EU members has been used around the construction of other infrastructural components elsewhere in Europe, like Piraeus, where tensions have flared.

Seaways

The "road" in the Belt and Road is, somewhat counterintuitively for non-Chinese speakers, a seaway that is no less important than the overland routes, and indeed, is designed to connect with them at various ports to form a web of infrastructural connectivity. The Maritime Silk Road is being made manifest with an eastern route that will stretch from the South China Sea to the Indian Ocean and north through the Suez Canal to the Mediterranean Sea. A western route could also connect China to the South Pacific. China's own major seaports—Dalian, Tianjin, Shanghai, Hong Kong, Shenzhen, Xiamen, Ningbo, and Qingdao—are to be complemented by a string of ports in other strategic locations:

Colombo and the new port of Hambantota in Sri Lanka, Gwadar in Pakistan, Kyaukphyu in Myanmar, and Piraeus in Greece. There is also talk of a Polar Silk Road, as climate change opens up the possibility of shipping, drilling for oil, and harnessing wind and tidal energy on a vast scale in the polar Arctic—another reason that China is not keen to weaken its long-term strategic partnership with Russia.

As President Xi noted in his 2013 Jakarta speech, the modern Maritime Silk Road recalls the voyages of Admiral Zheng He, who traversed similar routes. The new version will be linked by a series of ports, some already built and some, for now at least, existing only as an imaginary of a new century of Chinese-led trade and commerce. Buttressed by these historical echoes, the Maritime Silk Road serves a number of rationales at once. First is the rationale of economic development. The ports of the Maritime Silk Road, whether new or upgraded, are links to China's growing trade networks, as well as to the BRI's overland transport corridors, cities, and urban regions. China is using the Maritime Silk Road to alter the structures of the global economy by redirecting commercial activity, offering alternate routes for the flows of global goods into new channels.

It is possible to see the pieces of the puzzle start to come together: Gwadar Port linking the China-Pakistan Economic Corridor to the Persian Gulf; Kyaukphyu linking the Bangladesh-China-India-Myanmar Economic Corridor to the Indian Ocean; Piraeus linking the Mediterranean Sea to the Maritime Silk Road and the Maritime Silk Road to China's new spate of railway and highway building in Eastern Europe. China now has some kind of investment in more than two-thirds of the world's major container ports.[27] These ports, and others, boost trade by increasing the use of international sea routes and improving logistics, all of which helps to lubricate financial integration. This is a core aspect of the integrated infrastructural development model discussed earlier.

A second rationale has to do with resource security for China. These are the sea lanes through which most of China's oil and gas imports travel. To have greater access to, and control over, these maritime routes is thus an important strategic objective—and one that complements China's efforts to diversify its energy infrastructures, whether by developing new pipelines to Central Asia or moving into green energy technologies.

This brings us to a third, wider strategic rationale. The Indo-Pacific is a region that is central to the world's shipping, with routes running through key choke points: the Strait of Hormuz between the Persian

Gulf and the Gulf of Oman; the Strait of Malacca between the Indian
and the Pacific Oceans; the Suez Canal linking the Red Sea to the Mediterranean Sea via Egypt. By constructing or controlling key strategic
sites with its new port strategy, China is extending its ability to have influence in these regions.

Some are deeply suspicious of China's motivations in extending its
maritime interests and developing a blue-water navy. India has expressed
concern that some of China's key deepwater ports could also serve as
naval bases for the Chinese military, supplementing the actual naval base
that China now has across the water from the multi-purpose port of
Doraleh in Djibouti.[28] Such fears are not entirely unfounded. China has
been developing its naval capabilities over the last decade, shifting its
strategic thinking and ambitions toward becoming an outward-looking
sea power. China has also been enhancing its aircraft-carrier capabilities,
and official Chinese documents have noted ambitions for maritime bases
in the very same strategic locations where China has invested in the maritime element of the BRI, including Myanmar, Sri Lanka, Tanzania, Pakistan, and the Seychelles.[29] The ability to project power across space in
this way, and the capability to secure key sea lanes and channels of communication and trade, are core components of sustaining regional order.

Indian strategists talk of Chinese ambitions to create a "string of
pearls": a series of ports whose purpose, in their minds, is strategic encirclement of India. And indeed, suspicions of China have been bringing
traditional adversaries of China together in recent years, especially over
China's more aggressive stance in the South China Sea, its disputed territorial claims over the Spratly and Senkaku Islands, and tensions over
the island of Taiwan. China's newly assertive posture has generated forms
of power-balancing behavior, with the emergence of the Quadrilateral
Security Dialogue among the United States, Japan, India, and Australia,
and the AUKUS defense partnership involving Australia, the United
Kingdom, and the United States, through which they will now share and
collaborate more in the areas of nuclear submarine technology, intelligence, cyber tech, and artificial intelligence.

Two port projects offer gateways directly into two of the economic corridors: Gwadar Port in Pakistan and Kyaukphyu Port in Myanmar. Gwadar
City, located in Balochistan province, sits on an isthmus between the coast
of Pakistan and the Gwadar promontory. With little rain and consistent
weather across seasons, the area has long been attractive for those looking
to build a port. In fact, the project to develop a port at Gwadar predates the

BRI by some time—demonstrating once again how sometimes projects initiated at earlier times and by other agents have been cleverly enrolled into the BRI narrative. China first invested in the project in 2007. Its lack of profitability led to China Overseas Ports Holding Company taking it over in 2013, two years before the announcement of the BRI.

Gwadar's centrality to the China-Pakistan Economic Corridor is apparent, as is its proximity to the oil and gas reserves of the Arabian Gulf. BRI advocates and architects hope that new pipelines will eventually join the road and rail networks of CPEC, and that the port will eventually contribute to the extensive reshaping of Pakistan taking place. Gwadar is sometimes called a potential "new Dubai": a Chinese-financed coastal city with an international airport, new tourist facilities, tax and customs breaks for investors and developers, and new residential development aimed to appeal to an influx of Chinese expats. Even if CPEC fails to achieve China's wider ambitions for the corridor, China will have gained an important maritime base by investing in Gwadar.

Another deepwater port being enhanced as part of CPEC is the $9 billion project in Kyaukphyu, a small fishing town located on a natural harbor in Myanmar. Kyaukphyu offers a way to access the offshore oil and gas fields of the Bay of Bengal without passing through the Strait of Malacca, and it cuts almost 7,500 miles from the journey. It also offers links to the Sino-Myanmar oil and gas pipeline, and opens a gateway into the Bangladesh-China-India-Myanmar Economic Corridor.[30]

But perhaps the most important and successful port project now associated with the BRI is in Piraeus, next to the ancient city of Athens in Greece. Piraeus's success, under Chinese guidance, makes it a flagship for what China wants to achieve with its Maritime Silk Road ports. Its strategic importance for China is great: it offers entrée into the markets, and the politics, of the European Union, bringing Chinese influence, and an example of the reach of the BRI, into some of the heartlands of the Western world. Greece has had a particularly strained relationship with the European Union since its bailout following the 2008 financial crisis. China has been able to leverage these tensions, turning Greece into something of an ally in recent years by offering support and patronage. China has also enhanced its influence in similar ways in countries like Hungary, Serbia, and Portugal, and even generated tensions between the United States and the United Kingdom over now-shelved plans for China's Huawei to help provide critical infrastructure in the United Kingdom's proposed 5G network.

The history of Piraeus Port helps explain China's success in developing and operating commercial infrastructure. After the collapse of global shipping in the wake of the 2008 financial crisis, Piraeus Port was gradually acquired by China Ocean Shipping Company (COSCO), a state-owned enterprise and effectively an arm of the Chinese state. By modernizing the port and rationalizing its operations, COSCO has turned Piraeus into a thriving commercial success and one of the largest ports in Europe. Container traffic through the port grew from around 400,000 containers in 2008 to almost five million in 2018. During the last five years of that period, the connectivity of the Port of Piraeus to global shipping, according to one industry study, is estimated to have increased by more than 50 percent.[31] Most trade between Europe and China is done by Greek ships.[32] China's involvement in the port means that it has gained an important ally in Greece, access to the EU market, and a link to the infrastructure projects it has been funding in Eastern Europe, including the China–Central and Eastern European rail connection between Athens and Budapest. China's investment in Mediterranean ports such as Piraeus, Trieste, and Istanbul could begin to draw trade away from the traditionally dominant port cities of northern Europe such as Rotterdam, London, Hamburg, and Antwerp. The COSCO Shipping Port Company (CSP), the division of COSCO that manages port operations, also helps direct China's investments in a number of other European ports, including not only Rotterdam and Antwerp, but also Zeebrugge, Belgium; Savona, Italy; Valencia and Bilbao, Spain; and Kumport, Turkey.[33]

Some of China's other port investments have been less successful, at least in the short term. Consider Hambantota, in Sri Lanka. Like Piraeus, Hambantota did not originate as a Chinese initiative, and it predated the BRI. It was a project dreamed up by the Sri Lankan government, which contracted China Merchants Group, a Chinese state-owned enterprise, to build the port. When Hambantota opened in 2010, it was hoped that it could rival and complement the established port of Colombo, 150 miles away on the Sri Lankan coast. But the existence of Colombo has meant that Hambantota has remained unprofitable and, for some, a white elephant. Hambantota has also come to symbolize one of the key criticisms of the BRI: that it is a subtle form of debt diplomacy, whereby China funds projects that the recipient regimes cannot hope to pay back, in order to extract important strategic concessions when the loans go bad.

Such was the fate of Hambantota in 2018, when the Sri Lankan government's debt on the project was canceled in return for a deal in which

China would control the port and its connecting infrastructure on a ninety-nine-year lease, a term reminiscent of Britain's lease of Hong Kong in an earlier period of merchant—and eventually gunship—colonialism. This arrangement raised the alarm throughout the region and beyond. The deal inspired deep concern in India, which saw China as gaining a key foothold with its new strategic asset, and a fiery denunciation of Chinese "debt diplomacy" from then US vice president Mike Pence.

Despite these strategic implications, China's long-term hopes for the port may be more in line with the vision of peaceful commercial maritime trade that Xi evoked in his Jakarta speech, with its echoes of awe and respect for Chinese technology and centrality. China has not given up on Hambantota as a commercial success; instead it is attracting new investment that China hopes will one day turn the port into a successful transhipment and resupply hub along the Indian Ocean stretch of the Maritime Silk Road. Shipping traffic through the port is on the rise, and India and Oman have contracts to build a $3.85 billion oil refinery at Hambantota. As with all aspects of the BRI, China's vision is a long one; a hopeful gaze into a future, decades hence, in which the infrastructural assets being laid down now will create a new era of prosperity and cooperation for the peoples of Eurasia, under the guiding hand of Chinese leadership and patronage.

Take, as another example, the yet-to-be-built port of Bagamoyo, in Tanzania. Despite being an idea that has been on the drawing board for some time, also at the prompting not of China but of the Tanzanian government, it was at one point scooped up into the BRI brand. Construction on the port began in 2015, but later stalled when a new government in Dodoma came in—and it has yet to restart after disagreements between China and Tanzania. But perhaps Bagamoyo Port will be realized in the future. The newly elected president Samia Suluhu Hassan promised in 2021 that the project would be revived—and China is keen for the work to begin.[34]

As with the port in Piraeus, the Bagamoyo Port project draws on a long history of trade and commerce. The town was once one of the largest ports in Africa; a hub for the East African maritime trade routes between the fifteenth and nineteenth centuries, trafficking not just goods such as fish, salt, and ivory, but also slaves en route to the auctions on Zanzibar. The original plans for Bagamoyo, announced jointly in 2013 by the then president Kikwete and President Xi, would have had China Merchant Group head up the project, and turn the entire region around the town into a special economic zone, which in turn would facilitate the building of new industrial parks and other urban development projects.³⁵ Bagamoyo, in line with other BRI-style thinking, would be a gateway into the African continent, and its rich supply of resources, which China needs. (China has already funded pipelines in Tanzania, which has valuable gas reserves.) The new infrastructure around Bagamoyo would also provide links to minerals and metals mined in the Republic of Congo and Uganda, resources that have long drawn China's interest, and open up the possibility of infrastructural connectivity throughout the region.

China already had strong and long-standing patronage relationships in the region as the leader of the non-aligned movement in the Cold War, and will continue to be a big player in the region. In the 1960s, for example, China developed the standard-gauge railway system, and it has recently added to this with the Mombasa-Nairobi Railway in Kenya, one of the largest recipients of BRI funding to date. Mombasa is a regional economic hub, through which 80 percent of East Africa's trade passes. Another port project, at Lamu, farther along the coast, will add even more capacity. And more railway construction is extending northward in a bid to join up more of the East African coast; in particular, to connect Kenya with Ethiopia and South Sudan. The Addis Ababa–Djibouti Railway connects up the new African Union Headquarters, constructed in the Ethiopian capital with Chinese money and labor as a "gift to Africa"; a building whose design of interlocking hands symbolizes the increasingly tight embrace of China and Africa in the twenty-first century. The end game is a new transnational economic corridor—the LAPSSET—that will traverse the Port of Lamu, South Sudan, and Ethiopia.³⁶ This would then have the potential to link, via a land bridge through the African Great Lakes region, other corridors such as the East Africa Northern Corridor and perhaps especially the East Africa Central Corridor, which will eventually bring landlocked Uganda rail routes to the sea. Taken together, these initiatives show East Africa's pivot toward China's growing influence.

The port project of Bagamoyo, whether or not it is completed, reveals certain characteristics of the BRI infrastructure agenda. The BRI rolls up the hopes and aspirations of many other states, and many of the projects are not initiated by China, but rather are folded into the overall vision. This means that many of these projects are outside the control of China, and the vicissitudes of domestic politics in the states in which projects are constructed—or stall—make Chinese investments risky and sometimes prone to failure or rejection. China's control over a plan this big—or small, as we shall see in Chapter 3 in the case of the Kotokuraba Market in Cape Coast, Ghana—has limits. But the BRI is so new, with its revealed vision a mere decade old now, that it can only be evaluated in motion—as a wide-ranging attempt at international-order building on a gigantic scale and over a long time span. Some projects will not turn out the way they are currently planned. But the overall reshaping of geopolitical and geoeconomic flows and structures remains the long-term core of the vision. The port projects of the Maritime Silk Road are strategically placed gateways that are designed to open up entire regions that have been or could be reshaped by Chinese infrastructure projects, including the existing economic corridors of the BRI and the new ones that may emerge because of its impact. The vision has a coherent, if open, logic; and the infrastructural components are the ways in which the Chinese Dream will begin to become reality.

Digital Silk Roads

Although the Silk Roads evoke romantic images of centuries gone by, some of the pathways of the twenty-first-century Silk Road have little historical precedent. The concept of *wu tong*, or connectivity, that underpins the BRI does not refer simply to physical transport links, but also to communication and culture—and in the contemporary world, that means digital architectures.

In 2015, two years after his Astana and Jakarta speeches announcing the BRI, President Xi revealed plans for a Digital Silk Road. As with other parts of the BRI's infrastructure, the "plan" is sketchy and open-ended, offering general Chinese support, investment, expertise, and development assistance to those societies that want to be affiliated with the BRI. The Digital Silk Road has become a major part of China's industrial development strategy. But it is much more than this. It is also a mechanism to spread Chinese expertise and standards abroad, to win market share for its state-owned enterprises, and to develop governance infrastructures that incorporate Chinese norms and values—all in an effort to gradually tie in other states to China's evolving system of global governance. This work is already under way. Many cities in East Africa, for example, are experiencing significant expansions in both digital infrastructure—to include submarine and underground fiber-optic cables—as well as associated social and commercial ecosystems.[37] A decade ago, Kigali and Nairobi were dubbed "silicon savannahs" for their active approaches to enhancing their local digital ecosystems and their Smart City approaches, with Kigali home to more than forty startup accelerators. The technical objects, models, and standards that China is developing, if adopted by other states, have already shaped and will further shape the development of social norms, values, and mores across the globe, including in developing nations where urbanization is proceeding the fastest.

The older connectivity technologies of port, road, and rail are already becoming entwined with the new digital architectures, such as fiber-optic cables, 5G networks, data centers, satellite constellations, and e-commerce platforms. The Silk Roads of cyberspace are woven through the emerging urban landscapes, folded into the forms of digitally integrated Smart Cities, and so are generating new economic, political, and social spaces of interaction, value, and control. The Smart City is an urban form that is taking shape around the world in response to the convergence of these new technologies, but along the Digital Silk Road, China's use and development of new technologies will give these Smart Cities a distinctive flavor. Not simply an additional path through cyberspace, the Digital Silk Road is also providing the technical foundations for new forms of governance; not just connectivity, but also subtle forms of control.[38] Borrowing from the language of the Chinese Dream, the Digital Silk Road is framed as a "community of shared destiny in cyberspace." But what sort of digital destiny will it be?

The development of the internet and digital communications technologies has been central to a profound reshaping of politics, economics, and society over the past few decades. As with other technologies, such infrastructures are not neutral, but are instead shaped by the societies in which they arise or are implemented. In the 1990s, when the revolutionary effects of the internet on society were just beginning to be felt, the urban sociologist Manuel Castells made such an argument when he analyzed how the new digital information technologies were beginning to change economic and social practices. Castells described the emergence of what he called the "network society," which was rapidly reconfiguring the ways in which people live and work by generating the ability to compress space and time—that is, by offering new experiences of social simultaneity despite individuals being in physically non-contiguous locations around the globe. This generated a new arena for social interaction that he called the "space of flows."[39]

The new digital technologies, Castells was keen to point out, had a technical geography. Cyberspace did not float freely in the ether: it relied on technical objects and components rooted physically in the world: undersea cables, data centers, server farms, satellite networks (or, as a US senator put it, more colloquially, tubes). Importantly to Castells, given his background in urban form and social relations, these components were also threaded through cities and urban spaces, connecting certain high-value locales, such as the high-speed trading networks linking Wall Street and London, while disconnecting other neighborhoods. Specific geographies of connection and disconnection were thus created, often with international logics rather than national ones, as the new space of flows jumped territorial borders and scales. This new technical system was, in part, responsible for the new urban form of the Global City: a scale-jumping urban entity that generated new transnational networks, new forms of inclusion and exclusion, powered by the infrastructure of a new planet-spanning machine. In other words, the cities of late twentieth-century and early twenty-first-century financial capitalism, of both the apogee and perhaps the twilight of American hegemony, were very much shaped by digital connectivity and the way it was rooted in a particular political culture.

China's emerging Digital Silk Road should be considered in a similar fashion. It too is an evolving transnational machine, being constructed before our very eyes. It too will draw its shape and form from the society that designs its technical components, logics, and selective geography of connectivity. Its own "space of flows" may come to look very different from the internet that gestated and developed within American society, piecemeal and in stages from the 1960s onward, taking its networked form not only from the cultures of personal freedom developing in US university campuses, but also from the decentralized, networked technologies and economic models that looked to break down state hierarchies and controls financed by venture capitalists who funded early startups.[40]

The context for the Digital Silk Roads is more complex than that of the original internet, for it has as its underlying technical base this earlier technological model, shaped in the American context. China's society, in which such technologies are now being reshaped, is instead highly centralized, lacking a strong culture of personal freedom and liberalism, and missing the kind of private enterprise model that shaped the internet's early days. As China gazes westward, it hopes to build an infrastructure of digital connectivity that can extend the values and social practices of the Chinese state outward transnationally, across different regions and societies: shaping the ways people connect to the internet, the content they have access to, and even the very fabric of Smart Cities as they develop across Afro-Eurasia. How, then, will China's new efforts to construct digital networks outside of its own territory shape a new digital environment, one that integrates sensors, data, artificial intelligence, and algorithms? How will these infrastructures embed new values, principles, opportunities, and even subjectivities for a large swath of the world's population, millions if not billions of people, and with what consequences?

There is an unresolved contradiction lurking in the very foundations of the digital infrastructures that China is unfurling: technologies originally built on openness, freedom, and decentralization have now been yoked to a technical architecture based on a very different set of cultural and political values. It was once hoped in the West that the advent of these technologies would permanently weaken illiberal regimes, including China itself, as the increased availability of information to individuals undermined state control. But in recent years these hopes have been dashed. The Arab Spring became the Arab Winter. Early hopes for the emancipatory potential of the internet have turned to fear that the same technologies are being increasingly used for surveillance, control, and the spreading of disinformation, even in the Western heartlands where the technology first emerged.[41]

China keeps tight control over the flow of information and content that reaches its own domestic audience through what has come to be called the Great Firewall—named to bring to mind the Great Wall that once helped to secure China's borders from the nomadic tribes of the northern steppes. In effect, the Chinese domestic internet involves extreme network hierarchy. Access to the domestic network from outside is controlled by China's three big state-owned telecom companies: China Telecom, China Unicom, and China Mobile. These three companies control the internet exchange points, through which all incoming traffic must pass. Companies like Google, which dominate in other markets, are banned in China. The "big three" monitor and censor unwanted information and content. They are aided by two million state-employed censors, who in turn are augmented by an army of twenty million volunteers. New techniques based on machine learning are also being harnessed to control information flows, and weed out proscribed material, while an array of other sophisticated tools are being deployed to detect virtual private networks, hijack and redirect search requests, and examine individual data packets.[42] Furthermore, domestic search engines, such as Sina Weibo or Weixin, are subject to government oversight and restrictions. Research also shows that the citizens of large, linguistically isolated countries such as China tend not to move away from sites with domestically relevant content. All of this, in combination with the extreme network hierarchical structure of the Chinese internet, means that within China it is quite possible to control and shape the political narrative.[43]

This tight domestic control, however, is in tension with China's desire to grow its share of the global communications market and build its Digital Silk Road. The ambition to be at the heart of the "fourth industrial revolution," to export its own technologies, and to offer global leadership, presents a dilemma to the CCP about how to balance openness and control. More connectivity tends to make the tight control that the CCP wields at home more problematic. How to balance global engagement and influence, without opening up to all sorts of uncontrolled possibilities and new lines of flight? This fundamental tension is currently playing itself out—and is perhaps in an early stage. One possibility is that with its ambitions for the Digital Silk Road, China seems set to accelerate a technical fragmentation of the internet, splitting off its version from those of rival geopolitical systems.

The philosopher Benjamin Bratton refers to the technical systems of planetary-scale computation that have emerged in recent decades as "the stack." The stack consists of numerous layers and components that have become ubiquitous throughout society, including cloud platforms, Smart Cities, the internet of things, universal address systems, and sensor grids. These systems provide new layers and mechanisms of governance, but also, for Bratton, have begun insidiously to transform the very meaning of sovereignty itself. Different internets mean different stacks. The scale of the Digital Silk Road is transcontinental and qualifies as an emergent "stack," which in turn implies that Chinese-dominated governance and influence will extend well beyond its own territorial borders. This makes the Digital Silk Road perhaps even more significant than the other more traditional infrastructures of road, rail, and port that we have discussed so far. It also suggests that the Digital Silk Road could be the major conduit for dispersing the forms of transnational and tributary-style visions of world order that China wants to move toward with the BRI: *tianxia* in cyberspace. This is not some disembodied or purely ideational process: as we have argued, geopolitical power is expressed and extended in the relationships between dominant states and historically specific urban forms and infrastructures. Cities are the fabric through which governance is woven. Digitally connected and augmented Belt and Road Cities will be the material expression of any Chinese-led form of international society, just as in recent decades supercharged Global Cities were the expression and material framework for a system of highly financialized capitalism underpinned by US power.

But the stack has to be built, and immense effort, facilitated by a series of investments and agreements, has gone into constructing its foundations using the labor and expertise of Chinese state-owned firms and state-backed "national champions" (companies that get special support for extending their reach into foreign environments). Here companies such as Huawei have been instrumental in doing the hard and difficult graft, constructing new layers of digital infrastructure in often dangerous and inhospitable foreign locales and remote landscapes. They have shown a true pioneer spirit in developing the technical components, such as submarine fiber-optic cables and wireless networks, across much of the global South. By 2019 Huawei had been instrumental in building around 70 percent of Africa's entire 4G network.[44]

A key component of this strategy is to develop digital infrastructure in places that are currently communication "black holes," where no private providers have been willing to lay down infrastructure, and where local governments do not have the capacity. This is one of the benefits of China's state-driven approach—but one that is, of course, about politics as well as profit. So far, China has laid down $7 billion in loans and foreign direct investment for fiber-optic cables, $10 billion for e-commerce and mobile payment systems, and hundreds of billions more for smart-city projects. The funding has come from a combination of Chinese development banks (such as the Export-Import Bank of China, and the China Development Bank) and state-owned commercial banks. Chinese companies like Huawei, ZTE, Alibaba, or Baidu benefit directly from the Digital Silk Road umbrella: recipient states use the loans and investment to bring in Chinese companies to construct the telecommunications networks, smart cities, cloud computing, data centers, and digital payment platforms, areas in which they have developed significant expertise in the past decade. In return, they use the streets of foreign cities to experiment with new apps and collect data on users' experience. Russia has developed the Rostelecom network with a $600 million Chinese loan, Indian telecom operators received $2.5 billion worth of loans for hardware and equipment, while African states have borrowed over $1 billion.

Part of the rationale for this huge construction effort is that most new population growth will be in the global South. By 2050, around half of all global population growth is projected to occur in Africa alone. At the same time, in its *Agenda 2063*—the guiding strategic document for the continent's development—the African Union (AU) identified broadband development as an integral part of economic growth. The AU's associated Programme for Infrastructure Development in Africa (PIDA) is currently tracking over one hundred digital or information and communication technology development projects.[45] Such a focus on emerging markets increases the chances not only of Chinese companies locking in market share, but also of their products and technical standards becoming universal. There is a longer-term strategy at work here to disseminate China's own technologies and technological standards abroad, and thus to lock large areas of the planet into a technological system in which it has centrality. This is a parallel system to that which has been developed in the West and with which the West has locked in current technical standards and the very significant revenue streams that accrue with such control. This battle for the future of planetary-scale communications and computational systems will help to define international governance and the nature of international society in the decades to come.

Many countries in the West are unable to construct such technical systems on their own—and here China has tried to enter these markets, generating recent diplomatic tensions. For example, the Chinese firm Huawei became involved in the construction of the United Kingdom's 5G network, a situation that led to serious diplomatic and policy divisions between the United Kingdom and the United States, with the United Kingdom eventually bowing to pressure to remove Huawei's technology from its system and from future plans.

For countries in the developing world, the appeal of using Chinese investment and expertise to build these infrastructures is even more compelling. Western states have missed an enormous strategic opportunity by leaving much of the developing world open to China to come in to fund and construct its critical digital infrastructure systems and, in the process, entrench its own technologies, models, legal norms, and standards. Chinese companies also benefit from concessional credit lines that allow them to undercut foreign competition. Across the BRI, Chinese companies such as Huawei have been building out such infrastructures in countries such as South Africa, Egypt, Nigeria, Zambia, Uganda, Tanzania, Zimbabwe, Kenya, Indonesia, and Tunisia. These are the kind of trends the West will need to counteract if it is to compete successfully with China in the infrastructural geopolitics of the global South.

The basis of transnational digital connectivity today is submarine fiber-optic cable networks. China has come late to this party, but is now busily constructing a number of major submarine fiber-optic cables that can form the basis for its alternative internet. Huawei Marine is central to many of these projects. Already completed is the China-Pakistan Fiber Optic Project that runs along CPEC; the next step is to finish the Pakistan–East Africa Connecting Europe (PEACE) System, a 7,500-mile set of subsea connections from Pakistan to countries along the East African coast. Other submarine cable projects include the 3,600-mile South Atlantic Interlink (SAIL) Cable System, which joins Kribi in Cameroon with Fortaleza in Brazil and was completed in 2018; the Kumul Domestic Submarine Fiber Cable, which runs through Indonesia and Papua New Guinea; and the 2,800-mile fiber-optic Guinea Backbone Network, which will link together Guinean cities and make the African nation the digital gateway for the interconnection of West Africa, as part of the larger Smart Africa Project.[46]

Additionally, China is developing a constellation of over thirty satellites that will provide China with an alternative to its reliance on the three main global navigation systems (US-led GPS, the European Union's GALILEO, and Russia's GLONASS). The BeiDou Navigation Satellite System now has coverage in over 165 cities worldwide. China aims to extend this system to more than sixty of its BRI partners.[47]

China's move into global navigation systems is vital because of the integration of global positioning into so many components of the emerging "internet of things": from military applications, to Smart Cities, autonomous vehicles, smart power grids, and personal devices. Without its own system, China would have to rely on other Great Powers for these critical capabilities—a position that it could not accept. Instead, China's global positioning system also aligns broadly with the emerging BRI core—Pakistan, Russia, and Nigeria are all host reference states, and BRI infrastructures will integrate Chinese satellite navigation systems into their operations. Close partners that buy these systems may well be enrolling in a network on which they will be dependent for decades to come, and China will gain structural power and political and economic leverage as a result. As China breaks free of dependence on Western-dominated technological systems, other states are increasing their dependence on China.

Indeed, the United States, for so long the dominant force in developing the internet and thus benefiting from global flows of data, technology, talent, and trade, is now waking up to the fact that it is in a battle over the future of the internet's architecture.[48] The US government recently put pressure on Google and Facebook to adjust the planned route of their new 11,000-mile Pacific Light Cable Network that connects Los Angeles to Taiwan and the Philippines, so that it does not pass through Hong Kong as had been originally planned. The recent crackdown in the city by the Chinese regime over pro-democracy protests, and the advent of the new Hong Kong Security Law, have led to fears that the new infrastructure will be vulnerable to Chinese espionage.[49] Hong Kong, a former lynchpin of the Global City network that provided technical support for the liberal globalization that began in the 1990s, now finds itself facing disconnection from those past linkages, and pressure to reorient to the Belt and Road model. This shift in Hong Kong, perhaps the most striking example of a core city in the liberal world's Global City network transforming into a Belt and Road city as a result of Chinese power, illuminates the growing fault lines between openness and control, between personal freedom and the gaze of the authoritarian state.

This is a new age of competition in the realm of geopolitical infrastructure, and the stakes are high. But technology does not stand still. China's huge effort to lay the submarine backbone of an alternative internet over the past decade may soon be superseded by new developments in satellite systems. In particular, there is now a move to develop huge constellations of low earth orbit satellites (LEOs), which have the potential to provide broadband connectivity to large swaths of unconnected or difficult-to-connect populations. Elon Musk's SpaceX, in collaboration with the US space agency NASA, has plans to develop a twelve-thousand-strong constellation of LEOs by 2027. What is emerging here is a competition over very different models—profit-driven market capitalism led by private enterprise, in looser association with government and universities, versus state-led and directed capitalism, with firms and institutions tied tightly into national political agendas.

Alongside the physical infrastructure—the submarine cables, satellite systems, data centers, and telecommunications networks—there is the increasing possibility that different technical architectures and standards than those that prevail now will dominate the twenty-first-century version of the internet. Engineers and technicians from Huawei have been working on a new internet protocol (IP) system that offers a very different model of connectivity. Whereas the original internet that emerged out of North America and Europe is a largely unregulated, bottom-up, adaptable, and modular system—one largely constructed and shaped by big private companies such as Google, Facebook, Apple, and Amazon, and funded by venture capital—the system proposed by China is its very antithesis. It would be state-led, top-down, emphasizing control and placing state power and national sovereignty at the heart of its paradigm. China calls this model "cyber-sovereignty," and it aligns with its model for governing Chinese society, which includes much higher levels of censorship, surveillance, monitoring, and carefully controlled access.

In China, the eye of the state is everywhere—and it is watchful. Privacy and freedom are in short supply. China's urban surveillance system, Skynet, is composed of tens of thousands of cameras and sensors that can track citizens going about their daily lives, viewing them from rooftops, doorways, intersections, and public squares. China's cities are increasingly dotted with a multitude of sleepless eyes. And it is not only the state that can observe through these portals—many of the system's feeds are open to residents, who can observe their neighbors' behavior and report on undesirable activities.

Also in operation are tools for facial recognition, gait recognition, crowd analysis, and temperature sensing. These tools could help to spot symptoms of disease, people gathering for political protests, or unusual behavior from individuals. Used in service of the Chinese state, these technologies are, collectively, being pitched as a foundation of the so-called Safe City—a form of digital Smart City that is increasingly marketed abroad by Chinese companies such as Huawei, ZTE, Hikvision, and Dahua as offering a suite of urban "solutions." And there is no doubt that there is great potential for using sensing, monitoring, big-data gathering, and analytical technical tools to improve urban life in many ways, including more efficient use of resources; greater public safety; improvements to public health; traffic regulation; energy consumption and sustainability; and crisis management and response.[50] Many countries are struggling to balance these benefits of the Smart City and the implications for privacy. In the wake of the COVID-19 pandemic, however, the doors have swung wide open for deeper penetration of these technologies into urban spaces and social life in many countries, and here the Chinese state, and others, have taken full advantage. As has often been the case in history, a state of emergency or state of exception has been used to override long-held norms—in this case facilitating the greater encroachment of the state ever further into the realms of the community and the individual.

Another disturbing example of the use of these surveillance and control technologies has been the fate of the majority Muslim population of Kashgar, in China's western desert province of Xinjian. Kashgar, a vital trading outpost of the ancient Silk Roads, is today situated at a critical strategic point along the BRI, as a gateway to the regional neighbors of Central Asia that the BRI hopes to cultivate. But as a showcase for a Chinese-led future order, the city offers a dystopian warning. Home to around half a million people, 85 percent of them Muslim Uyghurs—a Turkic-speaking minority whose cultural differences China has sought to suppress after terrorist attacks in 2008 and 2011—Kashgar has become an extreme example of a surveillance city. Surveillance cameras, facial recognition scans, checkpoints, ID cards, and digital-control centers have become part of the fabric of everyday life, while the texture of the city, an ancient holy site full of mosques, has been disrupted and reconstructed to facilitate control.[51]

Indeed, the same technologies used in Kashgar can now be found in many cities around the world. Chinese firms have exported Smart City–style technologies and services to more than one hundred countries, including the United States. The Pakistani city of Lahore, and the Kenyan cities of Nairobi and Mombasa, have bought systems that include thousands of surveillance cameras. Hikvision and Dahua have managed to capture over 40 percent of the global market for surveillance cameras. How these technologies will play out in other contexts is an open question. The contradiction, if it is a contradiction, remains. At home, as Jonathan Hillman argues, "the CCP is building a society in which any challenge to its rule, including protests of any scale, can be cut down before it grows. Every tool—next generation networks, connected devices, cloud computing, is being aimed at that goal."[52] At the same time, China wants to be the world's supplier of these technologies, and aspires to lead an international society of which they will be part of its socio-technical fabric. China's 14th Five-Year Plan for the period 2021–2026 laid out the ambition to build an "integrated network of communications, earth observation and navigation satellites." Such an ambition, should it be realized, would immensely enhance China's ability to spread its norms, values, and influence abroad. Will other states buy into this offering—which increasingly looks like not simply a commercial choice, but a political one about the future socio-technical basis and foundations of international order? And how will other powers, with other values, respond to China's push to build much of the world's digital infrastructure?

The ongoing experiences and lessons in the development of this model in Chinese cities are now being deployed in diverse ways in cities across BRI corridors and beyond. In 2017, Huawei and the government of Malaysia agreed to cooperate to develop public security and Smart City programs for Malaysian cities, including the development of an associated technology lab in Kuala Lumpur. In 2018, when Alibaba's cloud-computing arm announced the first overseas implementation of its Smart City platform, the so-called ET City Brain, it was also to Kuala Lumpur. In 2019, Serbian officials announced the installation of a thousand cameras with advanced facial and license-plate recognition software at eight hundred locations in Belgrade, a city of fewer than 1.5 million residents. The program, under the Safe City Project, was to be conducted in cooperation with Huawei. Over the past decade, Huawei, ZTE, and other Chinese firms have deployed security and surveillance technology in Ecuador's largest cities, including Cuenca, Guayaquil, and the capital, Quito. The more than 3,500 cameras associated with the program are reported to have facial and license-plate recognition capability. Ecuadorian experts and officials have also traveled to China to visit surveillance laboratories.

The deployment of digital urban surveillance remains, in part, a local project. Local municipal governments in Belgrade, Quito, and Kuala Lumpur, even when preempted by their national governments, operate alongside the programs. But the use of such surveillance systems, which are tied to Chinese firms in nations with strong links to the BRI, is also part of a larger effort to remake international order. These technologies change the facts on the ground when it comes to privacy and individual rights. But China is also working to change the relevant rules of the road at international organizations. China has held leadership roles in the International Standards Organization / International Electrotechnical Commission Joint Technical Commission 1 working group on Smart Cities, and has hosted at least three of the organization's meetings. In recent years, too, China has increased its diplomatic activity in and attention to the International Telecommunications Union (ITU), the United Nations agency charged with establishing common standards for telecommunications technologies. It has increased its participation and donor funding to the agency, and is now seeking its stamp of approval for its new internet protocol. This is a play for international recognition: the legitimacy conferred by the ITU is an important consideration for countries adopting these systems. The ITU was previously dominated by North America, Europe, and Japan, but in the past few years it has had much more involvement by China and South Korea. China sees its participation as an important part of its bid to convince the world to accept its capacity for global leadership.

China has moved from a defensive stance in relation to the internet—seeking to block access to, and censor content of, foreign websites through its Great Firewall—to actively promoting an alternative internet system as an international standard. Already China has helped to develop systems for Russia, Iran, and Saudi Arabia that offer the ability to partially disconnect from the global web. Russia has tried to make use of this feature to control information domestically in the wake of its invasion of Ukraine.

The Digital Silk Road, then, offers states a choice: the older, more chaotic and decentralized, largely privately run internet, and a Chinese-constructed system that emphasizes digital sovereignty; state control over service providers, content, and access; as well as new censorship tools and the capacity to monitor individuals and the devices they use to connect. For many authoritarian regimes, the Chinese version is an appealing prospect, given that control over the narratives, discourses, norms and values of society are now heavily influenced by digital spaces. Given the digital infrastructure investment gap in large parts of the developing world, and, indeed, in some parts of the developed world, there will be many ways for China to spread this system.

It was once thought—hoped, perhaps—that the opening up of China to global flows of information would result in a liberalization of Chinese society and politics. This was one of the tenets of US foreign policy for decades, and one of the great analytical errors of the past fifty years. It is not just that the assumptions about liberalization never came to pass. In their belief in the gospel of liberalism, multiple US administrations, and major Western companies—such as Nortel, Cisco, and IBM—partnered and collaborated with Chinese companies in ways that enabled the Chinese to learn from them; to transfer the technology, intellectual property, and business models; and then, with the aid of Chinese state backing, undercut and outcompete those companies in markets around the world (including, in some cases, the US domestic market). Decades of openness based on faith in the free market has now led to a new and unexpected peer-level competitor for geopolitical dominance. In retrospect, it seems that an incumbent hegemonic power has provided the conditions and assistance to generate its own challenger.

So we seem to be moving in a direction unanticipated at the height of US unipolarity and globalization in the 1990s—when the Clinton administration actively encouraged technical collaboration with Chinese firms as a way into China's vast developing domestic market. Authoritarian regimes are using these capacities for greater social control of populations, and new technologies of surveillance and control, such as facial recognition and social credit rankings, are being embedded in the urban infrastructures of evolving Smart Cities. What the BRI offers is the possibility that models of technological social control developed in domestic Chinese society will be adopted by other states as a way to control their own populations. There are already examples of the extension of these technologies to states such as Egypt, Zambia, Zimbabwe, and Ecuador.[53] In this context the current travails of Hong Kong are being carefully watched.

There is the distinct possibility that these trends will take us in the direction of a "splinternet"—a carving out of two distinctive sociotechnical systemic blocs, each dominated by very different Great Powers, with very different domestic political, social, and economic models—of which digital connectivity is a fundamental component. Analysts talk of a potential "splitting of the root" of the core global internet, which is built on thirteen root servers that house the Domain Name System—the internet's address book. This would occur if China stopped using these global servers and migrated to its own system. This "splinternet" would be a world of diverging technical systems, each enclosing its own flows of information and data—and, potentially, its own universe of alternative narratives, where power and control can generate their own truths.

In the early years of the original internet, a US-based group advocating for self-government of the growing network issued a Declaration of the Independence of Cyberspace. From the vantage point of three decades later, their hope for a virtual space that would remain free of state control and corporate and financial power seems hopelessly naive, even if their fears were prescient. Corporate power underpins the original internet, while in other states its openness is increasingly opposed in the name of "cyber-sovereignty." China is the one state with enough power and resources to try to develop an alternative system.

Toward an "Ecological Civilization"?

The new infrastructures of the BRI, and the cities that they connect, will need to be powered. The billions of lives across the Afro-Eurasian lands are hungry for energy and resources. But it is now clear, as the threat of anthropogenic climate change looms ever greater, that for developing nations today to follow the same developmental path forged by the West as it industrialized would be catastrophic for all. Indeed, this has been long recognized within Chinese policy circles, and today there is a realization that the past decades of rapid economic development have come at great cost to China's own environment. A new model must be found that secures the energy that China and its neighbors need, while steering clear of the carbon-extraction based models of the past; a new model that recalibrates the relationship between modern society and the earth's physical systems and its biodiversity.

It is in the search for such a model that China has been developing the concept of an "ecological civilization." This idea emerged in Chinese policy thinking in the early 1990s, appearing in government white papers. It was then mentioned by President Hu Jintao in 2007 in a speech that argued for the concept to be a guiding principle for the future of Chinese socialism.[54] It first became one of the core goals of China's development plan at the 18th National Congress of the CCP in 2012, and was affirmed ten years later at the 20th National Congress. Part of *Xi Jinping's Thought on Socialism with Chinese Characteristics for a New Era*, this concept overlaps existing ideas of sustainable development; for example, it has been offered as part of China's contribution to meeting the 2030 United Nations sustainable development goals (SDGs). The ecological civilization idea, however, is considered much more than a contribution to the SDGs. China also means it to be something more; something that draws uniquely on not only Chinese philosophy and experience, but also what it sees as its own unique political system. It consciously breaks with Western development discourse and ideology around sustainable development to stress Chinese "characteristics." It has been linked specifically to the BRI—sometimes the term Green Silk Road has been used. And importantly for our argument here, cities are at the core of this vision (as, indeed, they must be, for any solution to the climate crisis must focus on cities, where most people live, most energy and resources are consumed, and most emissions are generated). Ecological civilization "pilot cities," such as the subtropical city of Guiyang, have been experimented with, alongside larger ambitions to transform whole city regions.

But perhaps today the ecological civilization idea is most important for its potential to showcase Chinese leadership within an emerging international society and, by extension, to begin to shift the norms of that international society to be more in line with those of Chinese domestic society. If China can get its strategy in this area right, it will have gone a long way toward developing the leadership and legitimacy it craves.[55] The concept, as it develops in both theory and practice, could become embedded in its vision for a "community of common destiny" that is guided by a core of Chinese wisdom and placed at the heart of a co-evolving international system of mutual development (more on this in Chapter 5). Successfully navigating the transition to a post-carbon economy and forging a new relationship between modern society and the natural world will be key—just as it will be for China's peer competitors. This is a litmus test for China's leadership ambitions. If the BRI can be a vehicle to truly build an ecological civilization—and, as yet, there is still a great deal of conceptual vagueness about what this might look like—then this would be a great boon to the world.[56] But this aspiration is still a long way from becoming reality. The present state of affairs is still one of voracious carbon extraction, and China, like all states, is caught somewhere between the unsustainable present and an unknown future.

China is, for its vast size, a resource-poor country. One of the strategic motivations for the BRI is to secure energy supplies, via access to the vast energy reserves and raw materials of Eurasia. Among the BRI's many infrastructural projects are new pipelines, new dams, and new power grids. There are BRI-related hydroelectric dam projects in Cambodia, Pakistan, Uganda, Tajikistan, Georgia, Myanmar, and Indonesia. There are solar- and wind-farm projects in Kazakhstan and Pakistan. There are new coal-fired power stations being constructed in BRI-associated countries, although a recent pledge has been made to stop investing in new coal-power stations. As noted earlier, too, China has built new infrastructures to tap into and reroute older Soviet energy infrastructures, and secured supply deals with a number of Central Asian countries. New pipeline projects are proliferating: the Central Asia–China Gas Pipeline traverses multiple countries; and natural gas pipelines are being or have been developed in Bangladesh, Tajikistan, Azerbaijan, and Pakistan. In Russia, China has collaborated on the Yamal LNG project, while the Russian invasion of Ukraine will likely create more opportunities to syphon off Russian energy that was previously bound for Europe.

Much of this engagement is with legacy systems of the carbon economy. Currently 55 percent of all global greenhouse gases are produced by countries along or touching the routes of the BRI, and this is expected to rise to 65 percent by the end of the decade. Cities and urban areas, meanwhile, consume more than two-thirds of global energy. At the same time, there is a growing desire for countries to make their post-COVID recovery strategy a green one. Many of the countries that China is courting in Southeast Asia and Eastern Europe have populations that are prioritizing sustainable development. China is responding to that demand. It has recently realized that if the BRI is to truly become a successful transnational infrastructure for the twenty-first century, with technological forms that lay down patterns of living for decades to come, it must be a sustainable one, across its many components. China's leadership, then, is promoting a growing emphasis on a Green Silk Road and on promoting harmony between humanity and nature.

China, given the size of its domestic emissions and its growing global linkages, will play a central role in how the world adapts to climate change. The BRI will be intrinsically woven through this response, both within China and in the many states it touches. Because BRI projects will form the backbone of many other states' infrastructure projects and urban spaces, the values embedded in these projects will reflect China's influence: through its ideas, preferences, investment, expertise, and via the firms that build these projects. In the once-in-a-generation level of construction and investment represented by the BRI, China has the opportunity to lead in creating infrastructures that are more sustainable for the world's natural systems. The scale and significance of this effort are enormous. The projects of the BRI, it has been estimated, will impact more than 142,850 square miles of critical habitat.[57]

More than most states, China is suspended between two worlds. China is currently the world's biggest emitter of carbon dioxide. Between 2000 and 2018, during years of booming growth, China's emissions tripled. China burns a staggering half of the world's coal, and is also busy building new coal plants. Between 2000 and 2019 the China Development Bank and the Export-Import Bank of China doled out $183 billion for energy projects, with most of that money going to coal-power stations and hydropower. Only about $6 billion went to solar and wind energy investments.[58] These have been years of voracious resource extraction, characterized also by pollution from the waste products of heavy industry, threats to marine conservation due to overfishing, and wildlife trafficking—all of which undermine China's latest messaging on protecting nature and biodiversity. China's vast state-owned enterprises are often extremely wasteful and inefficient.[59]

Yet despite its current dependence on carbon, China has many advantages as it makes the transition to new renewable energy sources.

China is the world's leading energy financier and energy market, which gives it considerable leverage in the world's energy markets. In the wake of the COVID-19 pandemic, China has been shifting its investments into renewables, so that by 2020, wind, solar, and hydropower made up 57 percent of its $11 billion investments in energy infrastructure.[60] In just three decades, China has built three times as much wind, solar, and hydropower-generating capacity as the United States has. China also has the biggest domestic market for solar panels, wind turbines, and electric vehicles, and is pushing the development of hydrogen-powered vehicles. It has expertise in the construction and running of nuclear reactors at home and abroad, playing a key role in the development of England's Hinkley Point C reactor. And China holds the largest share of the green bond market, which aims to prioritize sustainable projects with cheaper financing—a share that rose rapidly from 2.4 percent in 2015 to 23 percent in 2017. China is continuing to develop new "green" financial tools and products.[61]

Criticism of the environmental and social risks of the BRI have stung China recently into attempting to associate the BRI with sustainability. There is now a recognition that a fast transition away from carbon will need to happen. China joined the Paris Agreement in 2015, and in September 2020, at a speech at the UN General Assembly, President Xi committed China to carbon neutrality by 2060. Aiming to make 2030 the year of peak emissions for China, Xi proclaimed that "humankind can no longer ignore the warnings of nature."[62] Clearly Xi has decided that his flagship foreign-policy initiative, in which he has invested so much political capital, cannot be seen as backward looking when it comes to climate change.

China also has pressing internal motivations for shifting to a more sustainable relationship to the natural world. China's urbanites suffer daily from some of the worst air quality in the world. Low-lying coastal urban mega-regions are at risk from sea-level rise. Fragile ecosystems face destruction from warmer temperatures. Periodic flooding of the Yangtze River in central and southwest China has already cost many lives and displaced millions. And it is not just flooding. During the summer of 2022 there was a prolonged drought that caused the Yangtze, the world's third largest river, to lose over 50 percent of its normal water flow, and for many of its tributaries to dry up—which interfered with agriculture and shipping, and caused a crisis in Sichuan, which derives 80 percent of its electricity from the generation of hydroelectric power. The lack of preparation for the impacts of climate change—the so-called adaptation gap—that exists in most cities and regions around the world is a reality in Chinese cities as well.[63]

But China also sees in this crisis an opportunity to step into a leadership role that other major states have failed to offer. The dramatic policy U-turns and swerves of the United States during recent administrations have created a vacuum of global leadership on this issue that China has ambitions to provide under Xi. The Chinese Dream is one in which China reasserts its historical role as the moral leader of a community of shared human destiny. This is where the concept of an ecological civilization comes into play, as a structural shift away from industrial modernization and toward a new form of Chinese socialist modernization that will harmoniously balance economic and environmental objectives.

Building an ecological civilization, and expanding it abroad, represents a major shift for China from the past forty years of helter-skelter and inward-looking industrial development focused primarily on Chinese GDP growth. The concept has been enshrined in the constitution and in *Xi Jinping's Thought* and built into the 13th and 14th Five-Year Plans that guide policy. As mentioned earlier, the idea is consistent with the United Nations' own sustainable development goals, has been presented as such in speeches by Xi at the UN General Assembly, and has had influence at the United Nations Environment Programme (UNEP). China's contributions to the 2015 UN Framework Convention on Climate Change used the term, and emphasized its importance for not only shaping the urbanization process, but also creating a green, low-carbon model based on wind, solar, and low-pollution vehicles and transportation systems, as well as developing circular and sustainable economies.

But the concept of ecological civilization goes further than existing ideas about sustainable development, and represents a break with Western-led thought, instead bringing in distinctively Chinese cultural and political ideas, as well as philosophical ideas drawn from the canon of ancient Chinese thought about how to develop a harmonious relationship between humanity and the natural world and its resources. The political dimension of the concept appears to draw heavily from Chinese Marxism, stressing the importance of the model of centralized authority and the benefits brought by a vanguard elite, such as the CCP, as both an orderer of domestic governance, and the purveyor of international leadership and developmental wisdom. This is where it breaks with recent decades of thought on sustainable development in the West, and what it sees as the failure of liberal market models and governance approaches.

Instead, it seems to lean toward the figure of the "Green Leviathan"—and aspirations for an authoritarian state that can offer new models, tools, and leadership to try to break the impasses that hinder the multi-lateral system from dealing with climate change.

The aspiration to international leadership can be seen in the way that China is consciously linking the concept of ecological civilization with its other big idea about how to transform international society: the "community of common destiny." In Xi's virtual address to the UN General Assembly in 2020, as the first wave of the COVID-19 pandemic was breaking over the world, he called for all nations, as they came out on the other side of the pandemic, to try to build a "green recovery," one that was "innovative and coordinated."[64]

But if this concept of ecological civilization is to have the resonance and impact outside of China that China hopes for, it will need to be clearly communicated to other states. International legal scholars have emphasized that if any Chinese-inflected idea of ecological civilization is to have a chance of generating influence internationally, then it needs to be articulated in ways that can be readily understood and implemented by willing and like-minded foreign governments. It needs to be more than a slogan, requiring refinement of its definition and scope, and the technical and legal instruments that underpin it.

So far China has created goals for pollution reduction, biodiversity protection, low-carbon and "circular economy" models (systems designed to use fewer resources, and to capture as much waste as possible for reuse), protection of natural resources, and low-carbon cities and urban regions. Mechanisms to achieve these goals by 2035 include financing schemes, changes to taxation and legal systems, and the diffusion of new knowledge and technical skills. A set of priority areas have been identified: urban and regional spatial planning, technological innovation, land management, water and other natural resources, regulatory reforms, environmental protection, monitoring and supervision, public participation, and organizational implementation.

In the meantime, China has continued to work on developing these ideas at home, particularly in urban contexts, via experimental ecological-civilization "pilot cities," and by plans for entire eco-city regions. Zhen-jiang province, for example, has been designated an ecological-economic system, with the ambition to steer it toward the circular-economy model. Fujian, Guizhou, and Jiangxi provinces have all been earmarked as sites for ecological-civilization development, with pilot cities that include Shenzhen, Xiamen, and Guangzhou.[65]

Among the most interesting urban projects have been Guiyang and Xiong'an New City. Guiyang, the capital of subtropical Guizhou province in the mountains of southwest China, has gained plaudits as a showcase ecological-civilization city. With a population of 3.5 million, Guiyang sits on the banks of the Nanming River, surrounded by verdant hills and valleys. Over the past decade, it has tried to become waste-free, low-carbon, and to emphasize ecological living and well-being. As with many such attempts at developing eco-cities, however, both within China and elsewhere, the rhetoric often outstrips the performance. Although Guiyang has certainly improved its environmental quality and earned much praise, research shows that it still has a way to go to realize its carbon-reduction ambitions.[66]

Xiong'an, meanwhile, is a new city built from scratch in the Baoding area of Hebei province—and it is intended as a model "city of the future" for other Chinese regions and for the world. Located about sixty miles from Beijing, it is envisioned as a green high-tech development hub for the Beijing-Tianjin-Hebei economic triangle. The emphasis is on green finance, sustainable energy, and large, open green spaces for ecological living. It will be a city of parks and tree belts, and will be surrounded by newly planted forests—74,000 acres of new trees have been planted so far. At least half of the city's power will come from renewables, solar power, and geothermal energy—and it will all be managed by a smart grid. The city is also intended to be an intelligent city, or Smart City, with driverless vehicles offering public transportation, and with every physical building and infrastructural component mirrored on a "digital twin" city that is represented on an ever-evolving virtual map. While it is meant to be the size of London and New York combined, Xiong'an's urban diagram is also predicated on the idea of the "fifteen-minute life circle"—where all the goods and services needed for an urban citizen to live their lives should be available within the radius of a fifteen-minute journey. This idea has also taken form in other cities around the world, such as Paris, Barcelona, and Melbourne, illustrating how quickly new ideas about urban development travel around the world today.

Both Guiyang and Xiong'an, as pilot model cities, represent China's moves to develop urban manifestations of the concept of an ecological civilization, with Xiong'an in particular pointing to a new model of urban development that might be copied elsewhere in China, and, via the BRI and other mechanisms, beyond its borders.[67] There are also many other innovations coming out of the Chinese context, such as the

"Sponge City," in which low-lying and low-density urban areas within cities, and even across whole urban corridors, are redesigned with parks and wetlands that might absorb heavy rainfall linked to urban flooding, then recycle and rerelease that rainfall, gradually, back into rivers.

Renewable energy, it is increasingly clear, will be at the heart of China's ambitious plans for gaining international influence. It is in this area that we see some of the more far-reaching and dramatic possibilities of the BRI for the future of international order and for urban development. One of the most ambitious and potentially transformative ideas is a long-term ambition to link up the Eurasian space and beyond with a series of globally integrated energy grids.[68] The Global Energy Interconnection (GEI), if realized in its current vision, would be an eighteen-line global backbone of ultra-high-voltage transmission connections that would link over eighty countries in continent-spanning networks of clean, renewable energy flows. It would incorporate smart-grid technology, and link areas with ample sources of renewable energy—windswept steppes, sun-baked deserts, ocean tides—with distant centers of urban demand. In order for this vision of continent-spanning clean energy to become a reality, it would need continent-level integration—no easy task in regions where energy trading is generally low.

The GEI, as a concept and ambition, was floated in 2015 by State Grid Corporation of China (SGCC), the world's largest energy utility company, and the operator of almost all of China's domestic energy-transmission network. President Xi has thrown the state's weight behind the scheme, and linked it to China's international leadership ambitions on climate change and ecological civilization. In 2015 he gave a speech to the UN General Assembly at its Sustainable Development Summit, in which he proposed discussions on establishing a global-energy network to meet global power demand with sustainable and clean alternatives.

China has pushed for the development of GEI in the discussions for the UN Framework Convention on Climate Change, the UN 2030 Agenda for Sustainable Development, and at the Gulf Cooperation Council, among other forums. If realized, the GEI's continent-spanning energy grid would be composed of national transmission and distribution grids; energy bases in the polar region, equator, and on each continent; and a digital platform for allocating resources and facilitating market exchanges via digital communications networks. The ambition here is immense, with a half-century time frame to integrate all of these elements.[69] SGCC has proposed a three-step plan: an initial phase would integrate national grids, construct new smart grids, and hasten the move to renewable sources of energy, while the second phase would connect continental grids together by the end of the decade. The third phase, from 2030 to 2070, would involve the development of "Afro-Eurasian" transcontinental grids linked by ultra-high-voltage systems.

China's interests in driving the development of such a system are multiple. First, as mentioned earlier, China is resource poor, with large, energy-hungry, urban concentrations along its heavily populated coastal regions. Stretching its energy reach well beyond its own borders is imperative, and the GEI would be a secure and stable mechanism for doing so. Second, China, as a result of robust, long-term state funding for research and development, has become a world leader in the development of technologies related to energy grids and ultra-high-voltage transmission—similar to its leading position in 5G. China is clearly hoping that its standards will play a central role, and so place it right at the core of global energy governance, where it can influence an immense energy infrastructure that it has played a key role in constructing, and that is integrated into the BRI and the Digital Silk Road.

The moves to integrate these ideas with the United Nations' SDGs, and to push Chinese standards and technologies in multilateral international institutional forums, show the evolution of Chinese thinking: it now wants to participate in the global governance of climate change and the transition to more sustainable energy use—and the GEI seems to have been embraced by the UN system. China signed a collaboration memorandum of understanding in 2016 with the UN Economic and Social Commission for Asia and the Pacific, and was the host state for the 2017 High-Level Symposium on Global Energy Connection with the UN Department of Economic and Social Affairs. The GEI organization was a nongovernmental organization partner at the UN COP24 and COP25 climate-change conferences.

The ambition is breathtaking in scope, and some industry experts remain skeptical that it can work.[70] But the GEI is indicative of the globe-spanning gaze that China has been developing in the last decade. China's vision of developing global norms, and bringing its concept of an ecological civilization into existence, stretches south, from the deserts of the Middle East and North Africa, or the hydropower of Southeast Asia, northward to the vast plains of Russia and beyond, to the melting ice of the polar region. The renewable energy potential of Russia's immense empty steppe and its access to the Arctic regions has not gone unnoticed, with China, as mentioned earlier, forging plans for a Polar Silk Road in part because of the huge energy potential. Chinese investment and expertise could also potentially unlock Russia's vast offshore wind potential, incorporating Russian resources into the GEI and helping to feed Eurasia's expanding, power-hungry urban centers.[71]

CHAPTER THREE

Urban Spaces
Transformed and Contested

HROUGH THE PRODUCTION OR obstruction of cities and urban areas—which include everything from public spaces to electrical systems, public art, lampposts, memorials, monuments, offices, homes, and buildings more generally—power is applied, resisted, and altered. Great symbols of urbanization, such as the London sewage and water system, the Moscow subway, the Parisian boulevard, Mumbai's Dharavi slum, Shanghai's Bund, and the character street art of the King of Kowloon, speak to such power and associated disputes, as do, frequently, seemingly mundane urban components like lighting, public benches, and bike racks. In dense cities, where space is a commodity that can affect wealth, health, and safety, few spaces are uncontested. Some of these contests have achieved an iconic status in the urban planning world and beyond, not unlike famous boxing matches: imagine a Moses versus Jacobs headline, with an undercard of Le Corbusier versus Nehru, and Bloomberg versus Occupy.

But the historical fight card of urban planning and architecture—full of knock-down, drag-out bouts featuring big egos, capital, eccentric characters, and passionate communities—obscures the wider historical and geographic view of urbanization. Today, for example, multilateral institutions, including regional development banks, play a significant role in how urbanization plays out around the world, through international plans and agreements that are meant, in theory, to shape sustainable development more broadly and urban development more specifically.

Over the course of 2015–2016, member states of the United Nations adopted a series of outcome documents that together amounted to an international development agenda for the post–Millennium Development Goals era. These agreements included the seventeen goals of the 2030 Agenda for Sustainable Development, adopted in 2015, and the New Urban Agenda (NUA), adopted during the UN Conference on Housing and Sustainable Urban Development (Habitat III) in 2016. Thanks to ingenious branding and ongoing campaigns, the 2030 Development Agenda and the SDGs can be seen in everything from the pins worn by diplomats to the social-responsibility efforts of major corporations to the development strategies of major donor states. The New Urban Agenda is significantly less well known, and has been mostly influential as a reference point for global urbanists, urban-focused diplomats, and development experts.[1]

These agreements, as well as those of the Sendai Framework for Disaster Risk Reduction and the Addis Ababa Action Agenda, both forged in 2015, share an approach to stakeholder engagement that details who will do what. And curiously, while the agendas have been adopted by groups of states, and while all four agreements, including the New Urban Agenda, envision implementation by an expansive tent of stakeholders, they are mostly domestic in focus. Within these frameworks, the Westphalian international order—specifically, sovereignty within one's own borders, as well as competition and collaboration between states—remains the context in which the urban future is going to be shaped.

Such a focus on the state is not entirely misguided. As much as the United Nations remains the central body of global governance, its creation and many of its current practices are conducted under the wider umbrella of, or even in the service of, sovereignty. And as the urbanization that occurred after World War II in Europe, the Soviet Union, Latin America, and parts of Africa showed, national governments can be indispensable actors, particularly around housing and networked infrastructure.[2] Yet today the core activities of urbanization, including the planning and construction of housing, transportation, and urban infrastructure, have also been brought squarely into the sphere of geopolitics and globalization. That is, although in the past Great Power competition, and resistance to it, have guided attempts to shape urban spaces, more recently globalization—and the more disembodied forces of trade, finance, soft power, and climate change—have altered or transformed urban dynamics. In all of these cases, cities and urban areas are grasped at and competed over as platforms for the exercise of power and influence. And this may be more true now, in the context of the BRI, than at any time since the beginning of World War II.

States and empires have, to differing degrees, understood urban development to be an instrument of national wealth creation, stability, and regional and global standing. The most powerful among them, whether intentionally or not, have influenced urban forms far beyond their borders. Given China's remarkable urban rise, and leadership in innovation and experimentation, it is tempting to look for a universally implemented Chinese model for the cities along the BRI that are being built or redeveloped. Indeed, we can see important patterns there that align with Chinese goals, including approaches to special economic zones, mass housing, industrialization, and digital surveillance.

But most cities, especially those growing today, do not have master planners, and neither do those along the BRI. This chapter, then, offers a close look at the development of parts of respective BRI cities such as Cape Coast in Ghana; Gwadar City in Pakistan; Vientiane, Laos; Sihanoukville, Cambodia; and Addis Ababa, Ethiopia. The history of these components, and of these BRI cities, is one of their most fascinating features. They are almost always developed, even when built in green fields, on top of preexisting plans—that is, they enter history in stream, and their history, or better, histories, occur in particular geographic and social contexts.[3] Finally, these components—railways, stations, housing, ports, green areas—like so many Chinese local experiments, will have various futures. Some will quickly fade, while others will likely shape the lives of millions over the next century.

Power, Influence, and Built Environments

Urbanization and urban spaces have long been strategic areas of focus for foreign policymakers. Turning the process of urbanization and the built environment more generally into an instrument of influence is, however, another step altogether. The processes through which power, operating across borders and large geographic distances, becomes urban space are myriad, complex, and often indirect. Here the close readings offered by urban planners, architects and architectural historians, and even landscape planners are particularly helpful. Histories focused on cities, neighborhoods, even individual projects and buildings, can not only move us beyond national data, but also take us to levels of detail often beyond the analysis of those focused on geopolitics. Such histories and case studies guide us through the material impacts of policy and influence, and so can move us beyond rhetoric to explore questions about intentionality. The connectivity of transportation, commercial, and energy infrastructure addressed in Chapter 2, which connects urban settlements both within and across borders, offers a global perspective of interdependence. But in the case of urban life, and the cityscape itself, we can benefit from the approaches and practices developed by urban planners and historians, as much as those from infrastructure experts, when considering how BRI projects and processes are shaping urban development—from railway projects in Vientiane, to digital connectivity in Nairobi; from shipping in Piraeus, to housing in Gwadar.

Consider the colonial influence of Britain on the nineteenth-century development of Adelaide, Australia. Nicholas Phelps, dean of architecture at the University of Melbourne, has provided a helpful overview of the sites, scales, and approaches that informed this particular urban influence. His analysis includes legal frameworks, but remains place-based. The places and processes of influence used by colonial officials included deliberate urbanization; the allocation of land rights; advance planning; the development of wide streets in geometric order; the creation of public squares; the standardization of plot sizes; the reservation of plots for public purposes; and the formal distinction between town and country.[4] The imperial project zoomed down to the scale of street width, and out to questions of legal systems related to property ownership.

Consider too the case of American influence—both commercial and imperial—in Havana after the Spanish-American War of 1898. Jeffrey Cody, an expert in both US and Chinese architecture, has outlined a useful and intuitive scale of urban interventions taken by the United States and American firms in the city at the turn of the century. American influence on the built environment, according to Cody, came in four broad categories: the development or alteration of buildings by US firms; the establishment of industrial workplaces sponsored by US companies; the construction of urban infrastructure, often using American design and done by American engineers; and indirect influence in the form of transnational planning advice.[5] Looking at the work conducted by the influential American firm Purdy and Henderson across Central and South America, Cody identified similar scales of influence: specific buildings, harbors, elements of urban infrastructure, and company towns.[6]

Finally, moving from informal empire to globalization, consider Dubai, Abu Dhabi, and Doha. The rapid, seemingly miraculous development of these Gulf cities has sparked no small conversation about urban development, global architecture, and global capital, but as Davide Ponzini has shown in his detailed explorations of project development and implementation, the actual processes, and in particular the interaction among design, finance, global networks, and local influences, are inevitably complex. Even the most celebrated and sparkling of urban development projects from the turn of the twentieth century, Bilbao and the Guggenheim, were less about a new signature museum than about the interaction of those efforts with long-standing local and regional initiatives. In a template that would seem to resonate with Phelps and Cody, Ponzini argues that urban transformations should be interpreted according to four dimensions: design projects and built forms; the urban context; the actors and networks that enable, shape, or prevent projects; and, finally, how such processes change over time.[7] An understanding of such processes, he argues, can be found only in careful analyses of means of exchange, networks of influence, and project development. Today, as China bids to redefine international and urban order, these historical dynamics are all in play again in diverse urban spaces across Afro-Eurasia. And just as American influence in Havana and the Americas was distinctive from that of the British in Australia, Chinese influence in cities from Pakistan to Ethiopia is taking its own forms.

Cities often share similar features, and are shaped by "the more or less universal elements of urban planning," to use Phelps's phrase, though sometimes these similarities wilt under close inspection.[8] Every city is both different, and the same. This is the fundamental urban truth captured in Italo Calvino's 1972 classic novel *Invisible Cities*. Urbanists, anthropologists, and scientists, then, have categorized cities into types, and it is each group of cities' rough similarity within scales, and the idea of scale itself, that has informed many of the efforts to influence "similar" cities and urban areas even across nations, continents, and oceans.[9] Indeed this rough similarity in scale continues to inform the efforts of NGOs, international organizations, and nations seeking to shape urban futures. As will be explored, China, as well as nations like Germany, South Korea, Japan, and, further back in the pack, the United States, are increasingly engaging city networks as they seek to influence large numbers of cities on priority issues such as transportation and construction. Regardless of the city, those seeking to influence urban spaces meet with a wide array of actors.

Attempts by the USSR, and socialist states more generally, to shape urban development in West Africa in the 1960s illustrate many of the complex dynamics involved in projecting influence into cities from afar. In 1960, Ghana and the Soviet Union entered into a formal agreement to promote new urban developments in Accra and Tema. The macroeconomic structure of the agreement was complicated enough, involving a credit line extended from the Soviet Union to Ghana to enable payment for industrial goods, machinery, and the work of architects and engineers, with repayment flowing in the other direction in the form of local Ghanaian goods and agriculture. The formal agreement between the nations included allocation of credit to design and construct two residential neighborhoods, one in the capital and the other in the harbor town. Soviet planners at the State Institute for the Planning of Cities outlined new urban developments in Accra to support twenty-two thousand residents and laid out plans for new housing communities, an industrial zone, and a town center in Tema. Expertise and resources were deployed. Time for planning was taken. The plans, developed from 1962 to 1964, included the placement of trees, football fields, wading pools, and car parks. As the historian Łukasz Stanek has shown, Soviet engagement in the planning and development extended to the tiniest detail, including a visit by a group of Soviet specialists from Giprogor to examine the feasibility of raising the height of rooms.[10] After years of planning involving formal agreements, an array of institutions, Soviet experts, local experts, and leaders, the 1966 coup in Ghana ushered in a change of political leadership that began its own planning. Over the course of five or more years, and working within the framework of formal collaboration, everything from the height of rooms to the viability of the project came under question, with local and national politics eventually trumping all.

Scales: basements and buildings, trees and parks, alleys and streets, neighborhoods, municipal infrastructure and regional services, and more. Stakeholders: amorous teenagers, athletes and weightlifters, families with small children, taxi unions, street merchants, city officials and national policymakers, diplomats and financiers, and the elderly, among many others.[11] How these parts and players came together within China in the early twenty-first century during one of the intense urbanization periods in history is destined to inform, for decades to come, the shape of urbanization for many both inside and outside of China.

Shaping Urban Spaces

Cities are products of power. They also produce the basis for power. Since their inception, they have produced wealth; fomented intellectual advances; provided shelter, security, and resources to individuals; and offered sanctuaries for worship.[12] Power shapes urban life in some essential ways: the built environment and use of space carry with them a grammar of power—center/periphery, open/closed, accessible/gated—while the material world, along with the life and history of a city, shape its identity, purpose, and communities.[13] Grounded in theory this can sound abstract, but the relationship between the city and power has proven remarkably intuitive over the years. The great fire of Rome in the year 64 ultimately ushered out Nero and his dynasty and ushered in new urban practices around concrete and domes.[14] Indeed, in his *History of the Decline and Fall of the Roman Empire*, Edward Gibbon offers a kaleidoscopic history of urban transitions, as cities have moved between empires and faiths. The revolutions of early modern, Renaissance, and industrial Europe all brought with them new approaches to utilizing urban space to resist, maintain, or enhance power and influence. Sometimes the approach was violent, such as in Paris in 1871; sometimes it was symbolic, such as the refashioning, in places like Lisbon, of religious buildings into law courts, army offices, and senates. More recently, Cold War power consciously deployed democratic and socialist architecture in West and East Berlin, respectively, while newly independent postcolonial governments in Africa and Asia sought to reshape capital cities, such as Algiers, Cairo, and Delhi—or establish new ones, in the cases of Brasilia, Islamabad, and Dakar—to reflect national identities.

In our own time, climate scientists, economists, and sociologists have increasingly come to recognize the role of the built environment—and in particular cities and urban areas—in shaping our collective, but locally differentiated, futures. In 2018, the IPCC released its groundbreaking *Special Report on Global Warming of 1.5 °C*. The report, part of the then-ongoing *Sixth Assessment Report* of the Intergovernmental Panel on Climate Change, remains one of the more rigorous, and subsequently scrutinized, scientific documents of the past decade at least. The review and drafting process included the assessment of over six thousand recent scientific papers and documents, and more than forty thousand responses from stakeholders, including national governments and city officials. The report made clear that to limit warming to 1.5°C, or even catastrophically higher levels, significant action in cities would be needed. These actions, as laid out earlier, fell under the broad systems of energy; land and ecosystems; industry; and urban areas and infrastructure. None of these systems, or the conditions needed to enable them, are easily separable. Many of the actions needed—from the financing of infrastructure development and construction, to the development of new smart grids and building standards—are already shaping the future of cities, and that of the planet more generally.

But who gets to determine the shape of the urban future, and within it identities, opportunities, communities, and future histories? The term multi-stakeholders is thrown around both casually and frequently by urban experts and diplomats alike. It has come to include national actors, subnational actors, the private sector, civil society groups, nongovernmental organizations, and others—including organized crime and cartels, such as the water cartels in Nairobi and taxi gangs in Cape Town. In his history of the exercise of power in capital cities, the sociologist Göran Therborn grouped these participants slightly differently, to include political authorities, possessors of capital, the privileged classes, and the popular classes. Who you see depends on where you look, not just historically, but also geographically. The influential urbanist AbdouMaliq Simone looks toward the periphery of cities in Africa and Asia and describes the dynamics differently: "Urban politics will largely be a peripheral politics, not only a politics at the periphery, but a politics whose practices must be divested of many of the assumptions that it derived from the primacy of 'the city.' "[15]

China has helped finance the construction of Astana's central business district. But what is a central business district? Simone's definition—"a compost machine peopled by strangers"— seems far afield from the multi-stakeholder and multi-governance model advanced by the United Nations, regional development banks, and many overseas development assistance programs.[16] It is this breadth of operators and operation that prompted Michel Foucault to note in 1977 that a "whole history remains to be written of *spaces*—which would at the same time be the history of *powers* (both of these in the plural)—from the great strategies of geopolitics to the little tactics of the habitat."[17] These tactics and strategies, according to the French postmodernists and IPCC scientists alike, are bidirectional. While dictatorship over the urban space is a rarity, resistance to power is embedded in urban practices. But even then, power is not shared or exercised evenly. The state, particularly in the twentieth century and especially after

World War II, played an outsized role in many of the sectors and systems—housing, transportation, public health—that shaped cities. Even the IPCC reports, with their insistence on our shared future and attention paid to the action of individuals, are largely meant for policymakers at the national and international levels. This is not a surprise, because the IPCC falls under a broad UN umbrella, and because it is national governments that have long taken the lead when it comes to shaping urban development within their borders. Consequently, when considering the past and future of influence in the built urban environment, and the lives built around it, the city's role cannot eclipse that of the state. The urban spaces of Belt and Road Cities will be no different.

National Projects

The decades after World War II were a high point for sovereignty. Even the Universal Declaration of Human Rights, which was adopted in 1948 by member states of the recently founded United Nations, and which rooted rights not in one's membership in a political community but in one's being human, did not undermine the nation-state.[18] The Universal Declaration instead affirmed state and national welfare programs as necessary vehicles for securing rights and ultimately alleviating poverty.[19] Beyond rights and development, too, particularly in the wider space of security, the nation-state and sovereignty remained at the core of the post–World War II order.[20]

If the state was to be the guarantor of security and rights—even if those rights transcended states—it was also meant to deliver growth and prosperity. Economic development models in the postwar years recognized national economies, and, by extension, the state itself, as both the fundamental governance institution and the unit of analysis. Cities, or more precisely, urbanization, had integral roles to play in the development of national economies around the world. In the decades after the war, for example, Mexico City became the hub of Mexican development efforts. Between 1940 and 1980, while the population of Mexico grew from twenty million to seventy million, that of the capital grew from two million to thirteen million.[21] Mexico City was the focal point of postwar economic development, with the national government and private sector encouraging investment and infrastructure development in the capital. By 1970, the city was home to nearly half of Mexican industrial production, and almost 60 percent of its transportation activities.[22]

In postwar Britain, urban development and planning were explicitly undertaken as part of a national project. Industrial parks, though dating back to the nineteenth century, were created in the middle of the twentieth century to stimulate employment. Shopping precincts and council housing areas, too, were introduced in the 1940s, 1950s, and 1960s to encourage development of new towns and cities and to alleviate housing shortages.[23] These urban spaces, now so familiar in British cities, were part of a state-led modernization effort that stretched well beyond London.[24] More than a million public homes had been built in the interwar years, with most of the growth in London and Liverpool.[25] After the war, the growth in public housing, driven by the state, prioritized density, community, urban redevelopment, employment, and the management of consumer demand. By 1980, after more than two decades of intense development in housing, particularly apartments, and with Thatcher-led privatization around the corner, nearly one in three households was a tenant of the state.[26]

In France, meanwhile, another social and political transformation was occurring that also affirmed the centrality of the state and the importance of urban spaces. The *trente glorieuses*, three decades of sustained economic growth and expansion of the middle class, coincided with an intense period of urban growth. One in five French buildings was damaged during the war, and even those that were left unscathed lacked utilities. In 1946, nearly 50 percent of French homes did not have running water, and almost 80 percent did not have an indoor toilet. Over the next three decades, cities became an instrument of modernization and national economic development. "In less than three decades after World War II," writes the architectural historian Kenny Cupers, "France transformed from a largely rural country with an insufficient and outdated housing stock into a highly modernized urban nation."[27] In 1959 alone, for example, according to Cupers, 320,000 new homes were built, with nearly 90 percent of that construction financed in part by the state.[28] In France, as in Britain, collective housing—*grand ensembles*—outpaced single homes, while delivery of utilities—water, heat, and energy—became central concerns of national governments. In these postwar cities, the relationship between the urban resident and state was significantly different from that of city-dwellers decades later in the Global Cities. Social housing was commonplace and urban residents readily relied on the government for the delivery of basic services. Indeed, this arrangement was at the core of the economic miracles that rebuilt much of the West after the destruction of the 1940s.

Another kind of city-making as national project happened after World War II in former European imperial territories. These newly independent nations often used the development of new capitals as a way to knit their country together, manage domestic politics, and assert independence. The arcs and approaches to city-making differed by region, and by the long or short histories of the respective cities, but in almost all cases, politics and power, as much as economics and commerce, gave shape and identity to these capitals.[29] State formation in sub-Saharan Africa, for example, often involved the reshaping of colonial capitals, while most of the capitals of North Africa and Asia—Algiers, Cairo, Baghdad, Delhi, Seoul—preceded Western empires and thus followed different processes. In many cases, too, national leaders got personally involved in the effort to develop their capitals. Kwame Nkrumah and Jawaharlal Nehru, for example, both of whom took an active interest in modernism, engaged in architectural decisions and debates. New capitals offered even more opportunities for state-shaping. Brasilia, Islamabad, and Dakar were designed explicitly to represent and influence their respective newly independent states.

In all of these examples we also see the connections between urban development and the broader international context in which it takes place. In particular, after World War II, as the European empires were dismantled, the international order was reshaped to include new models of social and economic development in both the United States and Europe. This historical pattern—whereby shifts in the composition of the international environment find their expression in a transformation of urban form—is present today in China's influence across Asia and Africa and beyond.

The Cold War Empires

Although the state drove economic development and geopolitics in the initial decades after World War II, other forces that transcended national borders also influenced the transformations of cities at this time. The subsequent influence of globalization on cities has been so profound that it sometimes obscures the significant impact of the Cold War, and the Soviet Union in particular, on urban spaces. Culture was an instrument of the Cold War, and design, architecture, and urban planning were no small part of that.

American urbanists played minor, if notable, roles in the Cold War cultural competition.[30] In 1943, Jane Jacobs, perhaps the most influential

American urban thinker of the twentieth century, went to work for the US Office of War Information. After the war, she wrote about housing and cities for *Amerika*, a Russian-language cultural review funded by the State Department. In the late 1940s, Walter Gropius, the Berlin-born co-founder of the twentieth century's most influential design institution, the Bauhaus, who had during the interwar years sought to reshape German society through urban interventions, accepted an advisory role with the US government on the reconstruction of Berlin.[31] In the early 1950s, US policymakers vetoed the selection of Le Corbusier as architect for the forthcoming UNESCO headquarters in Paris owing to his previous dalliances with communism and the Soviet Union. In the late 1950s, Gropius and his design firm, the Architects Collaborative, were enlisted by James Conant, US high commissioner in West Germany, to develop innovative housing for the still-rebuilding West Berlin. Over the decades that followed World War II, the United States maintained initiatives to encourage home ownership in West Berlin. US foreign policymakers thought explicitly about spaces—including those related to home ownership, consumption, and transportation—and their relationship to democratic practices.[32]

Meanwhile, major urban-transformation efforts and signature urban developments in the domestic United States were also being framed by the Cold War ideological context. "For a moment in the late 1940s," writes the historian Samuel Zipp, with his eyes trained on New York specifically, "the concerns of liberal internationalism and urban renewal dovetailed, providing a link between the state of world affairs and the urban situation."[33] Urban renewal projects such as New York City's Stuyvesant Town—the largest housing project undertaken in the United States during and immediately after the war, built in the former Gas House District of Manhattan's East Side—were described by the *New York Times* as an effort to buttress the developing middle class in the face of class-driven ideological competition. Lincoln Center, as both a cultural venue and an urban renewal project, was even more explicitly framed as a Cold War instrument. "Lincoln Center," declared Wallace Harrison, one of the architectural leads for the development of the UN headquarters on the East Side and Lincoln Center on the West, "is a symbol to the world that we so-called monopolistic, imperialistic degenerates are capable of building the greatest cultural center in the world."[34]

While these developments were often described as being part of the US Cold War effort, a number of the influential thinkers and ideas were in fact shaped by experiences and experiments outside of the United States. Ed Logue, for example, was an instrumental figure in the development of the post–World War II American city, particularly along the Eastern Seaboard. But before Logue turned his attention to the liberal project of reshaping New Haven, New York, and Boston, the future-planner spent an influential year in India focused on, among other things, community engagement through development of the built environment. The work, supported by the Ford Foundation, sought to use physical infrastructure to promote democracy, self-sufficiency, and, at least implicitly, resistance to communism.[35] "The roots of Logue's life-long concern with improving America's urban environments," writes historian Lizabeth Cohen, "grew deep in the soil of rural India."[36] For Logue, as for fellow diplomat Bernard Loshbough, who returned from India to work on urban development in Pittsburgh and Washington, DC, this global influence was felt not merely in the general principle that localized development matters, but also in specific practices, including, most importantly, coalition and multi-stakeholder building, and the integration of social programming and infrastructure development.[37]

But the city is in no way the exclusive domain of the capitalist, and the influence of the Soviet Union on urban design was perhaps even more significant than that of the United States. In October 1917, the Bolshevik Revolution catalyzed ongoing debates about the future of Russian cities. The built environment is stubborn, and resists immediate, widespread change. But over time, many buildings in the capital were repurposed: merchants' clubs became workers' clubs, buildings for aristocrats became buildings for unions.[38] Shared housing, such as Ivan Nikolaev's Communal House, was developed with the idea of dissolving the family unit. Iconic buildings and streets, including the Cathedral of Christ the Saviour, were torn down, and as the 1920s turned to the 1930s, new iconic towers and lanes were built in their place.[39] In the decades after the Revolution, the Russian urban population rose by nearly 60 percent, with an increase of fifteen million urban residents between 1926 and 1933.[40] This domestic urban transformation was informed, however, by robust exchange with the wider world, and American experts in particular. Boris Iofan, chair for the Administration for the Construction of the Palace of the Soviets, dispatched numerous delegations of architects and planners abroad, and Soviet experts visited Detroit, Washington, DC, and Chicago, among other American cities.[41]

The ambition to reshape Russian cities during the interwar years—captured most symbolically in the ambitions for the Palace of the Soviets, the Moscow Metro, and the capital's 1935 master plan—took on a different tenor after World War II and during the Cold War. In 1947, amid the wreckage of war, Soviet architects began work on a series of seven skyscrapers across the capital (though the original plan was for eight) that were meant to attest to the USSR's modernity, its superpower status, and the arrival of Moscow as a world-class city.[42] The approach to these towers differed notably in both tone and process from interwar building strategies. Internationalism gave way to ideological competition.[43] Reversing course from the interwar years, the addition of skyscrapers to the Russian skyline was to be an endogenous affair, done without collaboration or technology transfer. Both the process and the product were an exercise in geopolitics: this was architecture as a global statement about national achievement. Stalin and the Communist Party leadership turned to urban development and architecture in Moscow as a means to memorialize the Soviet victory in World War II, erect monuments of cultural achievement, and demonstrate proof of Soviet global power. The seven skyscrapers, begun in 1947 and finished in the 1950s, were, as the historian Katherine Zubovich puts it, conceived as "examples of both Soviet world supremacy and Russian national achievement."[44]

Given the many actors and forces involved, the long periods of time required for design and construction, and the durability of the built environment once it is made, urbanism doesn't lend itself to sudden change. When such rare ruptures do occur, they often indicate a shift in the tectonic plates of international order and political competition. In this case, it was the acceleration of superpower rivalry in the early Cold War, and the emergence of rival visions for social, economic, and political life, that would be expressed in different urban forms. The 1950s in the USSR proved to be a dramatic turning point in urban development that tracked a political change. In a historic speech at the National Builders Conference in December 1954, Nikita Khrushchev, who had played a pivotal role in the development of the Metro and was replacing the recently deceased Stalin as Soviet premier, offered a striking denunciation of Stalin in urban and spatial terms. The new premier was familiar with the neoclassical ornament, pillars, and marble that in the mid-1930s had replaced the modernist visions of the Constructivists and Rationalists.[45] And he was intimately familiar with the soon-to-be-completed skyscrapers. It was with this knowledge, and in the context of architecture, that he launched an early anti-Stalin speech. In this speech, Khrushchev commented on the interaction between dirt and concrete, the overuse of iron, as well as construction costs per square foot. He also, most famously, denounced architectural "excess." Khrushchev praised prefabrication, criticized ornamentation, and argued for a reduction in architectural styles, all in the context of delivering mass housing. To be sure, influential Soviet architects and planners, such as Alexander P. Ivanitskii, lead planner of Nizhny Novgorod, had recognized the complexity of cities and the limits of buildings as mere symbols. But Khrushchev was no mere architect or planner, no matter how influential some were. He was outlining a new vision for how the built environment would represent the Soviet Union and deliver for its people. Functional, mass-produced block housing, not skyscrapers or ornamentation, was needed in response to the war's destruction.[46] Tracking the dramatic postwar expansion of housing in the United Kingdom and France, the turn against excess and toward industrial mass production led to nearly half of the Soviet population moving into new housing between 1956 and 1966.[47]

The definitive Cold War metaphor was one of materiality: the Iron Curtain. To be sure, during the 1940s, 1950s, and 1960s the Cold War divide thickened in real, material senses, no more so than in Berlin—as well as in a metaphorical sense, with the Soviet Union turning away from technology transfer and expert engagement, and the United States looking suspiciously at architects and planners who had worked previously with the Bolshevik regime. Even as US cities became the device of choice by which to communicate the threat of communist ideology—as captured most strikingly in the solitary lions of the destroyed New York Public Library represented in *Life*'s November 1945 story "The 36-Hour War"—and as the Stalinist Moscow enterprise rejected US technology, Soviet and American approaches to urban planning, housing, and domestic consumption remained in dialogue.[48] Sometimes this dialogue took the form of propaganda and intelligence, such as Jacobs's US State Department essay "New Horizons of the Architecture of the U.S.A.," which drew the attention of Soviet critics, who in turn rhetorically attacked not only Jacobs's criticism, but American cities themselves.[49] At other moments it involved more subtle forms of knowledge transfer, such as when, in 1955, after Khrushchev's reversal of Stalinist urban practices, a Soviet housing official touring the United States purchased a full prefabricated house, including its furnishings, and shipped it to the Soviet Union.[50] As historian Greg Castillo has definitively shown, in the cases of the various world expos, this knowledge transfer included the use of design and home appliances to project wealth, success, and freedom.[51] Churchill's "Iron Curtain" metaphor—first introduced in the small town of Fulton, Missouri, in 1946—was prescient with regard to Berlin's future, but when it came to design, consumption, and some planning practices, it was a curtain through which toaster ovens, kitchens, and prefab houses could still pass.

Within the Soviet sphere, this meant influence on cityscapes across Eastern and Central Europe, as well as in China and parts of Latin America and Africa. Soviet urban-planning experts arrived in China in Beijing as early as 1949, and returned in 1953 and 1955, drawing on the 1935 Moscow General Plan to guide Beijing's growth, including its industrial development. "Self-contained, largely self-sufficient live-work compounds were established, again closely following Soviet models," writes historian Thomas Campanella. "This is the origin of the work-unit compound, or *danwei*, that would become the basic unit of Chinese urbanism in the Mao era."[52] Across China, public squares and space were further developed for Communist Party rallies and gatherings. In Beijing, conservation-minded architects like Liang Sicheng, who envisioned preserving the historical city, lost out to those, most notably Mao, who understood the utility and site of traditional Beijing as a potential political symbol. Tiananmen, in particular, metamorphosed from an insular, imperial quarter into, in the words of Wu Hung, a political space that served both as the "architectonic embodiment of political ideology and as an architectural site activating political action and expression."[53] Over the 1950s, the size of the square increased fourfold.[54] And beginning in 1958, the monumental architecture of Moscow's skyscrapers was replicated, with Chinese details, in the capital: the "Ten Great Buildings" campaign, which celebrated the upcoming anniversary of the revolution, included the construction of Beijing's Great Hall of the People.[55]

The Opening of Chinese Cities

Chinese urbanization in the latter half of the twentieth century is one of the great migration events in human history. In 1978, on the precipice of the nation's opening, just 20 percent of China's population lived in cities and urban areas. This figure now stands at over 60 percent. Over the coming three decades or so, it is estimated that 200 million more residents will locate in urban areas, and by midcentury, urban dwellers may well reach 75–80 percent of the total population of China.[56] While a handful of nations have urbanized at faster rates—including both Korea and Japan in the wake of World War II—none have seen as many people located anew in urban settings. In a thirty-year period, 260 million rural residents in China became urban. Since 1983, more than 200 million farmers have left the countryside for cities, in what has often become a seasonal and circular migration. Populations have moved to follow investment, resources, and economic opportunity. Almost 50 percent of Shanghai's population today is made up of migrants to the city. A number of inequalities at the intersection of space and governance have emerged as this rapid urbanization proceeded, most notably the limited access to urban services for those with nonlocal *hukou* status.[57]

During the urban turn in the late 1990s, a particular state-led form of urban development trumped a more entrepreneurial, rural, market-driven approach—leading to massive developmental efforts going into urban regions.[58] As the urbanist Xuefei Ren has argued, China's economic boom since 1990 is an urban boom; the Chinese miracle is being realized in its largest urban regions.[59]

The Chinese urban experience not only conforms partly to the Western experience, but also has features that confound that experience. The central government has played a key role in the development of Chinese cities since the 1980s, managing regional development, redesigning and devolving the fiscal system to more local levels, and empowering municipal governments; in more recent years, too, it has reallocated resources away from rich and heavily populated eastern coastal cities.[60] Cities have become the main driver of the Chinese economy—a far cry from the anti-urbanism that afflicted the Mao years—although scholars of Chinese urbanism still believe that their agglomeration potential has yet to be fully realized, in terms of productivity or energy-efficiency gains, for example. China has its share of the world's megacities now, too: Shanghai, Beijing, and Tianjin all have well over the 10 million population threshold, and the advent of the BRI is likely to help to generate new megacity dynamics in the interior, such as at Chengdu, Chongqing, and Wuhan. Vast new regional networks of cities are emerging as a result—the Chengdu-Chongqing region, or the Qingdao-Jinan region—to rival the older coastal agglomerations along the Pearl River Delta, or the Lower Yangtze River Delta. China's opening to the world means that these models for urbanization will be shared and applied abroad.[61]

China's urbanization is also one of the great construction events—and thus climate-change drivers—in human history. China now has the largest construction market in the world, surpassing, in 2010, that of the United States.[62] Indeed, 40 percent of the newly urban population in the early twenty-first century did not move at all; cities arose around them, as nearby urban settlements expanded to encompass rural areas.[63] In the final two decades of the twentieth century and first decade of the twenty-first, the development of China's built environment—including skyscrapers, condominiums, parks, and squares—may have exceeded that of the rest of the world combined.[64] In one year at the beginning of the century, as Thomas Campanella points out, new housing construction in China exceeded more than 10 percent of US housing stock.[65] Almost one-third of global urban land expansion in the first fifteen years of the twenty-first century occurred in China.[66] Here too, spatially determined inequalities, often exacerbated by governance decisions, have developed. Millions of formerly rural residents now surrounded by cities—many in the *chengzhongcun*, or urban villages—find themselves without access to basic urban services. While agglomeration of industries, particularly in large cities, was a notable feature of this urbanization, density has none-theless given way to sprawl in low-density peripheries. "The urbanization of families has lagged behind the urbanization of jobs," concluded a 2014 report published jointly by the World Bank and the Development Research Center of China's State Council, "while the urbanization of land has happened faster than the urbanization of people."[67]

Historically, urbanization has occurred around the world without the intentional direction of national—or colonial—governments. But this is not the case in late twentieth-century China. Rather, this intense, un-precedented urbanization has been shaped by a shifting set of national strategies.

National Policies

Statements, declarations, and constitutional changes by China matter. They reflect philosophical, intellectual, and ideological shifts, and have bureaucratic and policy implications. The urbanization that both under-girds and has created the need for the BRI, and focused attention on en-vironmental issues, was a vision of the state. The concept of the ecological civilization, too, became a party goal in 2012 and was incorpo-rated into the national constitution. And the BRI itself, as previously noted, was written into the constitution of the People's Republic of China in 2017.

The paths from plans to implementation in China are bureaucratic, and are more complex than can ever be summarized, but national guidance on building efficiency and urban congestion—two critical elements in urban development across the global urban spectrum—offers some insight into the control over urbanization exercised by policymakers and policy guidance. In the 13th Five-Year Plan (2016–2020), one of twenty parts was dedicated to "New Urbanization," with the subsections: promote urban residency for people with rural household registration living in urban areas; improve the distribution and layout of urban areas; improve the housing supply system; and promote coordinated urban and rural development.[68] In the section "A New Style of City," the plan declared the government's commitment to harmonious and pleasant cities, and related it to the growing ecological concerns driving the policy direction of ecological civilization: "We will build green cities by adjusting the scale of cities in accordance with their resource and environmental carrying capacities, using eco-friendly planning, design, and construction standards, and carrying out initiatives to build ecological corridors and restore ecosystems."[69] One method identified for achieving these new cities was "promoting the construction of eco-friendly buildings." To this end, the government established the goal of 50 percent certification of new building construction by China Three Star, the green building evaluation program administered by the Ministry of Housing and Urban-Rural Development. From the national level, this ministry additionally provides technical guidelines and standards for energy-efficiency codes and for new technologies.[70] While at times the lack of regular review and ongoing evolution of policy has hindered the uptake of these standards, some local governments developed codes that exceeded the goals or ambitions of the national government. The city of Beijing, for example, developed a code for buildings' energy efficiency that is stricter than that of the central government, as well as an action plan with financial incentives for certified ultra-low-energy buildings.[71]

Sometimes, such metric-driven development leads to unintended consequences. The 2013 announcement and 2014 plan to reduce the use of coal and replace it with gas led to ambitious efforts by local leaders to retrofit millions of homes. "The percentage of coal in the national energy mix dropped to 60.4 percent [with a goal of 65 percent]," noted Yifei Li and Judith Shapiro in *China Goes Green*, "because of overenforcement at subnational levels. In people's homes, as in factories, old coal-burning equipment was destroyed in the enthusiasm to make the switch."[72] Ultimately, the lack of sufficient natural gas to meet the unexpected demand from homes and factories led to an absence of heat for homes that had transitioned. Nonetheless, national policies and goals continue to work as central ideas around which local leaders can demonstrate their capacity and innovate. The Ministry of Transportation's 13th Five-Year Plan for Urban Public Transport included recommendations for mitigating congestion and transportation-related pollution in urban centers that ultimately resulted in, among other developments, a partnership between the Beijing Municipal Government, China's Ministry of Transportation, and the World Resources Institute to develop the capital city's, and the nation's, first low-emissions zone and congestion-charge policy.[73] But new eco-cities, or districts, don't always succeed. The Sino-Singapore Tianjin EcoCity, located on China's northern coast, has developed innovative green tactical practices, while other new green developments, such as Dongtan, have met with limited success as coherent or functioning urban areas.[74] While it might be easier to make new cities "green"; it is not always easy to make new cities.

In March 2021, the National People's Congress approved China's 14th Five-Year Plan (2021–2025). It guides economic and social development, and, as with the 13th Five-Year Plan, provides signposts and indicators around which national ministries can plan. Given the continuing urbanization in China and its implication for social stability, economic development, human welfare, and climate change, such strategic visions, explicitly focused on the particulars of urban development, remain of immense importance. The 14th Five-Year Plan included a Climate Change Special Plan—to be implemented, in part, by local leaders—and outlined a vision to "improve the new urbanization strategy and improve the quality of urbanization development."[75] It also offered details:

> We will scientifically plan the layout of urban green rings, green corridors, green wedges, and greenways, promote ecological restoration and functional improvement projects, prioritize the development of urban public transportation, build a slow-moving network such as bicycle lanes and walking paths, develop smart construction, promote green building materials, prefabricated buildings, and steel structure residences, and construct low-carbon cities.[76]

The plan also signaled a shift away from sprawling urbanization toward more centralized, so-called human-centric cities:

> We will promote urban design and style management and control, implement the new era of building policies that are suitable, economical, green, and beautiful, and strengthen the management and control of newly constructed high-rise buildings. We will accelerate the promotion of urban renewal, renovate and enhance the functions of existing areas such as old communities, old factories, old blocks, and urban villages, promote the renovation of old buildings, and actively expand and construct parking lots and charging stations.[77]

The urban visions of the respective Five-Year Plans touch on everything from transportation and leisure practices within cities to connective links between them, as well as their regional balance. Ambitious in scope and detail, the Five-Year Plans will shape cities across China, and, via influence and emulation, within China's BRI partners—leading to China's ambition being implemented in an incredibly diverse array of city typologies in different regions.

Shenzhen and Shanghai: The Opening

The economic reform outlined by Deng Xiaoping in his 1978 Chinese Communist Party's Central Work Conference began taking legislative and material form in 1980. The "Provisional Regulations on Promoting Economic Cooperation" authorized four special economic zones in Shenzhen, Zhuhai, Shantou, and Xiamen. Shenzhen has become perhaps the most well-known of the original SEZs owing, at least in part, to its vertiginous increase in population from around thirty thousand residents at the time of the opening to more than ten million by 2010. This rapid population rise was matched by historic development in the built environment, both in terms of urban land cover and vertical construction. The Shenzhen SEZ included both the old market town and more than eight hundred square miles of the surrounding Bao'an County. Municipal borders were no match for the new vision of economic development and urbanization: the urban area is now six hundred times larger than the footprint of the original town.[78] Looking up as well as out, the total floor area under construction in the 1980s and 1990s expanded enormously:

the total floor area under construction in 1980 was double that of 1979, just one year earlier; and whereas between 1980 and 1987 sixty-six towers standing over three hundred feet had been constructed, barely a decade later the city contained 753 buildings over eighteen stories tall.[79] Policy innovation and experimentation accompanied urbanization. Shenzhen experienced radical reforms in housing, the first property auction in the PRC, a new stock exchange, and the first privatization of a state-owned enterprise. The extraordinary development of both the built environment and of the policies that helped shape it held import beyond the initially envisioned SEZ. "From the very beginning," architect and scholar Juan Du observed, "Shenzhen was to fulfill this threshold function in two ways: as a model for the rest of China and as an example for the rest of the world to see China's capability and commitment to reform."[80] Even today, the nodding to a larger audience continues. Shenzhen continues to sprawl and operate around a car culture, yet the city has also developed a capillary infrastructure: an expanding under/overground railway network and eco-tourism resort with references to Swiss retreats.[81]

The story of the Instant City contains a couple of crucial threads that are not immediately visible from a quick glance at the emergent skyline. First, the existing market town and topography, while small in scale compared to the eventual city and urban area, did influence Shenzhen's development. While Beijing did seek out relatively undeveloped urban areas for the initial SEZ experiments, Shenzhen was not a tabula rasa. Early investment, both national, international, and from Hong Kong, found its way to existing industries, as did new arrivals to existing housing. The earliest Master Plan, completed in 1982, built on existing geographic and environmental considerations, as well as features of the existing housing stock.[82] Even the population figures have been mythologized to celebrate the breakneck urbanization. Although in 1979 there may have been only tens of thousands of residents in the old market town, the population of the Shenzhen city region was much larger, over 314,000.[83]

Second, the Shenzhen story really is a regional story, with SEZ twists. Connectivity to neighboring Hong Kong, international talent, and the global economic system proved crucial. Indeed, a good portion of Shenzhen's early success is attributable to its proximity to Hong Kong. Between 1986 and 1994, nearly 80 percent of the foreign direct investment that flowed into the SEZ was from Hong Kong investors.[84] Hong Kong had money but needed the land and cheap labor that was readily available in Shenzhen. According to Weiping Wu, a specialist on urban China, during this initial period labor costs in Shenzhen were 50 percent to 70 percent lower than those of Hong Kong, while factory rent was nearly 70 percent cheaper.[85] Reflecting this complementarity, Hong Kong's direct investment in Shenzhen was concentrated around labor-intensive sectors such as textiles, garments, dying, rubber, and plastics.[86] Shenzhen was also well positioned to be a cultural crossroads, bringing together ideas from Hong Kong, Northern China and Mandarin speakers, Southern China and Cantonese speakers, and influences from the wider world.[87] While urbanists and development experts have often pointed to the value of regional approaches, this regional approach came with the added SEZ dimension. This zonal strategy was explicit, and would indeed be replicated. By 2003, less than twenty-five years after the initial four SEZs were inaugurated, the number of development zones in China had reached more than seven thousand.[88]

As historians and planners examine the early years of Shenzhen's opening, it has become clear that any coherent ideology or philosophy of urban development, municipal or regional, came after the fact, or likely oversimplifies the process. Yes, there was master planning, including with regard to population; but population growth continually outpaced official planning.[89] Law-making powers were distributed, according to the SEZ ideal, from Beijing to the provincial government of Guangdong, but even then many of the experiments in urbanization actually occurred "at the local level, in real time" as Du has put it, and involved plenty of trial and error.[90] Ultimately it was central control, both from Beijing and within the city government itself, that reified the narrative of Shenzhen's rise, going so far as to remove the "special" in SEZ for its case, as the so-called miracle became an example rather than an exception.[91]

Shanghai's outward turn involved a similar patchwork of governance coupled with an intentional development of urban areas as instruments of connectivity to the wider world. Shanghai has long held a unique administrative status within China, allowing the Shanghai municipal government to operate with many of the authorities of a provincial government. For Deng Xiaoping, and other party leaders, including Party Secretary Jiang Zemin and Premier Zhu Rongji, the city's financial, commercial, and spatial development was a priority. Support for Shanghai's development has come in many forms, some regulatory, some more material. Development of the Pudong New Area, in particular, began with plans launched from 1984 through the 1990s that would draw from diverse approaches to city transformation through connectivity.

The so-called Head of the Dragon resulted from a number of intentional policies, including development of a stock market, a free trade zone, and strong links between Shanghai and Beijing that allowed for substantive annual loans. Indeed, not unlike Shenzhen, a rather intricate governance structure—involving local government, businesses, state bureaucracies, state-owned enterprises, and diaspora investors—informed the transformation of both Shanghai and Pudong.

The relationships between the city and the world—as a destination for capital, as a symbol of China's global role and of modernity itself—remained of central concern. "Pudong is best understood," writes Anna Greenspan, "alongside Le Corbusier's City of Tomorrow, Baron Haussmann's Paris and Robert Moses's New York—as one of the great projects of modern urbanization."[92] If the Oriental Pearl Tower, completed in 1994, spoke to modernization and openness, the 2010 World Expo in Shanghai spoke to global standing and optimism, while being used within the city to alter urban behavior, in particular dress and fashion.[93] "Pudong," Greenspan notes, "is better thought of as an economic strategy than as an urban design. It was intended as a mechanism through which the city could transition from a rigidly top-down bureaucratic system to the more flexible and open networks of the open market."[94] The *lilong*, or larger neighborhood compound with long alleys and courtyards that as late as the 1940s covered more than 70 percent of Shanghai, was replaced by housing patterns more familiar to inhabitants of the late twentieth-century Global City.[95] High-rise luxury compounds, surrounded by green areas and wide streets, have taken the place of the *lilong*, while repetitive housing blocks have expanded the city's edges outward.[96]

These moves were part of an urban strategy that was very much of its time, and now is being rethought, as China turns away from reliance on global capital markets and Western models of urbanism, and develops its own alternative economic model. The Shanghai of the 1990s and early 2000s now seems like a city of an era slipping away in Xi's China—with its new relationship to a form of controlled globalism within the BRI, and recent moves toward decoupling from some of its interdependencies with US and global financial markets. Shanghai now bears the marks of a Reform Period flirtation with the Global City form and its starchitects, a remnant of a time when its urban morphology mimicked that of the great Global Cities of the world and optimism remained that China would merge into the liberal international economic and political order.

The patterns of this initial development, too—the razing of older, historical housing and buildings, the construction of signature buildings with limited regard for pedestrian transport, the focus on external appeal and symbolism—while driving Shanghai's remarkable growth, have not proven to be as productive as the livable, people-centered, green cities extolled in the most recent Five-Year Plan. As the policy goals and rhetoric have shifted—at both the national and local levels—so too have the approaches to urbanism. The Shanghai municipal government's latest "Measures for Urban Renewal" have sought to preserve and restore older areas, to develop Shanghai versions of the trendy Fifteen-Minute City concept, and to pursue approaches to new development that are low carbon and "put people first."[97] The helter-skelter boom years of Reform Period Shanghai are becoming a memory. And while these latest shifts may seem localized, they reflect larger strategic forces, including the BRI.

Xi'an: Turning Westward

The particulars of urban development outlined in the 14th Five-Year Plan—small, medium, and large cities, green seemingly all the way around and throughout—also include a vision for balancing urbanization and economic development across China. Smaller cities in western and central China are meant to be integrated into BRI corridors. Medium-sized cities in the same regions, too, will be developed with an eye toward balancing the economic strength of the East and South: "We will promote the coordinated development of urban agglomerations in the middle reaches of the Yangtze River, accelerate the construction of the Wuhan and Changsha-Zhuzhou-Xiangtan metropolitan areas, and create an important national growth pole."[98] And consistent with BRI strategies, central elements of development will be corridors and connectivity, in particular the Beijing-Harbin, Beijing-Guangzhou, and Baotou-Kunming railways.

Shenzhen, coastal cities, and SEZs more generally, all home to myriad overlapping experiments in governance and economic growth, drove China's opening to the world. From the opening in 1978 until 1998, roughly 85 percent of foreign investment was directed toward coastal areas, with less than 5 percent flowing to central or western China.[99] Concern with, and approaches to, balanced regional development differ by countries and regions. While in the later years of the twentieth century the US federal government ceded regional development plans to larger economic forces, earlier, after World War II, the United States used intentional strategic interventions to balance development across the country. Between countries and regions, the European Union has made use of infrastructure investment as well as publicity campaigns—the European capital of culture, for example—to bring regional development into greater balance. None of these efforts, however, likely match those deployed by China to expand its economic growth model westward, including beyond China's own borders.

The "coastal turn" was followed by a turn inward and westward, including the establishment of seventeen new economic zones, mostly in the central and western regions. But inward did not mean less connection with the world. To the contrary, development of urban and economic centers in central and western China opened new opportunities for connectivity.[100] As we have seen, corridors were developed that extended to the Indian Ocean, and overland through Central Asia and Europe from western China, with cities such as Xi'an serving as anchors in China. While the turn westward predated Xi's premiership and the BRI, it has accelerated under the strategic framework.

Although its launch in 2011 preceded the BRI, the China-Europe Freight Train (CEFT) has over the past ten years become one of the BRI's signature projects. CEFT routes pass through approximately two hundred cities in nearly forty countries in Europe and Asia, not to mention key cities in central and western China, including Wuhan, Zhengzhou, Chengdu, and Urumqi.[101] As Xiangming Chen has detailed, the central location of Xi'an within China and as a spoke for CEFT routes fundamentally altered the city's urban form: connectivity, and in this case logistics, transformed the metropolitan region of nearly nine million people. Long home to a diverse population representative of the ancient Silk Road trades, and still home to one of China's most significant Muslim populations, the ancient city is now surrounded by dense sprawl and congested streets. In the first decade or so of the twentieth century, the urban area around the city center expanded from about 72 square miles to around 132 square miles.

The International Trade and Logistics Park, a center of the logistics-based urbanization, occupies roughly a thirty-five-square-mile area northeast of central Xi'an.[102] The park was meant to bring together a bounded zone with an inland port and rail container center; or, as one provincial party official later put it, to be a "hub, gateway, and flow space."[103] More CEFT rails depart from or return to Xi'an than any other city, with more than 3,600 trains passing through the metropolitan area in 2020, easily exceeding the rail traffic in Chengdu and Chongqing. Many of these include domestic freight, but increasingly they include trains moving goods across Central Asia and into Europe, to Italy, Germany, and the Netherlands.[104]

The development of the park, including its location outside the city center, was explicitly conceived of as a point of not just connectivity, but also urbanity: a model of a new, fixed city cluster that facilitates connectivity with the world. If Shanghai became the urban symbol of the "entrepreneurial state," Xi'an now serves that same symbolic role for the "logistics state" of the BRI. Hotels, movie theaters, and restaurants cater to visiting executives (including then Facebook CEO Mark Zuckerberg in 2016, pictured running along the old ramparts with high-rise housing in the backdrop). Urbanists draw an important distinction between cities and metropolitan regions. Cities are discrete territorial units. Their boundaries match those of their political authorities, and so they can make statements that represent both governments and residents.[105] Metropolitan regions, meanwhile, link urban spaces that often have shared economies, transportation routes, and climate-change challenges, but do not necessarily share a governance structure. Increasingly, often at the advice of sustainability experts, economic and business advisers, and international organizations like the Organization for Economic Cooperation and Development (OECD), neighboring cities and towns are working to develop or improve their metropolitan or regional planning and governance structures. Important instances of this in China include, most famously, Beijing-Tianjin-Hebei (Jing-Jin-Ji), the Yangtze River Delta, and, in the case of Shenzhen, the Pearl River Delta. These urban agglomerations account for almost 40 percent of China's GDP and require regional planning. While Shaanxi has been a dynastic home (and birthplace of President Xi's father), it has also long been one of China's poorer provinces. Now the park itself, and the connectivity offered by Xi'an, has led to export-focused electronic companies relocating to, or investing in, the area.[106] The nine-hundred-mile trip via rapid passenger train to Shanghai takes around six hours. Hundreds of companies from coastal cities have moved to the area and, according to Chen, the free trade zone has attracted more than three hundred border-crossing e-commerce companies. And luxury goods, from cars to clothes to cosmetics, pass through Xi'an storage facilities before moving on to destinations through China.

The CCP, beginning after World War II, but especially from the late 1970s on, has recognized the value of urbanization as a tool for both economic development and social control. Yet urban development, and even zones within cities, have been undertaken as much with an eye to connection and the development of place. SEZs in eastern China have long facilitated movements in capital and labor, while their architecture and spaces have signaled openness, standing, and strength to the outside world. More recent urban transformations in central and western China have also connected China outward, through BRI projects. This is a selective form of openness, married to control and patronage, and in the service of a larger geopolitical and geoeconomic vision. In all of these cases, the urban form preceding the BRI framework has informed the current urban development. And importantly, in cities like Xi'an, but also in the eastern cities, this connectivity has itself altered the Chinese urban environment. The life of cities is hard to dictate, and even more so amid dynamic connections and flows of goods, capital, and people.

Connected Urban Forms: BRI Cities

The new corridor-based network of cables, infrastructure, goods, supply chains, and shipping routes that is the fundamental strategic focus of the BRI uses cities as depots, nodes, and hubs. And just as the BRI is influencing the form of cities within China, the material effects of connectivity are giving rise to new urban shapes beyond China too. But because the BRI stretches across continents and defies easy definition, and because of the agency of local actors and the importance of local history and context, there will likely never be a singular urban form associated with the BRI cities. Global and regional development, whether American-led or Chinese-led, is never as successful as its critics maintain at melting away local nuances and histories.

There are, however, to borrow from Nicholas Phelps, partial convergences and universal elements of the urban environment that have been brought about by, and represent, the globalization that has developed under the carapace of US geopolitical power and hegemony.[107] As Phelps, Stanek, and others have demonstrated, urban influences and impacts also develop at various scales, from buildings to blocks, from roads to highways, from light rail to freight rail, and from the neighborhood to the regional. Given the simultaneity of so much BRI development and its regional and global connectivity, portraits of urban developments, from the smallest in scale to those encompassing whole regions, allow us to identify some emerging patterns. Next we trace some of these dynamics, from the market squares and new towns of West Africa, to glittering ports on the Arabian Sea, to new railway hubs in Southeast Asia.

Cape Coast, Ghana

Cape Coast, a sixteenth-century Portuguese trading post and once the capital of Britain's Ghanaian colony, is now a secondary city, home to fewer than two hundred thousand residents. The Kotokuraba Market, the city's economic heart, is located near the southwestern border of Ghana's central region, about half a mile from the coastline and from Cape Coast Castle, a material, architectural reminder of the trans-Atlantic slave trade. Cape Coast served as the capital city of the British crown colony for seventy years after slave trade was banned in Britain, until the capital was moved to Accra in 1877. In the late 1930s and 1940s, as British rule approached its twilight in much of Africa, and nearly half a century after Cape Coast lost its standing as Ghana's primary city, the governing powers worked with local residents to build the Kotokuraba Market. The new market was meant to serve as a shopping and economic hub for British officials and residents and to enable the relocation of beachfront stalls away from the shore and from new administrative areas.[108]

In the years since Kotokuraba's construction and Ghanaian independence in 1957, the market's effective space has moved beyond its initial footprint, with stalls and stores opening in the adjoining Kotoka Market, and transportation hubs—Mankessim Station and Edina Station—emerging to serve the commercial ecosystem. Vibrant and yet formal—requiring licenses, taxes, rents, and rules—the market's physical structure eroded over time, and when a failing roof exposed stalls to rainfall and weather, the renovation of Kotokuraba became a political issue. Having made the market's refurbishment a feature of his presidential campaign agenda in 2008, President John Evans Atta-Mills, along with the Ghanaian ministry of finance and the appointed mayor of the Cape Coast Metropolitan Authority, looked to China for financing.

Here the details can read a bit like dry diplomatic and financial history, but it is through such details that the projection of international power can take form as a local built environment. On the advice of the representative Chinese diplomat, the government of Ghana, as the guarantor, applied to the Export-Import Bank of China for a concessional loan. The $200 million request, as detailed in Lewis Abedi Asante and Ilse Helbrecht's micro-history of the project, featured plans for stores, stalls, supermarkets, banks, medical clinics, toilets, and a car park. When approval arrived for a reduced, $30 million redevelopment loan, it came with caveats, some on the scale of geopolitics, others as detailed construction plans. In addition to having to adhere to a One China principle with regard to relations with Taiwan, the borrowers would have to work with a Chinese construction firm, China Railway Construction and Engineering Group Limited, and use material sourced in China. Once signed in November 2012, the financing was to be repaid by the municipality over a twenty-five-year term at 2 percent annual interest, through market rents.[109] In other words, international financing from the China Export-Import Bank was secured through the promise of rents from trading spaces located in a market in a secondary city on the coast of West Africa.

For shoppers, as well as shop-and-stall keepers at the Kotokuraba Market, this meeting of local development needs and Chinese foreign policy had material implications. To begin with, the local design firm was replaced by a Chinese firm, consistent with the terms of the loan. Redevelopment of the market in a way that reduced commercial opportunity while changing the feel, process, and look of shopping was perhaps even more broadly felt. As Asante has detailed, vendor engagement in the design process was extremely limited and it showed: there were not enough trading spaces to accommodate existing merchants; stalls were too small for vendors; trading lanes of similar groups were broken up; and a mall-style, antiseptic feel of porcelain-tiled floors and even superstores was deployed. The material implications of the removed design process were matched by economic decisions that rendered precarious the viability of the stalls for merchants. Rents, set significantly above pre-improvement levels to match the financing requirements, threatened to push out stall- and shop-keepers.

It is the rare exercise in globalization—whether Chinese, British, or American led—where terms dictated are the terms that determine outcomes. Merchants pressured Ghanaian politicians, often outside of the bureaucratic processes meant to determine rents, to lower prices. And Cape Coast leaders, fearing that the well-organized market would give way to something more informal as merchants moved to the streets, worked to ensure the construction of further commercial spaces, including into entranceways, public open spaces, and fire exits. Mean-while, enterprising merchants with newly renovated spaces adapted them ad hoc, building vertically and closing off the fluidity of the space. The design and feel of Cape Coast's economic center, Kotokuraba Market, now speaks to the material implications of the projection of power and influence, and its limits. Make no mistake, the market is different because of Chinese intervention, and by extension, China's geopolitical strategy—only not exactly in the ways that the Export-Import Bank had dictated or planned. A colonial space has been updated for a new world. Though different from the local vision, the space has been localized.

Kilamba, Angola

In Kilamba, Angola, some 2,485 miles southeast of Cape Coast and the Kotokuraba Market, a much more ambitious Chinese intervention in urban form can be found. Kilamba is a so-called New Town, located on the outskirts of Luanda, the nation's capital. Following independence in 1975, and four centuries of Portuguese influence and rule, the capital city—modeled in part on plans by Portuguese planners—experienced extraordinary growth. Between independence and the beginning of the new century, the population in Luanda expanded from around 600,000 residents to more than five million.[110] Since the conclusion of the country's civil war in 2002, the Angolan government has undertaken the development of a number of housing projects, as well as satellite towns, including Kilamba, to meet the housing demands of a population that largely resides in informal settlements. The scale of the housing development in Kilamba, as Sylvia Croese has pointed out, is rivaled in recent sub-Saharan history by post-apartheid South Africa, and was advanced, in part, by special state agencies sitting outside of the established bureaucracy.[111]

Construction on Kilamba's first phase began in 2008. The Chinese CITIC Group Corporation Ltd., a state-owned enterprise, took the lead as part of an exchange of construction material and expertise for Angolan resources. As Łukasz Stanek has demonstrated, such in-kind exchanges have a long history in urban development, especially when the country on the receiving end of prefabricated housing faces limitations in currency exchange or debt facilitation, or is rich in resources such as oil. Two years later, Xi Jinping, as vice president, made an official trip to Angola, while construction continued in Kilamba.[112]

New Towns, or in many cases New Cities, are to be found in development, or more likely being planned for development, across Africa and
Asia. Some such urban areas, like Kilamba, border preexisting cities.
Almost all of them, like Tatu City, near Nairobi; Waterfall City, near
Johannesburg; and New Town projects near Khartoum, seek to take advantage of urban agglomeration as a strategy for undertaking green
development while linking to, and driving, existing economies and addressing existing housing crises.[113] In certain cases, like Konza Smart
City in Kenya, the government and developers utilize parts of the SEZ
model—such as granting or leasing the land to private holders—to try
and jumpstart innovation. (As Andrea Pollio points out, such efforts
often occur side by side with other international efforts, such as, in the
case of Konza Smart City, a South Korean–financed and built university
and roads that are Italian built and EU financed.) In many cases, the
New Towns and urban areas are meant to show both a domestic and international audience that a new era has arrived, with new rules. Consider
Egypt's New Administrative Capital, where the China State Construction Engineering Corporation is building the central business district,
rail infrastructure, as well as the tallest skyscraper in Africa.

In something of a natural experiment, Kilamba was developed at
roughly the same time as other Luanda-adjacent New Towns, in particular Zango and Panguila. In those new developments, as Rachel Keeton
has detailed, residents have adapted spaces to their own commercial
and residential purposes. Kilamba, meanwhile, was intentionally designed to prevent such organic adaptation.[114] Composed of dozens
of towers offering condominiums with parking spaces and Chinese-
designed interiors—aluminum door frames, tiles, drywall—Kilamba offers relatively spacious housing. Yet without commercial and mixed-use
spaces, the urban areas lack dynamism. Kilamba, which has now gone
through multiple phases of development, and could eventually house
more than 750,000 residents, has also gone through multiple stages: an
infamous "ghost city" to which Western journalists parachuted in; a
high-priced, exclusive area subject to accusations of patronage and corruption; and finally, a destination for aspiring middle-class Angolans. In
expanding the housing supply, Kilamba and other state-led projects may
also have made housing more accessible and affordable elsewhere.[115]
Kilamba does not capture the full story of Angolan urbanization, which,
as Croese has recently demonstrated, includes presidential control and
patrimonialism. But while Kilamba remains somewhat exceptional amid

the informal housing at its borders and the complex, ongoing development of centuries-old Luanda, it still offers a glimpse of the Chinese
vision for urbanization in distant places like Africa.[116]

Gwadar Port City, Pakistan

Located on the Arabian Sea opposite Oman, Gwadar Port is the oceanic
endpoint of the China-Pakistan Economic Corridor, making it a vital
strategic urban space and showcase for the BRI's most important corridor as yet. For landlocked countries and economies in Central and East
Asia, the port offers the promise of access to the Middle East and Africa.
Such ports, and their adjoining urban areas, have become among the
more visible BRI projects. As we saw, the Sri Lankan port of Hambantota
is perhaps the most notorious example of the so-called debt trap of BRI
financing. BRI-associated projects and financing have also advanced in
the ports of Hamburg, Germany, and Piraeus, Greece. And the deepwater port, special economic zone, and residential housing developed at
Kyaukphyu, on the Bay of Bengal, provides an outlet for oil and natural
gas, as well as agricultural products.

    Amid these and other developments, Gwadar Port offers numerous
advantages over other regional ports, from its depth, to its natural break-
water, to its desert climate that means there is little change in weather
throughout the season. In 2007, through an agreement with the Gwadar
Port Authority (GPA), the Port of Singapore Authority acquired respon-
sibility for development and operations. In 2013 those rights, including
over 2,280 acres of land for the free port zone, were transferred to China
Overseas Ports Holding Company Limited (COPHC)—which holds a
memorandum of understanding for financing with the China Development Bank—for forty-three years.

    But of course, for Gwadar to be the port envisioned by both China
and Pakistan, it must also be a city. The ensuing city-port split, as well as
the administrative structures that shape urban development in Pakistan,
have led to a patchwork of governance. While the GPA holds responsi-
bility for supervision of the areas leased to the COPHC, a separate entity, the Gwadar Development Authority (GDA), is charged with
developing the rest of the city where, in theory, tens of thousands of port
employees will live. This division is significant. The port authority is a
federal entity that reports to the Ministry of Maritime Affairs of the government of Pakistan. The city's development authority, meanwhile, is

regional, reporting to the government of Balochistan.[117] These divides in governance influence—or just as often, muddle—everything from development policy to tax regimes.

Despite this governance divide, planning for Gwadar as a city is being approached somewhat holistically, much like that for other new BRI cities under consideration or development, such as New Yangon City and Yatai New City in Myanmar. The city's master plan—Gwadar, "the smart port city where you're always welcome"—has been drafted by a subsidiary of the China Communications Construction Company, Ltd. A small town previously driven by fishing is envisioned as expanding to around two million residents over the next thirty years, with dormitories located near the port, as well as hotels, shopping plazas, and a cruise-ship docking area populating the isthmus. The plan for the city itself includes a cultural experience zone, a tourism center, a seaside resort, and a number of hotels. Ecological corridors and green streets are meant to run throughout the city, in keeping with the steering vision of ecological civilization. The plan itself captures the complicated governance of Gwadar, with the offices of the GDA, GPA, and the municipal authority situated mere blocks away from each other.[118]

The port, despite heavy investment, has yet to meet with heavy shipping traffic, and the city's development is lagging, demonstrating some of the challenges of BRI-driven urban spaces. The local population, most of whom were there before the project began, still struggle to access basic services, especially water (a situation made worse by drought), and electricity, access to which has been hindered by a lack of connection to the national grid.[119] Chinese workers, brought in to help develop and operate the port, have also become a lightning rod in the middle of long-standing tension and violence between Balochistan and the federal government of Pakistan. And as health, education, and other basic services have fallen behind, economic tensions have increased. Rumors and official announcements of development have driven up land prices, while, according to the local population, the traditional fishing economy has come under pressure from Chinese fishing trawlers.[120] In November 2021, thousands took to the streets in Gwadar to protest checkpoints, the lack of services, and, most visibly, the emergent challenge to the local fishing economy. While the Chinese Ministry of Foreign Affairs dismissed the fishing concerns, the provincial government entered into a new agreement with the local population, with the region's chief minister affirming that "providing people the opportunity for growth, as well as the provision of fundamental rights, are our priorities," and with Pakistan's prime minister backing, at least rhetorically, the concerns of the fishermen.[121]

Boten and Vientiane, Laos

Connectivity changes cities and urban areas, in both the short and long terms. The China-Laos Railway (CLR), with a northern terminus in Kunming, China, and southern terminus in Vientiane, Laos, was officially opened in December 2021. (The broader project, the Laos-China Economic Corridor, was introduced as a concept in 2017 during a visit by President Xi to Vientiane, with the Laotian portion of the larger project estimated at $5.8 billion in 2018.) The connection will be one of many rail lines linking the major urban centers of Southeast Asia as part of the Kunming-Singapore rail network. The launch of the railway, true to the times, was virtual: President Xi joining from Beijing, and President Thongloun Sisoulith logged on from Vientiane. But the railway, and its repercussions, remain very real.

Run by the Laos-China Railway Company, a joint venture between the two countries, the China-Laos Railway runs over six hundred miles, with about four hundred miles of rail in China and two hundred miles in Laos. The associated infrastructure is significant. In Laos alone, the railway passes through 75 tunnels and over 165 bridges.[122] The CLR is among the most sectorally integrated of major BRI projects. It has brought together expertise in large-scale engineering, finance, construction, economic development, design—and, notably, plans for long-term capacity development to enable local maintenance of the railway. All of these features, but particularly those focused on commerce and the development and maintenance of the built environment, have had a direct influence on urban spaces along the railway's route.

At the China-Laos border, Mohan and Boten offer an urban typology not unfamiliar to the BRI: a metro region with transborder agglomeration driven by infrastructure and supply-chain connectivity. Like Khorgos, the area on the Laos side includes a special economic zone as well as a logistics hub for clearing freight and a passenger railway. The Boten special economic zone, under development by a Yunnan-based real estate company, is a new town. Pictures taken in the 1980s of Boten, and the border-crossing in particular, include dirt roads and narrow streets lined by forest. The special economic zone predates the BRI, as it does with so many of the cities being altered by BRI-affiliated projects, and Boten experienced something of a boom in the early twentieth century as a gambling destination.

Following a feasibility study, the "China Mohan–Laos Boten Cross-Border Economic Cooperation Framework Agreement" was signed by the SEZs on both sides in 2010.[123] The former casino town is now transitioning to logistics and tourism. In the case of Boten, this includes an area meant to house 300,000 or more people and an economy that moves beyond transportation to include e-commerce and agriculture, much of it powered by Chinese companies. Boten, the golden land of gambling riches, has been rebranded as Boten Beautiful Land. As the IPCC has made clear, emerging cities and urban areas like Boten have significant options for developing in ways that mitigate carbon emissions, including through strategic patterns of land use and ecosystem engagement. In particular, the conservation of green and blue assets, the development of urban forests, and the use of green roofs, walls, and retrofits offer opportunities for emission reductions in emerging cities, whether they are compact and walkable or expansive and car-centric.[124] In Boten, the surrounding forest has given way to agriculture, while vehicle exhaust and the dust and dirt of construction have pervaded streets. Despite the presence of memoranda of understanding, major infrastructure investments, and planning, it can still feel like a borderland. Reporting from Boten, Jessica DiCarlo, a scholar of China and its borderlands, has described local labor gathering on street corners in pursuit of work, and fights between truck drivers.[125] Trade in illegal wildlife—including tiger bones for wine, elephant skin, pangolin scales, and bear bile—has been observed as recently as 2018 and likely continues. As DiCarlo reports, the wider governance system appears to cede significant power to China. Boten runs on Beijing's time zone, and allows for the use of both national currencies. A combination of representatives from the Chinese Haicheng Group and Lao government officials manage construction and operations in the area. Mirroring patterns seen in places like Gwadar City, the growth is outpacing service delivery. According to DiCarlo, the Boten SEZ Management Committee is, as of recently, still working on plans to establish offices for basic services such as health and public utilities.

Such independence and autonomy, while not an operating option in Vientiane, was still extended to some degree in Laos's largest city, located near the border with Thailand on the Mekong River. The route from Boten to the main passenger station in Vientiane, construction on which began in 2016 by the China Railway Construction Group, ultimately claimed roughly 33.4 million square feet of green space for rails and stations.[126] In the capital, the concession for the railway to the government of China granted the operators a wide array of privileges, including exclusive influence on design, construction, and telecommunications and data systems.[127] While the design of the station has been couched in the language of diplomacy and soft power, mediation between officials and the local population has been needed to arrange land-use changes. In sections of the railway, local residents have yet to agree to compensation for use of land, and in some cases, they have practiced a form of tactical urbanism seen in locations from Cairo to Caracas, constructing informal bridges to traverse the formal infrastructure.[128] In another area of Vientiane province, the planned relocation of an urban center will likely include the demolition of four hundred homes to make room for railway construction. While discussions of relocation remain in progress, these changes are couched in terms of urban benefits: reduced congestion and traffic, and improved local development opportunities. Localizing the rail maintenance is also part of the project. With training facilities and housing in Vientiane's Xaythany district, the Lao Rail Vocational Skills Academy trains conductors and engineers.

A number of joint China-Laos urban development projects have advanced alongside the CLR rail development. The Vientiane Saysettha Development Zone, an 4.4-square-mile experiment in low-carbon urbanization, was launched in 2020, and features current practices for emerging and rapidly growing urban areas: decarbonized streetlights; greenways; walkable layouts; urban forests; and transit-oriented development. The official rhetoric also reflects the "people first" approach to urbanization identified in official Chinese policy, transposed from the Chinese domestic urban context. Just as the Vientiane central train station's architecture has been described in terms of regional politics and friendship, so too have Chinese media and the Chinese lead on the Vientiane project noted the diplomatic goals of urban development: "the project will strengthen the consensus between China and Laos in addressing climate change and green and low-carbon transition, and boost the regional cooperation between China and countries in the Indochina Peninsula in tackling climate change."[129]

Sihanoukville, Cambodia

Freight trains originating in cities such as Shenzhen, Nanjing, Chengdu, and Huaihua can continue on to Vientiane.[130] But the CLR is also slated to extend farther into Southeast Asia. Trains from the Lao capital will continue on to Bangkok, the Thai capital, and then farther still, to Phnom Penh, the Cambodian capital, and the port of Sihanoukville, thereby connecting inland agriculture, manufacturing, and mining to the Gulf of Thailand and the wider Indian Ocean. In Cambodia, urbanization has historically advanced without central planning, and it continues today at notable rates. The urban population continues to grow at roughly 1.5 percent per year, while the capital's population grows at nearly 5 percent.[131] Nearly 10 percent of Cambodia's urban population does not yet have access to sanitation and roughly 40 percent lives in slums; the BRI projects in Sihanoukville have been couched in terms of not just economic, but also social, development.[132]

The Phnom Penh–Sihanoukville Expressway is the largest BRI project in a country in which China is by far the largest investor and trade partner. Running roughly 118 miles, and financed by the China Road and Bridge Corporation, the expressway seeks to cut in half the travel time between the two cities. As regional and global powers have repeatedly learned, building a road is different from dictating how it will be used. When it was first opened, according to local press, the expressway had speeding cars, slow motorcycles, cattle on the shoulder of the road, and drivers going in the wrong direction.[133] Nonetheless, the new infrastructure is facilitating movement between the port city and the capital. According to the Ministry of Public Works and Transportation, roughly 200,000 vehicles used the new expressway in the first two weeks of October 2022.[134]

The coastal city of Sihanoukville, meanwhile, has been undergoing its own transformation, one that predates this new connectivity. In concept and development, the Sihanoukville Special Economic Zone (SSEZ) dates back to 2006, when, as one of the original nineteen overseas special economic zones, it was designated a pilot development project in order to receive support from the Ministry of Commerce and the Export-Import Bank of China.[135] The SSEZ is located three miles from the airport, roughly twelve miles from the port, and ten miles from the city center. Its governance structure, as Mark Bo and Neil Loughlin have noted, is a complex patchwork of local, regional, and national; public and private.[136] Indeed, as it is in Mombasa, Addis Ababa, and Konza Smart City, Chinese investment is increasing and being applied alongside contributions of other international actors, including Japan, the Asian Development Bank, and the World Bank.[137] Chinese projects are not simply attempts to displace these preceding efforts, but are designed to work alongside them: as the National Development and Reform Commission puts it, industrial parks are to become "cooperation platforms," with existing efforts potentially "made use of."[138] Though the SSEZ began with a focus on manufacturing consumer goods, it is ultimately meant to produce materials for export, including hardware machinery, photovoltaic materials, and fine chemicals. The way in which new housing and commercial developments are built and powered will go far toward determining the future of the wider climate and of local air quality—despite rhetoric around green development, the SSEZ includes a 100-megawatt coal power plant. As of March 2020, 174 factories, mostly operated by Chinese companies and featuring more than thirty thousand employees, had opened in the zone.[139] Indeed, the model is being replicated. While Sihanoukville remains Cambodia's only deepwater port, additional BRI-related deepwater ports are under development. In May 2022, the Shanghai Construction Company and the China Road and Bridge Corporation began construction in Kampot, a southern city near the Vietnamese border, where the port complex, covering nearly 1,500 acres, will include not only an SEZ and warehousing, but also housing and green space.

Even though the SSEZ has been touted as a key BRI project, earlier and ongoing influence by local and national forces has done much to shape the zone. Indeed, as Neil Loughlin and Mark Grimsditch argue, understanding the BRI's effects in Cambodia and in the SSEZ in particular requires a firm grasp of not only Chinese policy and ambitions, but also Cambodian politics and history. In the case of the SSEZ, for example, local entrepreneurs, often with ties to the government, benefit from leasing land or acting as brokers to Chinese investors. The zone, of course, is different than the city of Sihanoukville, and while the SSEZ is a formal BRI project, Chinese influence is not limited to formal investment or to the boundaries of its areas of investment. In the later 2010s, Sihanoukville became infamous for its gambling economy and opportunities. In a short window from 2017 to 2018, the number of casinos in Cambodia grew by roughly 50 percent, with most of this growth occurring in Sihanoukville. In-person and online gambling exploded, and crime and gang activity grew. While distinct from SSEZ activity, the differences were often collapsed around xenophobia or fear of Chinese influence.[140] The gambling boom, associated crime, and the Chinese role in that crime became instruments for use in domestic Cambodian politics.[141] In contrast to the city itself, however, the Cambodian government has made a point of promising "stability and harmony" within the special economic zones. "This protection from the top levels of the Cambodian government provides a layer of stability for economic projects," write Loughlin and Grimsditch, "by providing tight political control, similar to the role the state and military played in earlier development initiatives by policing economic land concessions."[142]

Addis Ababa to Djibouti City

Some of the most intensive examples of China's engagement in Africa—both before and after the announcement of the BRI—have occurred in Ethiopia, where China's investment and interests have worked vertically across all scales, from discrete buildings to special enterprise zones, to major urban, regional, and national infrastructure projects. But just as in Laos and Cambodia, China's foreign-policy strategists' appreciation of the relationship between influence and the built environment in Ethiopia, including urban fabric and buildings, predates the BRI. China financed the new African Union headquarters in Addis Ababa, which cost nearly $200 million and opened in 2012.

The African Union is the continent's hub of multilateral affairs and its guiding international organization. It provides a training ground for Africa's leading diplomats, hosts negotiations around lodestar agreements such as "Agenda 2063: the Africa We Want," and now resides in a twenty-story tower that sits above the rest of the city. The marble and glass headquarters, designed by Chinese architect Ren Lizhi, was unveiled with the familiar diplomatic rhetoric of a "win-win" collaboration between China and African nations. Construction and maintenance of the building, however, remained a Chinese affair (a situation that has led to, among other things, charges of hacking).

The list of signature government buildings in Africa constructed with Chinese support is extensive and growing, including the parliament building and Palace of Justice in Maputo, Mozambique; a new foreign-ministry headquarters for Kenya; and a new foreign-ministry headquarters for the Democratic Republic of Congo. Indeed, even as late as 2016, the construction sector represented the largest share of Chinese direct investment in Africa.[143] In 2018, the Economic Community of West African States (ECOWAS) Commission signed a memorandum of understanding for a $32 million dollar grant from China to Nigeria to finance the Abuja headquarters of the region's leading multilateral organization.

At the diplomatic rollout, design was a talking point for both sides. The president of ECOWAS urged his Chinese counterpart and the design team to ensure that the complex would reflect "the culture and African-ness of ECOWAS Member States." Zhou Pingjian, China's ambassador to Nigeria and the ECOWAS, promised that the building design would take into consideration the regional culture. In addition to announcing the grant and the maintenance, an ECOWAS press release noted that "an ECOWAS designated authority and the China Development Bank Corporation will work together to verify records of account payments at regular intervals."[144] Back in Addis Ababa, construction on the Africa Centers for Disease Control and Prevention headquarters began in 2020.

The headquarters building, as well as the more recent projects, were themselves preceded by a wide number of endeavors, including so-called stadium diplomacy projects—with China-financed, and often China-built, football stadiums in Angola, Equatorial Guinea, Benin, Mozambique, Sierra Leone, and elsewhere. Indeed, like many communist and socialist states in the decades after World War II, China actively used building projects as a diplomatic tool, beginning as early as 1958 with the National Sports Stadium in Ulaanbaatar, Mongolia.[145] Notably, however, such efforts now plug into, or are developed alongside, a wider system of connectivity.

As Edgar Pieterse, Andrea Pollio, and Liza Rose Cirolia at the African Center for Cities have shown, most debt, including for infrastructure projects, is issued at the national rather than local level.[146] Meanwhile, bilateral lending outpaces that of multilateral organizations, including development banks, with China the leading lender to Africa. This has proven true in Ethiopia as well, with material implications in Addis Ababa. The light rail system, which opened in 2015, cost $475 million, was financed via concessional loans from China's Export-Import Bank and built by China Railway Group Limited, and now carries more than 100,000 passengers a day.[147] Given demographic and development trends, housing and transportation in sub-Saharan African cities remains a local, national, regional, and even global concern. While Ethiopia is still a largely rural country, it is also one of the most rapidly urbanizing countries in the world, with an annual growth in urban population of between 4 and 5 percent. Given the lock-in associated with urban development, especially infrastructure and buildings, the nature of this urbanization will go a long way toward determining the future of the country's economy, as well as its human and natural ecosystems. Even if compact urbanization is not always the best option, densification, transit-focused development, and co-located, mixed-use building will mean fewer emissions.[148] Smaller and medium-sized cities in sub-Saharan Africa are especially vulnerable to the impacts of climate change.[149] As is the case in many African cities with BRI projects, the development landscape is crowded with multilateral, overseas development-assistance and civil-society players. New York University's Marron Institute Urban Expansion Program, for instance, has partnered with Ethiopia's Ministry of Urban Development and Construction to open up new land for urban development, with an eye toward using systematic planning to deliver housing and economic growth.[150] The light rail project, meanwhile, offers a response to key urban concerns related to traffic congestion, air quality, and access to transportation.

China's engagement in the Horn of Africa offers a vivid example of the different scales and forms of connectivity that shape urbanization. From buildings to public transportation, to national and international rail, China's involvement is multi-scalar and multi-modal. A signature BRI project, the Addis–Djibouti Railway, runs from the capital of Ethiopia, Addis Ababa, to Djibouti's Doraleh Multipurpose Port (DMP). As with so many projects that are now part of the wider BRI narrative, the railway has a history of fits and starts that predates both China's involvement and the BRI itself. Ultimately developed by the Ethiopian Railway Corporation and the China Civil Engineering Construction Company, and financed by the Export-Import Bank of China, construction started in 2012, with commercial operations beginning six years later, in 2018. Even with a delay in opening after completion, the final paving of roads around the station, connecting it to central Addis Ababa, had yet to be completed: the capital train station of the new Ethiopian National Railway Network sat lonely, awaiting cars and congestion. As political scientists István Tarrósy and Zoltán Vörös have reported, the Addis Ababa terminus of the new line, Furi-Lebu Station, is designed using the same standards, colors, and displays as railway stations in China.[151] Costing nearly $4 billion, the Addis Ababa–Djibouti route runs approximately 470 miles, is the first fully electrified route in Africa, and is one of numerous East African rail routes financed and constructed by Chinese entities. These infrastructure projects are often developed concurrently. In May 2017, for example, as the Ethiopian railway was nearing completion, the Export-Import Bank of China financed, and China built, a passenger railway that runs about 290 miles between Nairobi and Mombasa, and is operated by a local Chinese subsidiary located in Kenya.[152]

The DMP, meanwhile, sits roughly 7.5 miles west of the capital city, Djibouti City. Although small in population—with roughly one million inhabitants, around 80 percent urban—and geographic size, Djibouti, located on the Bab al-Mandab Strait, a slim shipping route connecting Europe, Africa, Asia, and the Gulf, has increasingly become a site of regional and geopolitical chess. The US Navy maintains a base in the country, as does China's People's Liberation Army. The DMP was constructed by a number of Chinese firms, including the China State Construction Engineering Corporation, and was opened in 2017. Jointly owned by Djibouti interests and the China Merchants Group, the port provides a coastal outlet for the major railway project. In both development and operation, the port illustrates a tension in major infrastructure development: even those projects without intentional urban dimensions result in urban effects.

While the port itself, also financed by the Export-Import Bank of China, covers approximately 1,700 acres on the Doraleh littoral and can house over 114,800 feet of warehouse facilities, it has not driven economic growth or employment in the region. According to David Styan, most of the labor has come from China or other foreign countries.[153] In certain senses, the urban dimension of the port comes from its proximity to the capital, Djibouti City, as well as its long-distance connectivity to Addis Ababa. But as is so frequently the case with BRI projects, the port's developers have also eyed an additional urban dimension. The China Merchants Group, along with other companies from China, including the Dalian Port Group and the government of Djibouti, have an interest in developing the Djibouti International Free Trade Zone, which adjoins the port. The plan is to follow the "Shekou Model" (port, central area, then city), but begin with a series of clusters: a logistics industry cluster, with transportation, warehousing, logistics and distribution; a business industry cluster; a duty-free-merchandise retail cluster; a business support cluster, with financial services, information services, dormitories, office buildings, and training; and a manufacturing cluster.[154] The broader free-trade zone plan is not without implications for the old Djibouti port and the city itself. According to the developers, "the existing port has the required characteristics to be transformed into a business district. The district is expected to comprise residential areas, financial buildings, waterfront developments, and a cruise terminal to cater for the tourism activities in the city of Djibouti." In addition to a tourism hub, the new urban area will offer a "vital mixed-use city core of global stature" and "create a new urban lifestyle for the people of Djibouti."[155]

A new urban lifestyle for the people of Djibouti? They will have their say too, ultimately. For in the end it is people, whether middle-class residents in Luanda or fishermen in Gwadar, that are an essential, if not the defining, component of cities. Among the myriad tropes appearing in the 2016 New Urban Agenda adopted by UN member states is a commitment to develop "people-centered cities." This idea, to develop cities that serve the needs of people and their rights, rather than say, those of cars or economies or institutional interests, also appears with some frequency in the language of mayors and city-network leaders. Chinese policymakers, too, have attempted to make people a central concern of their national urban policies. But while it makes intuitive sense that cities should have a relationship to people, when it comes to BRI development, this relationship is less than straightforward.

The sheer scope of BRI projects within cities and urban areas, or connecting them, renders nearly impossible the idea of focusing urban development around people themselves. The parts are many: stations, railways, light rail, highways, housing, markets, ports, parks. The places, too, are many. And while the lock-in nature of infrastructure makes current development choices essential given the long-term development and climate implications, the extended time horizon of such projects hides another essential temporal fact: the development of all these component parts in all these different places is happening almost simultaneously. In the end, the BRI involves something akin to synchronized urban development on a continental and global scale. But the urban lives within are hardly synchronized. Cities have secrets. Tricks. Hacks. And those that don't, develop them. Operating in a city requires not only a sense for standard practices in urban spaces, but also knowledge of a particular city's quirks and customs. In New York City, pedestrians regularly step off of the sidewalk and into the street while waiting to cross; in San Francisco and Washington, DC, they rarely do. In Accra, walking down the street is an act of "improvisation," but one during which, as Ato Quayson vividly details in *Oxford Street, Accra*, pedestrians rarely listen to music.[156] This could not be less true of Oxford Street, London, or High Street, Oxford. And so, each Belt and Road City around the world, whatever the built environment, will in the end also be shaped by residents as they, individually and together, live their lives.

CHAPTER FOUR

Tools of Influence

Institutions, Diplomacy, and Culture

O N FEBRUARY 13, 1945, the final year of World War II, the *New York Times* printed a letter written by US president Franklin D. Roosevelt to Congress. In it, he presses legislators to adopt proposals made by an international delegation at Bretton Woods, New Hampshire, for several new international organizations that would be developed alongside the fledgling United Nations. As FDR explains:

> If we are to measure up to the task of peace with the same stature as we have measured up to the task of war, we must see that the institutions of peace rest firmly on the solid foundations of international political and economic cooperation. The cornerstone for international political cooperation is the ... proposal for a permanent United Nations.

He goes on to argue that

> international political relations will be friendly and constructive, however, only if solutions are found to the difficult economic problems we face today. The cornerstone for international economic cooperation is the Bretton Woods proposals for an international

monetary fund and an international bank for reconstruction and development. In this message I have recommended for your consideration the immediate adoption of the Bretton Woods agreements and suggested other measures which will have to be dealt with in the near future. They are all parts of a consistent whole.

He then closes his letter with a warning that lifts us out of that distant past, into a world of problems that we recognize today: the "point in history at which we stand is full of promise and of danger. The world will either move toward unity and widely shared prosperity or it will move apart into necessarily competing economic blocs."[1] The Bretton Woods settlement and the postwar international architecture that Roosevelt advocated in his letter did indeed come into being. So too did the world of competing ideological and economic blocs that he warned against, in the form of a great Cold War competition for power and respective spheres of influence.

More than four decades later, the core global institutional architecture that was born at Bretton Woods remains fundamentally intact, even if some of its original guiding principles and characteristics have become lost or altered across the intervening decades. Now, however, with the rise of China, and the fading of the US unipolar moment, the specter of competing geopolitical and geoeconomic blocs is rising once more. Struggles over the nature of the international institutional architecture are taking place at multiple levels and in multiple arenas. The BRI is at the core of Chinese ambitions to redraw the outlines of the very system that Roosevelt's endorsement helped bring to life.

China's largesse in funding the BRI is just one of the tools of influence that it wields in shaping the landscape of global governance today. It is symbolic of China's increasingly confident and assertive forays into reforming, reshaping, or perhaps, in the longer term, replacing the existing international institutional architecture. As China rises, as the balance of power continues to recalibrate, China has been pushing and probing the boundaries of that international institutional architecture, while also experimenting with its own role on the international stage. It is testing the nature of its own return to Great Power status, its own ambitions for international leadership, and its own taste for the traditional responsibilities that go with being a Great Power in the international system.

China consistently uses rhetoric designed to reassure other states that its rebalancing of power in the international system will be peaceful—that its goals of reshaping the international environment, in line with its growing status and reach, will not follow the many historical precedents when the restructuring of international order was achieved through conflict. Nevertheless, China's growing military strength, technological prowess, and strategic ambitions have alarmed neighbors and competitors, and, indeed, have begun to provoke the kind of strategic balancing that is part of a common historical pattern, and that is, indeed, predicted to recur by Realist international relations scholars.[2]

Yet the centrality of the BRI to Chinese Grand Strategy does suggest the possibility of a recalibration of international order that will be achieved primarily through economic and institutional change. The BRI's main emphasis has been economic development, connectivity, trading networks, and the export of Chinese culture and ideology. China appears to be engaged in a multidimensional strategy in which soft power, influence, and the various tools and mechanisms by which they can be projected are applied in multiple arenas simultaneously. This multi-level game of influence can at times appear contradictory, with China both trying to reform existing international institutions, while also simultaneously developing alternative institutional architectures, such as the Asian Infrastructure Investment Bank, which is seen by some as a potential rival to the World Bank. But in pursuing these multiple routes, China is giving itself room to maneuver, testing different waters, experimenting with different structures for influencing international governance. At the same time, it is forging its own identity as a (re)emerging Great Power.

China has multiple tools at hand for the projection of influence, including emerging models of economic development; international institutional architectures (old and new); transnational city networks; and cultural exports and influence. These arenas are, today, each part of a system of multilateral global governance that has characterized the post–World War II period, and that has developed increasing layers of complexity over the decades. Some of this system's core institutions have been with us since the 1940s, while other elements of the global governance ecosystem—such as activities carried out by representatives of globe-spanning, transnational city networks—are much more recent. Indeed, many scholars have advocated for restructuring our current institutions of global governance to deal with both the changing realities of power, as states rise and fall, and the many pressing governance challenges, such as the reform of the global economy and the existential threat of climate change. It may well be that the rise of China will point ultimately to new geopolitical and urban configurations beyond the limitations of the current institutional architecture.

Beyond Bretton Woods

The international institutions that arose from the ruins of World War II were designed to provide the basis for cooperation among states, and so avoid the catastrophic failures of the interwar years. The foundation of this system would be the United Nations, a replacement for the failed League of Nations, and would include institutions that have remained at the core of the international institutional architecture ever since, in one form or another: the International Monetary Fund, the International Bank for Reconstruction and Development (now the World Bank), and the General Agreement on Tariffs and Trade, which would later become the World Trade Organization. The Bretton Woods system, as this institutional architecture would come to be called, would fundamentally shape postwar international relations and global economic relations. And although for almost half a century the international system would be bifurcated by the Cold War, those institutions would continue to expand after the Soviet Union's collapse.

Now, however, the most significant shift in the international balance of power since these institutions were built—China's rise—places question marks over their future. China's relationship to these institutions has long been ambivalent, and increasingly so. The Bretton Woods system was built at a time of Chinese weakness, during the chaos of its own civil war. It was crafted by others, who imbued these institutions with structures that reflected their own values and power. China's engagement with these institutions, and commitment to them, has shifted over time: at different times it has defended them, or used them to fuel its own development, or advocated for their reform. But it has always remembered their genesis in a moment of Chinese impotence on the world stage. In the past decade, this ambivalence has only increased, as China seeks to wield more influence through the existing governance institutions and the UN system, in line with its growing strength, while also putting in place building blocks for a possible alternative governance system—looking beyond the existing structure of international society to the shadowy outlines of a different one.

In order to appreciate this ambivalence on the part of China, we must recall the intrinsic link between geopolitical power and the institutional architectures that have helped to shape international order in the modern period. For such architectures are never generated in a vacuum, nor are they the product simply of rational dialogue among states at international conferences such as Bretton Woods. They are always shaped by their historical moment, and take on the characteristics of the dominant ideas and power configurations of those moments.

Such was the case in 1919 at Versailles, with the birth of the League of Nations, a multilateral international organization aimed at sustaining peace and stability—but one constructed in a way that ignored not just the interests of defeated powers such as Germany, but the very reality of an enduring change in the distribution of geopolitical power after World War I.[3] So it was, also, with the United Nations and the Bretton Woods institutions, which sought to learn from the mistakes of the League, explicitly recognizing the balance of power as it stood at the end of World War II. The five permanent members of the newly minted UN Security Council (the United States, the Soviet Union, Britain, France, and China) were given special responsibilities to help preserve international peace and security; and new finance and trade organizations were created in order to learn from the economic collapse of the interwar period, which had fueled the growth of dictators and helped to pave the path to a second global conflict.

The domestic model of political economy of any Great Power seeking to shape the structure of international society matters greatly. In the 1940s the Bretton Woods architecture was shaped by the features of Franklin Roosevelt's domestic New Deal program. Indeed, it was explicitly viewed by Roosevelt as a projection of the New Deal onto the international stage: an attempt to engineer a new international order built around his progressive values, which aimed at greater economic and social justice, and the provision of international public goods. With this new framework, the United States sought to show that it embraced its responsibilities as a Great Power in ways that it had not when President Woodrow Wilson had failed to garner enough domestic support to ratify the League of Nations in 1919.

Bretton Woods, then, also represented the ascendance of a new set of ideas about how to organize economic and social life; a historic shift in the dominant patterns of thought. In particular, there was to be a new role for the state at the very center of economic life, and new ways for states to collaborate in smoothing out the instabilities of international capitalism. It was hoped that the Bretton Woods institutions would provide a rules-based system for global trade. And it did, though within a particular framework: the system was heavily imbued with the values of the Allied victors of the war, principles that scholars call, collectively, "embedded liberalism."[4] Despite its evolution over the decades, economic liberalism still underpins this system today, albeit in its more "dis-embedded," neoliberal form. The Bretton Woods institutions have allowed states to provide key international public goods; to underpin a stable monetary and exchange regime; to offer an international lender of last resort; to supply counter-cyclical and long-term lending, to provide the environment for open markets and balanced trade; and to coordinate international economic policy. All of this would pave the way for the great housing boom of the midcentury, and the sprawling suburbanization that characterized urban form in the mid- to late twentieth century. The institutionalization of these ideas represents a form of structural power that has lasted for decades.

Today, many voices are arguing for a reform of the institutions, because, for a variety of reasons, they have lost the impetus of social and economic equity that they were first constructed to provide. Although the Bretton Woods system helped to generate unprecedented economic growth, it is also now implicated in the creation of a world increasingly characterized by inequalities (both between and within cities and countries), economic insecurity and indebtedness, and increasingly severe climate-related breakdowns. Many of the progressive economic and social aims of the original Bretton Woods conference have been watered down or reversed; first, at the moment of its inception, by the pushback of the financiers, and, later, by the rise of the neoliberal economic paradigm. This new paradigm, which began to take hold in the 1970s, led to the partial restructuring of the system and changes to the operations of its key institutions, with the emergence of what has come to be known as the "Washington Consensus": neoliberal economic principles that favor open markets, free movement of capital, and a much reduced role for the state in guiding and regulating economic activity.

Voices calling today for the reform of the system, or for the construction of a "new Bretton Woods" to reconnect with those earlier values, and to retool these institutions to deal with the necessary tasks of rebalancing capitalism and tackling climate breakdown, may find their hopes for a new era of international cooperation, and the renewal of collective goals of global governance, dashed against the reality of growing Great Power competition and clashing value systems.[5] The Bretton Woods institutions came out of a time of clear US hegemony and were tempered in the fires of the Cold War. Today the international environment looks very different, with liberalism, democracy, and even US power itself on the defensive. One of the possible interpretations of the BRI is that it sets the stage not for a renewal of the kind of collective global governance envisaged at Bretton Woods, but for the possibility of its ultimate replacement by a new system of economic and social governance.[6] In other words, one of the biggest open questions is whether China's rise can be accommodated within the existing multilateral institutional architecture, especially given the Chinese Communist Party's firm rejection of Western-style liberalism and democratic values. During the past four decades of reform and opening, Chinese leaders had been content to use this system to facilitate China's economic development, often explicitly defending some of the primary, deep-lying ideological components that are built into the charter of the United Nations, such as sovereignty and territorial integrity. Since joining the World Trade Organization in 2001, China's economic growth skyrocketed within the existing liberal institutional array. In many respects, as US policymakers have come to belatedly realize, the post–Cold War period of rapid economic globalization has effectively been one in which an incumbent global hegemon has provided conditions favorable to the growth of a new systemic rival.

With the advent of the BRI, then, we may be witnessing the birth pangs of a very different institutional order, one that over the coming decades could lead to a bifurcation in the international system—perhaps one based on rival blocs that are undergirded by very different forms of infrastructure, urbanism, and technologies, and governed by competing sets of international institutional architectures.

China as an Engine of Global Trade

Perhaps the most important tool of influence that China has for reshaping its external environment today is its gathering economic strength. China's growing weight in global trade brings with it the ability to reshape long-standing economic patterns and flows. But perhaps the most significant trend for the longer term may be China's attempts to craft a distinctive model of economic development. This model diverges radically from the economic orthodoxy pushed by leading Western states over the past forty years or more. It is based around a central role for an interventionist collectivist state, which maintains a high degree of control over all aspects of policy, including the operation of markets. China is evolving its own distinctive form of state capitalism.

China's growth has reconfigured the very landscape of global trade. The Reform Period, which began in 1978, two years after the death of Mao, was one of four decades of sustained "opening" for China, both economically and ideologically, and both to the world and within China itself. At its core was the embrace of a market-oriented economy, after the failures of central planning in the Mao period.

The Reform Period's opening transformed the Chinese economy. As China embraced market forces, even in a controlled and limited way, including the reform of agriculture in its vast rural hinterlands, the inherent relationship between market forces and urban growth took hold, generating that vast wave of urban transformation that has forever changed the balance between urban and rural life in China (see Chapter 3). Along with the economic reforms came moves to decentralize domestic political authority. Regions and cities were given more power to shape policy, and more autonomy to let the crucial dynamic of urbanization and markets play out.

These decades of growth, then and now, have been driven by exports, and by China's comparative advantage in providing cheap labor. Between the 1980s and 2010 China grew at an average rate of 10 percent per year. A further export-driven growth surge followed its accession to the World Trade Organization in 2001, with exports quadrupling between 2002 and 2007.[7] This astonishing period of growth has begun to slow and the structure of the Chinese economy has begun to shift. Before the impact of COVID-19, medium to high rates of 6 percent growth had seemed set to help China overtake the United States in nominal GDP by the end of this decade—but the global slowdown and travails over its zero-COVID policy have hit Chinese growth hard. The IMF now forecasts annual growth for China of between 3 and 4 percent for the next five years, and China's aging population may mean that the years of very high growth are over. Playing into this climate of slower growth is the Xi regime's recent prioritizing of security over growth, with China also moving down a path toward greater technological self-sufficiency and economic self-reliance. That is, China has been attempting a decoupling: it has moved away from reliance on foreign investment, especially US treasury bonds, and it has been moving toward what it calls a dual-circulation economy, which means that it is trying to boost domestic sources of growth, and insulate the domestic economy

from external geopolitical and geoeconomic pressures, while simultaneously boosting demand for Chinese products abroad. Hence the crucial
significance of the BRI.[8]

Despite its slower growth, China's increasing centrality to the global
economy has been reflected in its rising share of global GDP: from
7 percent in the 1980s to 28 percent in 2017. China is now the primary
trading partner for over 120 states—and this has changed the map of
global trade. Its vast economic resources can now be directed to augment
its power in other ways, too. The size of its economy has enabled it to
pump huge sums into research and development, where its budget could
reach around $500 billion by 2025, as it seeks to become a world-class
economy and move up the global value chain. Such resources are also
being directed to the creation of a world-class military, and Xi has set the
goal of 2050 to achieve this ambition. Currently defense spending stands
at around $300 billion per year, second only to that of the United States.[9]

The economic model that has provided this growth, however, has
become increasingly hard to sustain. Being the workshop of the world in
perpetuity is not in line with China's ultimate ambitions. Western expectations that China will seek increasing openness and greater free-market-
style reforms have been disappointed, and since the 2008 global financial
crisis it has become increasingly apparent that China is now on a different path. Attempts to internationalize the renminbi in the mid-2010s
stalled, which leaves the BRI as the preferred policy response to the huge
glut of domestic savings produced by economic growth, which had at
one point become equal to half of China's national income.

China's own response to the global financial crisis, where it stepped
up to help stabilize the global economy via its own stimulus programs,
has also given Chinese policymakers confidence to take on greater roles
in the governance of the global economy. As Hu Jintao handed over
power to Xi Jinping in 2012, the crisis had come to represent both an opportunity and the need to find a different path forward. This path led,
rather unexpectedly for many observers, to the creation of the BRI. The
decision to pursue the BRI, and its implications, may come to be seen in
retrospect as an inflection point in the history of the international system.

The BRI, then, has at least a part of its origins in the shifting weight
and locus of Chinese trade, with implications for the future of globalization. At the turn of the century, the United States was the destination for
over 40 percent of Chinese exports. By 2013 this figure had dipped
below 20 percent. Additionally, China's trade with the rest of the world is

far more balanced than it is with the United States, with whom its huge trading surplus had reached $420 billion in 2018. This synergistic coupling of the US and Chinese economies, where earnings from Chinese exports were being used to undergird US debt, helped to power globalization for decades. It may now be coming to an end.

Strategic considerations and gathering geopolitical competition have compelled China to attempt to break its dependence on US technology and debt. The deep integration of the US technology sector with Chinese manufacturing has become a source of tension, as China seeks to develop its own national technological development policy, especially given the deep protection China affords its own domestic services industries, where the US comparative advantage would lie.[10] This tension was one of the motivations for the Trump administration's trade conflicts with China, and the steady deterioration of relations over recent years. A growing possibility is that decoupling may lead to a carving out of competing blocs, as like-minded partners that share suspicion of Western-style institutions and economic practices, such as Pakistan, Iran, and Russia, increasingly integrate with a Chinese economic and political core.

In addition to needing to break free of its economic relationship with the United States, the potential for trade in the Eurasian region, China's immediate neighborhood, is immense. Eurasian trade in Chinese goods is already double that of transatlantic trade in Chinese products, for instance, and given the chronic underdevelopment of the institutional and physical infrastructures of the region, the possibilities for even greater growth are immense if they can be improved. The BRI is the tool by which Eurasian trade is to be developed.

Of enormous significance here are new attempts to forge regional free trade, such as the recently signed Regional Comprehensive Economic Partnership (RCEP), which, from January 2022, became the world's largest trading bloc in economic terms, and which the UN Conference on Trade and Development claims will shift the center of gravity of global trade even farther eastward. RCEP includes fifteen East Asian and Pacific nations, including Japan, Australia, Vietnam, and Myanmar, and it encompasses 30 percent of global GDP. China will be the biggest player. The agreement will remove 90 percent of tariffs for members, but the considerable gains in trade will come at the expense of non-member states.[11] RCEP has the potential to facilitate greater Chinese economic leadership in the region, and to exclude the United States from influencing that process.

In 2016 China joined the TIR (Transports Internationaux Routiers, or international road transport) Convention, a multilateral treaty that removes administrative boundaries for the international transportation of goods in customs-sealed containers, a move that reduces border checks and so makes international trade more efficient. This provides a boost for China, because the majority of TIR participants are affiliated with the BRI. Indeed, some of China's border cities have become TIR "gateways," and have been transformed as a result.[12] The twin city of Khorgos/Horgos, mentioned earlier, is one such city. It straddles the border with Kazakhstan in the Saryesik-Atyrau desert, with a dry port on the Kazakh side, and, on the Chinese side, ambitions to bring in major tech, logistics, and robotics-manufacturing operations. In China's Inner Mongolia Autonomous Region, on the border crossing with Mongolia in the Gobi Desert, the small city of Erenhot fulfills a similar gateway function through its border market, the International Trade City. And on the southern tip of China's eastern Liaodong Peninsula, a TIR gateway to the Maritime Silk Road has emerged in the seven-million-strong port city of Dalian, which mixes modern high rises and a glitzy central business district with old Russian architectural influences.

These changes are helping to contribute to China's growing centrality in the global economy. Yet despite its ubiquitous "win-win" rhetoric, China now often uses its growing power in global trade as a political weapon. Increasingly, China is denying access to the huge Chinese market as a punishment for states and firms that have taken political stances that the Chinese regime does not like. In recent years, Norway, Australia, the Philippines, and South Korea have all experienced the cost of the Chinese government's displeasure by being shut out of key markets. In 2019, too, when the general manager of the US Houston Rockets basketball team tweeted support for political freedoms in Hong Kong, the team's licensing, television, and streaming deals were canceled by Chinese firms such as state-owned China Central Television and tech giant Tencent.[13]

State Capitalism

The Xi regime has been increasingly assertive in pushing toward an alternative developmental framework: an untried and distinctive model of state capitalism. Part of this assertiveness comes from the conviction that the Western model of neoliberal capitalist political economy is in decline, as is the historical period of Western international leadership and US hegemony. The increasingly dysfunctional nature of Western-style democracy only adds to that confidence. President Xi now appears to view this as the moment for China to offer its own authoritarian-inflected political economy as a developmental paradigm to other developing states, as a gateway to closer association with an increasingly Sino-centric economic and political order.

It remains to be seen if this model will be successful in the medium to long terms, or how appealing it will be to other states. China's decades of astonishing growth are slowing, and structural weaknesses in the economy have yet to be overcome. But there seems to be little doubt that Xi is banking on a future model of political economy that looks distinctly different from what we have seen in the present round of globalization.

China's challenge to the existing international institutional architecture is, then, partly a function of the fact that its domestic model of political economy is fundamentally different from the dominant norms and practices that are currently embedded within it. Although China has embraced capitalism in ways that have radically reshaped its cities and its citizens, it has not been willing to open itself fully to its tumultuous forces. And because the neoliberal model that has dominated Western intellectual life for almost half a century has seemingly run its course, China now seeks to engage only on its own terms, and, perhaps, only with those partners that will buy into its system and its leadership. Its own evolving model of political economy fundamentally rejects the idea—so important to the neoliberal capitalist mode of regulation—of a reduced role for the state. In fact it reverses it, so that the economy becomes a tool of the state, with its generative capacity harnessed to state-defined objectives. State control over citizens' economic and social lives is prioritized over economic and social freedoms, and the growth of private wealth is ultimately subordinated to the needs of the state.

China has reached that point in its own growth cycle where it is trying to move from being dependent on an external environment shaped by others to fuel its growth, to wanting to reshape that external environment to fit its own preferences. But in doing so, it will necessarily come into conflict with other powers, who will want to shape that environment in different, perhaps incompatible, ways. When President Roosevelt projected his own preferred model of domestic political economy onto the postwar international institutions, he was perhaps simply doing what all leading powers do. The problem for China, and for the world, is that it is rising within an established international order. It does not have the blank slate of postwar reconstruction, or the geopolitical power vacuum, that at once both challenged Roosevelt and provided his historic opportunity.

There are many mechanisms by which China hopes to spread its own model. But China hopes that the BRI, and the institutions that support it, can become the centerpiece of a new developmental philosophy. Given its size, and its decade-long head start, China may be very hard to compete with. As we have seen, the BRI produces its own space via the generation of new infrastructural components. The BRI, and the institutions that support it—such as the investment funds, and state-owned enterprises that go out into the world and physically build its components—are so important because they generate new forms of connectivity, and produce new forms of social space, and by so doing create greater economic integration across Afro-Eurasia. The new integrated spaces that are emerging are tied to the growing meshwork of Chinese influence, which also, as we have described, runs through the fabric of these infrastructural and urban forms, and becomes braided into their very structure and operations.

The emerging relationship between market and state in China is complex, and possibly contradictory. Unarguably, China's momentous economic growth since the beginning of the Reform Period has been driven by an embrace of markets. The Chinese state, led by the Marxist-Leninist-inspired CCP, considered the collapse of the Soviet Union, as well as its own historic economic failures, and resolved to embrace capitalism. But this capitalism was not the free-market version that has taken root in the West. Chinese policymakers have long been wary of uncontrolled market forces as a potential source of domestic chaos. Market forces, then, have been embraced only with care, and introduced slowly and experimentally, in tightly constrained ways. Initially the places where international capital was allowed into China were carefully demarcated and controlled special economic zones, such as Shenzhen or Guangzhou. And although in the West there has always been a hope, or even an expectation, that political liberalism would follow the forces of markets and capitalism, just as night follows day, today these expectations seem remote. Instead, there is increasing confidence within the Xi regime that China can offer the world a model of political economy that it claims is superior to the free market: a brand of state capitalism—one with Chinese characteristics, as the saying goes—allied to China's

increasing economic weight in the global economy, and its redrawing of
the patterns of international trade.[14] Such a new model of state capitalism is, perhaps, China's greatest tool of influence today, especially as confidence in the free-market model has been heavily eroded around the
world by the 2008 global financial crisis, and now by the impact of the
COVID-19 pandemic. It also chimes with the rise worldwide of authoritarianism, because state capitalism offers the kind of control that authoritarian regimes crave.

State capitalism isn't new. Many different states have sought to use
markets to pursue political aims, as well as to use their state power and
resources to derive benefits from international markets. The major oil-
producing states such as Saudi Arabia or Russia are examples. There has
also been recent empirical observation of a move toward forms of state
capitalism, especially in the global South, with governments engaged in
more intense steering and shaping of economic processes, including state
ownership and market interventions.[15] Such governments profess a lack
of trust in unfettered markets and liberalism, pointing to not only the
2008 global financial crisis, but also earlier events like the post-Soviet experience in Russia, or the Asian financial crisis of 1997.

Over a decade ago, the political theorist Ian Bremmer wrote, in *The
End of the Free Market*, of the growing threat to the international economy posed by the rising prevalence of state capitalism. Bremmer described the ways in which states were increasingly mobilizing their
resources to benefit from the free movement of capital and goods generated by the existing structures of global economic integration, skewing
markets to feed their own political ends. But this, for Bremmer, could
only be a short-term, parasitic relationship. He saw the free market and
state capitalism as fundamentally incompatible in the longer run, and
state capitalists as ultimately reliant on the dynamism of a global economy based on openness, and underpinned by liberal institutions and
states.[16] China's path and recent success now call this claim into question.

Bremmer defines state capitalism as a form of political economy
where the state dominates markets for political purposes. The balance
between state and market under contemporary liberalism, where markets
are allowed to generate wealth for individuals, is seemingly reversed.
State capitalism uses markets as tools for state elites to extend their own
political and economic leverage over society, both at home and abroad.
Of course, in all modern political systems there is always some mix of
state and market forces.[17] We might think of categories such as neolib-

eral capitalism or state capitalism as ideal types—in reality there will always be greater or lesser forms of state control, and greater or lesser forms of market activity. As Karl Polanyi reminded us long ago, there is really no such thing as the free market anyway: the free market is always an artifact of statecraft; a product of the state's power to create, sustain, and regulate market activities.[18]

Just as it is an alternative form to the free market, so state capitalism is also something very different from the command economies of the twentieth century, as practiced in the Soviet Union, or indeed, in China itself under Mao. In a command economy the state would decide what gets produced, by whom, in what quantities, and at what prices. Chinese officials learned from the failures of twentieth-century command economies, and embraced the generative and allocative power of markets. But they also retained their awareness of the socially destabilizing potential of lightly regulated markets, and have kept them under the political control of the state.

In many respects the development of Chinese capitalism has been extraordinary. Three decades ago, capital markets did not exist in China. The past ten years have been transformative, with rapid domestic development and internationalization. Today China has the second largest equity markets and futures exchanges in the world, and the third largest bond market. More companies are listed on the Shanghai and Hong Kong exchanges than on any other in the world. These markets are increasingly connected to regional and global financial markets, influencing investment patterns, and enhancing China's role both in the provision of development finance and in governing global financial practices.[19]

But again, these capital markets do not operate in the ways that they have traditionally operated in liberal market economies; they are yoked to the political goals and institutional logics of the Chinese state. They are "institutionally embedded"—meaning that Chinese capital is linked directly to national development goals set by the CCP. The growing weight of Chinese state capitalism in global financial markets, then, has led to unresolved questions over how China's growing influence can fit into the existing global financial architecture.[20] The rise of China's form of state capitalism now sits uneasily within a system built on free-market logics.

The ability to set the rules, norms, and procedures that underpin the global financial order, and that govern cross-border money and finance, is another form of structural power.[21] Exchanges are one important mechanism by which markets are organized and coordinated. One of the big open questions about the nature of Chinese state capitalism is whether it will ultimately lead to a rejection of the previous financial order, built around the Washington Consensus, and the pursuit of an alternative, or perhaps parallel, system. It is too early to say, but we should not make the mistake of conflating the historically specific circumstances that gave rise to the Washington Consensus with the global financial order itself. Markets are not simply abstract coordination mechanisms, but social phenomena embedded in particular institutions. China's adoption of market principles, then, takes place within its own distinctive economic model: although it includes the many thousands of decisions made by market participants, the state provides top-down control, ultimately guiding the sum of such activities toward its own objectives by monitoring, regulating, and managing the behavior of these bottom-up actors.[22]

The social shaping of capital markets in China is coordinated primarily through exchanges—the major stock exchanges of Shanghai and Shenzhen, the commodities exchanges of Dalian or Zhengzhou—and the regulatory power of the China Securities Regulatory Commission. These exchanges, and their regulators, are powerful forces of agency in their own right, generating the financial infrastructures that shape investment, and framing what counts as "rational" economic decision-making by market participants. Exchanges act as transmission mechanisms for government objectives. They are themselves deeply entwined with the political system; indeed, they are part of the regulatory apparatus of the state. They are also pathways by which key officials are able to further their careers within the party apparatus, and move on to other government posts.[23]

The BRI offers avenues by which these domestic institutions may project influence internationally. Here the example of Astana is interesting. The Kazakh city in which Xi first announced the BRI to the world has become, since 2018, the location of a regional international finance hub, the home of the Astana International Financial Center, and a key component of the BRI's financial architecture outside of China, connecting China, Central Asia, Russia, and the Arab world. Partly owned by the Shanghai Stock Exchange and the Silk Road Fund, the Astana International Exchange is an experimental move aimed at extending Chinese financial influence along the BRI. It also plays an important role in linking Chinese and Russian companies.[24]

Similarly, the Pakistan Stock Exchange (PSX), with physical locations in the major Pakistani cities of Karachi, Lahore, and Islamabad, has been heavily tied into Chinese capital markets. The Shanghai Stock Exchange took a 40 percent stake in PSX, and Chinese executives now exercise significant influence on its board. PSX has been integrated into Chinese stock markets through the China Connect Interface, allowing more Chinese investors to enter Pakistan's stock markets. Research has shown that as a result of this integration, Pakistan's stock market has begun to decouple from global markets and to align more closely with Chinese market dynamics—a development in financial infrastructural architecture that complements the development of the China–Pakistan Economic Corridor and the closer integration of the Chinese and Pakistani economies.[25] Johannes Petry has shown that a "patchwork" of alternative financial infrastructure is emerging along the BRI, where BRI-related financial infrastructure investments and arrangements grew significantly between 2015 and 2021, including in places as diverse as Abu Dhabi, Bangladesh, Laos, and Cambodia.[26]

One element of China's state capitalism, then, is its emerging financial statecraft: its use of international monetary or financial capabilities to achieve foreign-policy goals.[27] Financial infrastructure is one of the original "five connectivities" that underpin the BRI, and it is perhaps every bit as important as the hard infrastructures of railways, roads, and ports. Indeed, China's development of these new financial components and capabilities is a key indication that it is looking to build a parallel international financial architecture to the current one. The ability to set the rules of the game via the world's financial architecture has been, and remains, a core element of US structural power in the international system today. Nasdaq, the New York–based financial-service firm that owns and operates three of the major US stock exchanges, as well as seven European exchanges, currently also provides trading technologies, platforms, and services to fifty countries. China's strategy is to challenge this global dominance by helping its partner states build alternative financial architectures—especially China's growing roster of partners along the BRI, many of which are marginalized by the current order, require development assistance, and are opposed to Western dominance of the contemporary international order. Building new financial interdependencies and relationships can make China a central node in a parallel financial architecture that grows in the forgotten spaces, the forbidden and sanctioned realms, and the interstices of the contemporary order, integrating such markets into Chinese financial circuits and locking them into an emerging system. At the same time, the ability to shape the financial rules in such places gives China a modicum of control. Petry describes this as an essentially defensive move, despite its outward-looking approach, for it shields China's market practices from global scrutiny, pressure, and sanction. He argues that "individually Pakistan, Kazakhstan or Bangladesh is not an important market and a small rule-taker in the contemporary GFO [global financial order]. However, by integrating all these markets into Chinese financial circuits, connecting them to Chinese investors and potentially diffusing Chinese practices of market organization, China could in time create a 'parallel system of capital markets with Chinese characteristics.' "[28]

This emerging socio-technical system of financial architecture has helped to finance the BRI by providing access to Chinese capital markets—complementing the Asian Infrastructure Investment Bank (AIIB) and the big Chinese policy banks. Individually each state that signs up may be a relatively small player, but the overall logic is systemic—China is creating a parallel system that can begin to influence the shape and direction of global capital markets, lock in a core of Chinese practices and values, and advance the foreign-policy goals of the Chinese state. Whether this nascent system can eventually compete with the existing US-dominated global financial system is an open question.[29] But China's moves here mirror, to some extent, the kinds of developments we saw with its construction of an alternative digital architecture across Afro-Eurasia—which allowed it to shut out Western influences by substituting its alternative system, which takes hold in the gaps, failures, and resentments of the existing international order.

Another tool of influence has long been a key component of Chinese state capitalism: the state-owned enterprise. There are over 150,000 state-owned enterprises in China, forming the bedrock of Chinese economic influence and activity. The largest and most powerful are some of the most profitable and influential companies in the world: huge banks, such as the Agricultural Bank of China or Industrial Commercial Bank of China, and enormous industrial and commercial enterprises able to intervene in global markets with profound effects, like China Railway Engineering, China National Petroleum, China National Offshore Oil, Sinopec, State Grid, China Mobile Communications, and SAIC Motor.[30] And then there are the national champions—companies that are not state-owned, but are certainly heavily tied to the state, and given state backing that often distorts markets in their favor. The big Chinese technology companies such as Huawei, Alibaba, Tencent, Baidu, and Xiaomi, for example, are not state-owned, but they are seen as national champions, tied to the state and instrumental in facilitating its wider geopolitical and geoeconomic goals, as we saw with Huawei's build-out of submarine fiber-optic cables that may come to comprise the backbone of an emerging Chinese internet (Chapter 2).

Bremmer saw the emerging forms of state capitalism as ultimately likely to prove inferior to the unfettered operation of free markets. In his classically liberal view, the stifling of innovation, dynamism, and free thinking that occurs when markets are directed to the ends of a political regime, or skewed by the dead hand of officialdom, will ultimately bring about inferior results—consider, for example, failures of the command economies of the twentieth century. But China's orientation in recent years has confounded any expectations that it will adopt a more liberal path. Instead, the CCP seems to be banking on the possibility that it has alighted on a new historic variant of capitalism; one that might be superior to liberalism, that will enable it to continue to develop and take its place at the core of the world economy, while also allowing the CCP to maintain tight control over social forces at home.

Despite questions about the relationships between freedom, innovation, and state control—questions that also were posed for much of the twentieth century and had an important influence on the outcome of its geopolitics—this new form of state capitalism is becoming, via the conduits of the BRI, the centerpiece of an evolving Chinese developmental philosophy and foreign policy. It is further bolstered by the belief that the 2008 global financial crisis—a crisis that ripped through the real estate market and financial system and that originated in poorly regulated US credit markets, and an unregulated shadow-banking sector—represents a terminal structural failure of the free-market philosophy at the core of the Washington Consensus.

In other words, China has no faith in the theory of the self-correcting market that has fueled Western political and economic thought. Perhaps more critically, its core assumption is that finance should primarily serve the real economy. Whether the 2008 global financial crisis represents the beginning of the end of the US-designed global economic system remains to be seen. And where free-market states like the US have intervened on a gargantuan scale to prop up economies reeling from the financial crisis and from the damage wrought by COVID-19, such interventions are seen as firefighting responses, undertaken with the hope of returning to the "normal" operation of the free-market system. China's state capitalism is instead a long-term strategic choice.

Corridors of Power

It is from the conjuncture of state capitalism and world trade, then, that the BRI draws much of its significance. The BRI incorporates bilateral trade agreements that commit to significant policy coordination, the development of transportation infrastructure, the removal of tariff barriers, currency integration, and cultural exchange. But it is in the incipient material infrastructures growing along the BRI that the new model of political economy emerging in China, if it is to leave a lasting legacy, must manifest itself in both domestic and transnational space. It is these infrastructure projects that lay the tracks for new patterns of human activity.

The economic corridor, the heart of the BRI vision, is an established developmental model that draws specifically on the generative power of urbanism and urban agglomeration. The concept has been around since at least the 1980s—one of the earliest examples is the Asian Development Bank's effort to develop an urban corridor in the Greater Mekong Subregion in Southeast Asia. So in one sense, the BRI fits comfortably into existing global trends toward economic regionalism, urbanization, and logistics and transport integration along transnational corridors. This is the type of contemporary transnational territorial rescaling identified by urbanists like Neil Brenner.[31] Urban corridors bisect territories, jump scales, and forge new city forms and regions. As they do so, they alter the geographical contexts of each. Such corridors can be found in most of the world's regions. In West Africa, an urban corridor stretches from Abidjan, Ivory Coast, through Accra, Ghana, on to Cotonou, Benin, and Lagos, Nigeria. Urban spaces link Iraq and Iran, Pakistan and India, Saudi Arabia and Bahrain. In North America, Amtrak riders have come to know the stretch from Boston to New York to Philadelphia to Washington, DC, as, while not transnational, an extended corridor nonetheless.

Deployment of global infrastructure, as we have seen, is a way to reorder territory. The BRI, and the emphasis on urban corridors that underpin it, is a tool to prize the global economy away from its North Atlantic configuration. But at the same time, China's use of state capitalism gives its foray into corridor construction a distinctive tint. The corridors of the BRI draw on the power of markets, and of urban agglomeration dynamics, but they also serve the political and international goals of the Chinese state. The corridors of the BRI may lead to economic development for the states through which they travel, but they are also, at the level of political order, a tool in service to an evolving Great Power with a historical sense of destiny, and an ambition to bend the arc of history toward its own orbit and interests.

Here the most developed of the BRI's corridors, the China-Pakistan Economic Corridor (CPEC), demonstrates the scale of China's ambition. CPEC, on the face of it, and in official memoranda, is held up as an example of how the BRI provides a "win-win" for all involved: China invests, Pakistan gets a much-needed economic development boost, and so do, in theory, surrounding states such as Afghanistan and Iran as well as the Central Asian region more generally.[32] During the mid-2010s China-Pakistan trade rose rapidly, with annual growth rates of nearly 20 percent on average. CPEC forms the basis for a "China-Pakistan Community of Shared Destiny," tying Pakistan into China's broader vision for international order.

The CPEC incorporates China's Xinjiang Uygur Autonomous Region and the entire territory of Pakistan. It has a core trunk and several radiating smaller corridors, with key nodal cities forming the backbone of the transport routes. These include cities as diverse as Kashgar, a Chinese city in the Tarim Basin in Xinjiang, and a crucial oasis waystation along the Silk Roads with a two millennia history, swapping between Turkic, Mongol, and Tibetan rulers across the centuries; Gilgit, a city set in a valley of the Karakoram mountains, a key point along the Karakoram highway, and a famous major center of Buddhism on the historical Silk Roads; Quetta, a high-altitude city, city of orchards, and a trading outpost linked with Afghanistan and riven by conflict in recent years; Karachi, Pakistan's largest city with around fifteen million inhabitants, a cosmopolitan trading port on the Arabian Sea, and a critical financial and industrial center; and the newly emerging Gwadar Port City, a formerly sleepy fishing village on its way to becoming a new Dubai that, ultimately, may prove the final link in an infrastructural chain stretching from the western provinces of China to the Indian Ocean.

This kind of transnational urban corridor represents a fundamentally new model of economic development—one in which a powerful state effectively influences industrial development in peripheral states in line with its own core economic development goals. China sees itself moving away from the low-cost, low-value segments of the world economy, with Pakistan one of the countries slated to take its place. CPEC literally builds this vision into existence. Similar positions are earmarked for other recipients of BRI development, whether in East Africa, Southeast Asia, or Eastern Europe. These countries include Cambodia, Laos, Malaysia, Myanmar, Thailand, and Vietnam, in the China–Indochina Peninsula

Economic Corridor; Kazakhstan, Belarus, Czech Republic, and Poland along the New Eurasian Land Bridge Economic Corridor; or Mongolia and Russia along the China-Mongolia-Russia Economic Corridor. Because many of these are low-income countries, the BRI corridors have the potential to lift tens of millions of people out of poverty, cementing China's vision as a regional leader, and helping it realize the Chinese Dream.

As mentioned earlier, China needs to lift itself out of its "middle-income trap," and the BRI corridors pass through reservoirs of cheap labor, where China might relocate some of its more basic economic activities. This would allow China to position itself at the conclusion of production cycles for higher-value products. The national logistics network that China is helping to build across Pakistan, for example, represents a plan that can help bring this about, as do the new freight railways connecting China to multiple points across Eurasia. The transportation upgrades will cut travel times and increase trade and investment, giving the countries through which the corridors run an economic edge. But the success of the BRI vision will require new urban clusters to develop organically along the new lines of connectivity. This is where state-financed construction of transportation infrastructure can enhance the economic growth, division of labor, and specialization that comes with urban life. Belt and Road Cities will become key nodal points along these new networks, with the communications networks that tie them together becoming key conduits for the flow of information and ideas.

Such developments will change the fortune of cities around the world. New cities will rise, as they take advantage of new connectivity, while others may fall as they are left behind. Urbanists have long talked of global "urban hierarchies," where certain cities become key nodes or switching points in the circuits of global capitalism, defining flows of trade and communication. Under US-shaped neoliberalism, a specific configuration of the global urban hierarchy has developed, with first-tier cities such as New York and London playing a disproportionate role in shaping and directing such circuits.[33] China's rise will inevitably transform global capitalism—but it will also influence urban hierarchies at multiple tiers. Already we see a detrimental impact on Hong Kong, as China's new security laws and tightening of freedoms push investment and firms elsewhere. But we also see the fortunes of some cities prospering as part of the BRI and the new economic corridors, both within China and beyond its borders. Cities such as Khorgos, Alashankou, Kunming, and Ruili, for example, have been reinvigorated because of their positions as nodal points, or gateway cities, in circuits of global capital, information, and labor that are changing their routes in response to the BRI.[34]

Kunming, the capital city of Yunnan province and once an important center on the old southwestern routes of the Silk Roads, has been rejuvenated as a consequence of China's policy of opening to its Western neighbors, as well as its new high-speed rail connections to east coast cities such as Shanghai, about 1,200 miles away. The border town of Ruili, home to no more than 300,000 people at present, which sits near the border of Myanmar, has become an important cross-border trade hub and transit route for the new oil and gas pipeline coming up from an expanded Kyaukphyu, part of the new Maritime Silk Road. Meanwhile, Alashankou, located on the China-Russia border at the site of the famed Dzungarian Gate, an important historical mountain pass, has again become a gateway city as a result of the new freight trains that cross the Eurasian Land Bridge Economic Corridor—an important hub and transit center for the Europe-China freight line, as well as the Kazakhstan-China oil pipeline that runs through. Such cities take advantage of their nodal positions as gateways to China's growing influence in Asia to change their fortunes from formerly small and peripheral settlements to important waystations and switching points in a transmuting pattern of global flows.

China's moves into global infrastructure construction along these emerging transnational economic corridors, then, pushes toward a reconfiguration of the technological and territorial connectivity of global capitalism—and perhaps represents a new stage in the evolution of capitalism itself.[35] The urban corridor and the city node are two key infrastructural forms that act as mediators between territories and the global economy. But in order to work, such corridors require spatial, technological, and regulatory coordination, and in many cases, standardization, across a wide array of economies and nation-states. They require the creation of what Andrew Barry calls "technological zones."[36] A technological zone is a form of space that is neither global in extent, nor bounded by a particular territory or national borders, but in which the differences between technical practices have been reduced and smoothed out and common standards have been established, whether these are related to regulations, bureaucratic procedures, measurement, computer software, or transportation infrastructure. As an attempt to create enormously ambitious technological zones, the BRI has the potential to accelerate and intensify the agency of the Chinese state; to push outcomes that favor China's own international interests and preferences. New forms of bordering are being generated—being inside a corridor or technological zone has advantages and costs, as does being outside of one. Connectivity is a form of relational power. And as the BRI generates new connections, it places China more centrally in the global urban system—ushering in new forms of relational power. Developing states may be able to cherry-pick different technologies, but they may eventually be faced with having to choose between rival technological zones operated by competing geopolitical systems.

International Organizations

The investments of the BRI change the reality of connectivity for people on the ground, in their everyday lives, in the cities and towns in which they live, and in the new connections that are forged at national, regional, and global levels. But in the more rarefied diplomatic environment of international organizations and institutions, China is also using its weight to reshape the norms and rules that are used for global governance—the deep-lying practices, norms, and values that shape and constrain the behavior of states, organizations, and individuals. If the CCP remains true to its current course, this effort will involve the creation of an institutional environment more conducive to state control, authoritarian structures, and state capitalism, and less amenable to the continued dominance of the liberal norms and values that have shaped the past four decades of international relations. For example, the emphasis on the expansion of the international human-rights regime, which has been a key feature of the past two decades, is likely to lose its centrality because China and other similarly minded states oppose its extension.

As we discussed earlier, there is a notable ambivalence in China's stance toward international institutions. China's relationship with the United Nations has been difficult and ambiguous since the organization's founding. Although the United Nations recognized the special responsibilities and weight of Great Powers in maintaining international peace and security by creating the five permanent members of the Security Council, China's seat at that table, and in the UN system more widely, was initially given to the Kuomintang Nationalists, who at the time were still fighting a civil war with the CCP. It took until 1971 before that seat was transferred to the People's Republic of China. This decades-long gap

meant that the crucial founding years of the United Nations were beyond the influence of the CCP— causing a weakness in its structural
power that China now seeks to rectify.

Despite the historical contingency of these developments, and even
though China's domestic norms are at odds with many of the established
normative structures of the international governance system, China has
been seeking to work through the system, and influence its development
from within. As its interests have been changing, China, tied as it now is
to the successful ongoing development of global trade, is increasingly
aligning itself with the pursuit of the successful governance of globalization. Recently, under Xi, China has moved from engagement with international organizations to sometimes attempting to take a leading role.
This signals a broader shift in China's aspirations of global leadership, toward applying Chinese "wisdom and strength" to the task of twenty-first
century global governance.

Increasingly this strategy appears to be effective—to the extent that
China's drive to reshape international organizations is beginning to receive greater pushback from states that are alarmed at some of the CCP's
domestic agenda creeping into that of the core institutions of international society. The Sinologist Elizabeth Economy has noted how China's
rising profile in international organizations over the past decade has led to
important positions being filled by Chinese diplomats in key UN agencies. This has afforded them a platform from which to influence important UN agendas, as well as a way to gain experience in directly shaping
global governance and running key institutions.

As Economy argues, one of the strategies that China has been pursuing in its quest to reshape global governance is to seed key positions
within the UN system with Chinese representatives and experts. Over
the past ten years, Chinese diplomats have held leadership roles in the
UN's Food and Agriculture Organization, the International Communications Union, the International Civil Aviation Organization, Interpol, the
UN Department of Economic and Social Affairs, and the UN Industrial
Development Organization—important specialized agencies that can
shape international rules and interactions in their fields. In this way,
China can work to realign some UN institutional architectures from
within, to match up more closely with its own domestic initiatives and
policy preferences.

Not the least of these, of course, is the BRI. There are clear signs
now that the new institutional environment of the BRI is being slowly

aligned with UN sustainable development goals. Xi has been particularly
keen to give these goals rhetorical support. UN Secretary General An-
tónio Guterres, in turn, has spoken warmly of the potential of the BRI to
help the United Nations accelerate the achievement of the sustainable
development goals, and endorsed China's embrace of the "ecological civilization" concept. There are now many institutional linkages between
the BRI and multiple UN agencies, reflecting both the significance for
global development of an initiative of the BRI's size and scope, as well as
China's desire to give the BRI the international legitimacy that comes
with UN approval. The Chinese-led UN Department of Economic and
Social Affairs has funded the "Jointly Building Belt and Road Towards
Sustainable Development Goals Program," for example, while the UN
Industrial Development Organization has integrated Chinese technical
standards into some of its projects, giving Chinese firms a key advantage
in some markets in the global South.[37]

   The UN system has been a key arena in which battles for influence
over international standards are fought out. International standards
might sound innocuously technocratic. But the control of technical standards can have wide-ranging implications for the shape and balance of
the global economy—as we saw with Chinese attempts to define internet
standards (see Chapter 2). Control over global standards leads to influence over revenues from intellectual property, patents, and the adoption
of technologies.[38] It is a powerful form of path dependency, and is currently monopolized by the developed world (again, those states that were
instrumental in shaping the structure of the international system).[39]
China is seeking to break into this top tier of global industry chains as
part of its strategy to reposition itself in the global economy.

   This is a difficult proposition, because these positions will not be re-
linquished lightly. China's best bet is to build new value chains that are
more efficient, and that incorporate new technologies. It has been building its own new domestic technical standards quietly, with the potential
to internationalize these as its power grows. Its ambitious ten-year *Made
in China 2025* manufacturing strategy pushes in this direction. It seeks to
utilize the huge resources of China's state capitalism to rebalance the
global economy, focusing on Chinese strengths in sectors such as shipbuilding, infrastructure construction, information technologies, robotics
and artificial intelligence, autonomous vehicles, power generation, and
steel manufacturing. Its emphasis is on developing indigenous technologies and innovations, recognizing that the period when China can rap-

idly boost its development with technology transfers from more developed nations is coming to a close.⁴⁰ It may well be that an era of economic complementarity with those developed nations is also drawing to a close, and with it the emergence of rival socio-technical spheres.

But if China is to rise to the top of global value chains, it will entail a wholesale reorganization of the international division of labor. This is where the material construction of the BRI corridors and the new forms of urban life emerging along them become key. Economic growth has been driven by China's masses of low-skilled workers. If China moves into higher levels of the value chain, those workers will need to be found elsewhere in the global economy. This is where the BRI becomes inextricably intertwined with China's "global development policy": a holistic approach to the world economy as a single entity (and one resonant of the Chinese concept of *tianxia*, discussed in more detail in Chapter 5). The CPEC is emblematic here, representing nothing less than the spatial reorganization of an entire territory, and its development as a component of China's embryonic global value chain. Similar arguments could be made about the other economic corridors of the BRI.

It is with the example of CPEC in mind that the former EU diplomat Bruno Maçães has argued that the BRI might be viewed as the first transnational industrial policy, in that it goes beyond national-level strategy in an attempt to influence the industrial policies of other states. This coordinated approach to development links many states together under broad Chinese economic leadership, with economically subordinate states each taking their place in lower segments of the evolving value chain.⁴¹ Meanwhile, China supports this process with cheap finance and development experience and knowledge. As we saw earlier, this strategy also accelerates urbanization and industrialization, as well as the spatial reorganization of those transnational spaces. These interventions are likely over time to shift the spatial organization of urban hierarchies across the region, with profound effects for future trade and production.

Maçães argues that, ultimately, the BRI is about using the power of state capitalism to shift the global playing field, intervening to limit the control of unfettered markets in determining the flows of technology and commodities, and reorganizing the international division of labor in coordination with other states in order to shift China out of its middle-income trap—especially in an era of fast technological transformation in which Chinese technology is often now at the leading edge.

China is also working to change the landscape of international finance carved out of the post–World War II world. But here the emphasis is not just on working through and reforming UN agencies, but also on setting up alternative international institutions, or simply engaging in new bilateral agreements. China has good relations with the International Monetary Fund and World Bank, despite never fully committing to their agendas. But Chinese frustration over the slow pace of reform, and particularly US resistance to change, has led it to make perhaps the most eye-catching move so far: in 2015 it set up an alternative institution, the multilateral Asian Infrastructure Investment Bank (AIIB), mentioned earlier. Today its website says that the AIIB was created with the specific aim of helping recipients of its investments build the "infrastructure for tomorrow," with a focus on green infrastructure innovation and connectivity—and it has a target of $10 billion to $20 billion in annual lending. But when it was originally envisaged, it was very much linked to the BRI, and seen as a tool for aiding its development. The AIIB currently has over one hundred members drawn from around the world— and more recently it has been decoupled from this explicit BRI linkage to include investments beyond BRI partner states. The AIIB's member states represent almost 80 percent of the world's population and command 65 percent of global GDP.[42]

The AIIB competes with—and complements—similar initiatives like the Japanese-led Asian Infrastructure Bank, or the BRICS New Development Bank, in seeking to invest in infrastructure development throughout the region. The AIIB is notable, however, because it represents a rare foray into multilateral institution-building by China, which had generally been far more comfortable exerting bilateral influence.

The AIIB is new for China, but multilateral development banks have been part of order building and geopolitical maneuvering in the past. During the Cold War, the United States used the Inter-American Development Bank as a tool to keep states from falling into the orbit of the Soviet Union, while Japan uses the Asian Development Bank to augment its regional leadership and influence. So too the AIIB and China. Its actual lending is relatively small, but its significance is in what it signals: Chinese attempts to develop institutional leadership, to be seen as a provider of international public goods and a purveyor of international development expertise. By signing up so many members to the AIIB, Chinese infrastructure and order building are given much needed legitimacy. And as China develops its role in international leadership, such institutions can be used to project its own political values and economic norms—as the United States has done in recent decades via the World Bank.[43]

But the AIIB, despite gaining the headlines as an unusual foray by China into multilateral institution building, is small in comparison to the domestic Chinese policy banks, such as the Bank of China, Chinese Development Bank, and Export-Import Bank of China. These are much bigger players in the funding of the BRI, and, unlike the AIIB, they are less transparent, with most of the funding going to Chinese firms. A further important source of BRI finance is the Silk Road Fund, which has a focus on Russia, Pakistan, and Central Asia, and whose administrators are now seeking to incorporate post-conflict reconstruction in Yemen and Afghanistan into its remit, with some notion of the BRI as a new platform for such post-conflict reconstruction and development.

In addition to accusations that these Chinese policy banks have a lack of transparency and poor construction standards, these banks can also be less scrupulous in where their money is invested, which opens up BRI investment to all types of political regimes. This offers newer, rival geopolitical infrastructural schemes, such as the US-led Partnership for Global Investment and Infrastructure initiative, or the EU's Global Gateway, the opportunity to differentiate themselves by linking their schemes to higher investment standards—and democratic values. The Blue Dot Network, an earlier infrastructure alliance set up in 2019 between the United States, Japan, and Australia, assesses and certifies projects, and was also designed to provide an alternative to the BRI, with less risk and higher standards than many BRI projects are subject to. Although some have suggested that these new schemes can complement BRI projects, and, indeed, the infrastructure investment gap is huge in the global South, we may be seeing here the beginning of the formation of rival infrastructural blocs that incorporate competing values, technologies, and standards.[44]

Other institutional tools of influence have been developed in the security arena. Although the central role of the BRI in recent Chinese foreign policy has been to emphasize trade, commerce, and peaceful coexistence, China has also made moves to develop security institutions across the region. Its primary purpose here is to raise its own leadership profile in the region and beyond, and to circumvent and weaken the existing US-dominated security order. The Association of Southeast Asian Nations (ASEAN, whose members include Brunei, Cambodia, Indonesia, Laos, Malaysia, Myanmar, the Philippines, Singapore, Thailand, and

Vietnam) is also seen as primarily aimed at balancing against Chinese power. In the security realm, China has tended to work through existing institutions that have been around for some time, while reinvigorating them with renewed energy as vehicles for its own leadership.

Perhaps the most important of these has been the Shanghai Cooperation Organization (SCO). Headquartered in Beijing, the SCO builds on an earlier version—the Shanghai Five—which included Russia, Kazakhstan, Tajikistan, and Kyrgyzstan. In 2001 it expanded to its current form to include Iran, Pakistan, India, Uzbekistan, and Mongolia.[45] Some have compared the SCO to NATO, although it does not reach the level of a formal collective security alliance. With the exception of India, all these countries are also core BRI partners, increasingly tied to China's economic foundations.

Another security-focused institution that has been around for some time is the Conference on Interaction and Confidence-Building Measures in Asia (CICA), which China has led since 2014. In its new enthusiasm for CICA can be read the Chinese search for a vehicle with which to develop a longer-term vision for a new pan-Asian security architecture free of the domination of the United States and its encircling alliance system—one based on a Sino-Russian axis that is growing ever closer. Such a forum, which can provide a place to demonstrate regional leadership and give legitimacy to that leadership via multilateralism, can become key to Chinese ambitions here.[46]

Russia, with whom China shares a deep resentment of the postwar security architecture, including NATO and other US alliances, has deepened its strategic relationship with China in recent years. Increasingly the junior partner, it is now in danger of becoming thoroughly dependent. At a summit in Beijing in February 2022, exactly fifty years since Nixon's handshake with Mao realigned the balance of the Cold War, and just weeks before Russia's invasion of Ukraine, China and Russia affirmed their "limitless" strategic partnership. Indeed, the increasing integration of Russian infrastructures, energy networks, and economic partnerships with China and the BRI may well have played a role in President Putin's strategic calculus over the decision to invade Ukraine. The consequences of that war are likely to increase Russia's integration into a Sino-centric system.

It is also worth noting that, in recent years, China has played an increasingly active role as an observer member of the Arctic Council. Despite China's geographic distance from the region, China sees the Arctic, where climate change is opening up shipping routes and new resource opportunities, as strategically important. And although it is only an observer within the council, China clearly has big ambitions to shape Arctic policy: as mentioned earlier, there is talk of a Polar Silk Road, tied to its broader efforts to revive the Silk Road narrative.[47] This is all in line with China's maritime ambitions, including the development of its navy, and perhaps promises new maritime tensions for the future, in line with the problems caused by China's recent island building and territorial claims in the South China Sea.

Transnational City Networks

The traditional corridors of power offered by the core international organizations of international society are not the only avenues of diplomatic influence today. One of the leading trends in global governance in the past few decades has been the rise of transnational city networks, whereby the world's major cities have come together to improve the global governance of key issues such as climate change, security, or disaster risk management, as well as to share best practices in urban-development strategies. These increasingly significant transnational city networks sometimes act in concert with states, sometimes act in parallel with state diplomatic activities, and, indeed, in those cases where their interests diverge from policies pursued by their central governments, have begun to challenge states.[48] Here we see the diversification of contemporary global governance, and the importance of non-state and civil society actors and agencies in beginning to shape the international arena.

In the context of the climate crisis, geopolitics, cities, and diplomacy have come together. China's climate concerns in the urban context are significant. More than one in five of every Chinese urban dwellers lives in a coastal zone less than thirty-three feet above sea level. In terms of total urban land cover, the coastal cities and peri-urban areas do not represent a significant share, but they are home to high-value real estate and critical infrastructure.[49] While the relationship between climate warming and air quality is indirect, the links between air quality and a number of key urban-policy issues—transportation, heating, and cooking, for example— are very strong, as are the economic and human consequences of poor air quality. According to the Coalition of Urban Transitions, air pollution costs the Chinese economy roughly $40 billion a year in economic losses.[50] Meanwhile, as China looks to further develop cities, including smaller ones in the interior and to the west, low-carbon infrastructure, building, and transportation approaches will be crucial for cutting emissions more generally. Cities of fewer than one million residents, for example, represent more than half of China's urban-based emission abatement potential.[51] Plugging into global networks of urban expertise will be an important part of mitigating such urban challenges.

There is now a vast and complex diplomatic ecosystem of cities acting together on the world stage, including an immense array of city-to-city networks that goes far beyond earlier forms of city-twinning. Although this is not entirely a new phenomenon, many of these networks have emerged in the last few decades. Globally, there were slightly over sixty city-to-city diplomatic initiatives in the mid-1980s. Today there are somewhere between 250 and 300 formal associations of cities worldwide.[52] Some of these are large and important, and play an influential role in the UN system, as well as in multilateral fora like the G7 and G20. These include major international efforts like ICLEI (Local Governments for Sustainability), founded in 1990, which has been foundational in including a "local" emphasis on the UN sustainable development framework; the influential C40 Cities Climate Leadership Group, founded in 2005, which has had a prime spot in the development and implementation of the Paris Agreement on climate change; UCLG (United Cities and Local Governments), which dates its origins to the early twentieth century and plays a key role in many UN frameworks; and Metropolis, founded in 1985, which shares experience and best practices among the world's great cities. The recently disbanded Rockefeller 100 Resilient Cities initiative, founded in 2013, channeled over $100 million in direct investment to strengthen resilience planning in cities.[53]

The activities of such city networks are sometimes termed "subnational diplomacy." But given the immense expansion of urban life in the late twentieth and early twenty-first centuries, as well as the sheer scale and power of some of today's major world cities—which often dwarf many states in terms of population and economic might—this term may not fully capture their capacities and potential. Indeed, one of the motivations has been to engage in parallel diplomatic activities to their host states on the international stage on issues such as climate change. Such cities, especially those with elected leaders and representatives, often see themselves as representing the interests of their urban populations not just nationally, but internationally. Some of these city networks have a democratic legitimacy, even if they lack sovereignty. In 2022, when the presidency of the G7 was in Germany's hands, cities and urban expertise were integrated in a historically unprecedented fashion. This work was encouraged by German ministries, but was ultimately advanced by the Association of German Cities, ICLEI, and the Global Parliament of Mayors. Peter Kurz, the long-standing mayor of Mannheim, participated alongside national ministers in the meeting on sustainable urbanization. The communiqué emerging from the September meeting in Potsdam noted, "Today more than ever, cities are interconnected globally, nationally and regionally, and city networks are becoming major global players. Cities have the power to develop visions of their own future, to create innovations and to mobilize resources, and are key to implementing landmark international policy frameworks."[54] The development of this diverse ecosystem of hundreds of transnational city networks of various sizes that frequently interface with the UN system and other governance actors, and help to shape governance agendas (such as the SDGs, the Sendai Disaster Risk Framework, and the WHO Healthy Cities agenda, to name but a few), has opened up new avenues of influence on the world stage.[55]

Chinese cities are very much part of these developments. They are active in major transnational city networks, as well as in bilateral relationships, such as city-twinning.[56] A 2016 report commissioned by the United Kingdom's Foresight Future of Cities Project found that the number of twin-city relationships held by Chinese cities exceeded those of most British cities. A similar examination of sister-city relationships in the context of Chinese public diplomacy, partly funded by the US Department of State, also found widespread use of bilateral relationship-building by Chinese cities. More than one-third of China's sister-city relationships are in the East Asia Pacific region—and there has been a doubling of such friendship arrangements in the past twenty years, to almost a thousand.[57]

But unlike in the West, where city-twinning and transnational city networking and diplomacy are often undertaken without much interference by the state, Chinese cities engaging in these activities appear to be on a much tighter state leash, operating with state oversight and pushing toward goals set by the Chinese state. As an instrument of diplomatic outreach, sister-city relationships involving Chinese cities, for example, are more likely to be developed with cities in countries with which China does not have extensive security or strategic relationships. While city-to-city diplomacy never occurs entirely outside the context of national politics and international relations, and while the purposes and ties between national capitals and city halls do vary by country, it is clear that the city-diplomacy practices of Chinese cities operate within the context of China's national and geopolitical goals.

Beyond sister-city relationships, Chinese cities have also taken active roles in durable transnational city networks. As symbols, urban spaces, and nodes, Chinese cities have played an integral role in promoting subnational connectivity.[58] Beijing, Guangzhou, and others are members of highly collaborative and well-organized transnational city networks and have played a vocal role in the agenda setting of such platforms, including those that feed into the G20. Such diplomatic engagement has brought best practices and policies to Chinese cities and urban areas, but it also facilitates outward-flowing influence. Take, for example, the C40 Climate Cities China Buildings Program. The initiative sought to facilitate progress in green-building standards in Beijing, Shanghai, and other cities. The program overview also made clear, however, that flow of information was meant to be bidirectional: "International knowledge exchange will also be an important feature of the C40 [Climate Cities China Buildings Program], so as to ensure that best practices from China are highlighted and showcased to the world, and that inspiration from other leading Global Cities is readily available to an audience of Chinese practitioners."[59] A number of other collaborations with city networks have been experimented with or continue. Metropolis, a leading city network operating out of Barcelona, has a Learning Hub in Chengdu with the goal to "jointly develop, promote and implement an international learning curricula, onsite learning seminars as well as research works."[60] The center is itself a collaboration, supported by Metropolis member cities and the Chengdu Foreign Affairs Office of Chengdu Municipality. Chinese development experience, methods, models, and expertise may, then, also travel back through the conduits of these city networks: one more tool of influence in an increasingly complex and multi-layered global governance regime.

Indeed, if cities are to be central to any effective response to climate change, as they must be, the inclusion of Chinese cities, Chinese-influenced cities along the BRI, and new models of urbanism will be absolutely key. One new model is the Chinese concept of the "Sponge City," which, as we saw in Chapter 2, is designed to increase the resilience of southern and central Chinese cities prone to periodic flooding, in an era of breakneck urban sprawl. In some of these cities, such resilience may be a matter of survival as climate change bears down. The

Sponge-City concept, associated with the influential dean of Peking University's College of Architecture and Landscape, Yu Chongjin, endorsed by President Xi as a national policy, and rolled out to over thirty Chinese cities, such as Ningbo, about ninety miles south of Shanghai, is linked to the idea of China's transformation into an ecological civilization. It envisages clearing low-lying urban space—at the scale of whole districts, cities, and urban corridors—in order to install parks and wetlands that would act as a sponge in periods of heavy downfall, absorbing excess water that could then be recycled or released gradually back into rivers. Many cities in China are currently experimenting with these kinds of schemes as a result of top-down government directives that mandate that by 2030, no less than 80 percent of China's urban spaces must have Sponge-City adaptations and recycle at least 70 percent of rainfall. One successful example is found in the city of Harbin in northern China, where the 84-acre "Qunli stormwater park" collects, filters, and stores stormwater, while simultaneously helping to conserve the natural habitat.

These kinds of design ideas, developed at a scale not seen in places where similar ideas have been tested, such as in the low-lying Netherlands, are a possible Chinese contribution to urban development that might be amplified along the existing transnational city networks. And there are many others, including around technologically integrated Smart Cities, or so-called Safe Cities (see Chapter 2).

To some extent, the Chinese cities that are part of these networks operate on the edges of two worlds. As members of, or collaborators with, huge transnational city networks designed specifically for global cooperation and knowledge sharing, they are open to the world. And yet the Chinese state sees city diplomacy via such networks as still another conduit to project state policy goals and Chinese experience and technology developed in domestic urban contexts. So, where, in the West, the international activities of cities in transnational networks have established a space for the relative autonomy of cities from states, sometimes in ways that lead to a divergence between city and state, in China the state is very much in control.

Cultural Exports and Soft Power

A further source of influence on other states and peoples, one that is difficult to measure, is China's culture. China is the heir to a glorious history of cultural achievements. The cities of past Chinese dynasties, in particular, were famed in distant lands, an influence still felt today throughout East Asia.

This is the kind of influence that China seeks to re-create today. It is what Joseph Nye famously described as "soft power": the ability to shape the preferences of other peoples, institutions, and states because of the appeal of your own cultural and political values and achievements. Soft power bends the aims and ambitions of others to want what you want, and to want what you have, and so aligns the interests of those others with your own.[61]

The ability to project soft power is crucial for states with big international ambitions. Conversely, the inability to persuade others of your cultural achievements and to attract them to your domestic model of politics, economics, and society is a significant indicator of weakness. China has been self-consciously thinking about its own soft power for some time, since at least the Hu Jintao regime, putting in place steps that it hopes can augment it: international events to showcase its historic and contemporary importance—such as the spectacular 2008 Olympic Games ($28 billion), the 2010 Shanghai World Expo ($44 billion), the less spectacular COVID-hit 2022 Winter Olympics, and a variety of other major international expos on trade and investment—as well as the development of hundreds of Confucius Institutes, seeded around the world in partnership with foreign universities. The Chinese approach to soft power brings together the domestic and the international, seeking at once to promote Chinese power through images of domestic success, while also projecting power globally in a way that fosters stability and cohesion at home.[62]

China reportedly spends over $10 billion a year in promoting its soft power around the world, in part by presenting to the world, through an international communications strategy, a picture of China as a powerful actor on the global cultural stage, as well as a defender of globalization.[63] To make these points, this narrative focuses on Chinese "exceptionalism"—the elements of China's culture and history that make it not only unique, but also, in the Chinese view, a better source of ideas for how to shape international relations. The emphasis on China's alternative belief systems and philosophical heritage (including the influence of Confucianism, Taoism, and Buddhism on Chinese intellectual traditions), and the notion of a distinctive, and still coalescing, Sino-centric version of modernity, are both part of an attempt to counter the dominance of Western narratives about modernity, and Western discourses on international relations. But the crafting of such narratives is also a message from the CCP to the Chinese domestic audience about China's wider destiny—one that the CCP uses to shore up its own standing at home.[64]

Soft power is difficult for states to deliberately cultivate or control. Often it has to be built up over many decades, if not centuries. And it does not derive simply from state power, but from the whole cultural ecosystem of civil society. Real soft power happens through the development of appealing societal achievements, and is different from state-led coordinated projects to try to increase and to seed cultural influence around the world. There is overlap, but they are not the same.

The growth of China's material and economic power will inevitably bring in its wake indirect cultural consequences, though it is too early to know what those will be in the long term. International polling suggests that in many parts of the world today, China's cultural appeal remains low. Recent surveys by the Pew Foundation, for instance, indicate that China's global soft power remains fairly weak, with three-quarters of respondents across the major economies of North America, Europe, and Asia having an unfavorable view of China, and its record on foreign policy, including issues like human rights in Xinjiang and Hong Kong, its military activity in the South China Sea, and Chinese health diplomacy given the travails of its zero-COVID policies.[65]

Notably, major recipients of China's trade and investment do not have significantly more favorable views of the country. Soft-power-ranking schemes, for what they are worth, consistently place China near the bottom of the league.[66] China's authoritarian political system, its entertainment culture, and the brand power of its leading companies have not closed the soft-power gap with leading nations like Germany, the United States, Japan, or South Korea—although the reach and recognition of leading Chinese companies such as Huawei and Tencent and the unexpected runaway success of social-media platforms such as TikTok have clearly been recent big steps forward for China's global soft power.

The success of a country's educational establishments and its ability to attract international students are also crucial components of soft power. Chinese universities have been rising in the international rankings in recent years, with Tsinghua University and Peking University pushing at or near the top twenty in the Times Higher Education world university rankings in 2021.[67] (The top ten remain dominated by US and UK institutions.) But China has the third highest number of overseas

students studying in its universities, with only the United States and
United Kingdom having more. Notably, in 2017 many more African students chose to study in China than in the United States or the United
Kingdom. This trend may have significant implications for future connections between Chinese-trained African elites and Chinese elites, in a
world where the ties between the African continent and China are both
material and social.[68]

One of China's most notable moves in the last two decades, when it
comes to planting the seeds of soft power, has been the setting up of
Confucius Institutes, which are collaborations between universities or
schools within a host nation and China. The first was set up in 2004, and
by 2018 there were five hundred Confucius Institutes around the world
(with the United States hosting the most, over one hundred, including
some at Ivy League institutions). Such institutes promote Chinese language and culture. They also foster ties between a new generation educated in these host countries and China. There has been some tension
around Confucius Institutes in recent years because the curriculum
taught within them is tightly controlled by the Chinese Ministry of Education, and their governance structures are secretive. In some cases, this
has led to conflict with the host university over principles such as freedom of expression and censorship, and some institutions in the United
States and Europe have closed their Confucius Institutes as a result.[69]

At a more rarefied level of international collaboration and intellectual exchange, initiatives such as the Silk Road Think Tanks Forum in
2015 have been designed to foster international reflection on the shared
culture along the historic Silk Roads, by providing Chinese funding for
museums, exhibitions, festivals, and heritage institutes. Although the aim
is to celebrate the links forged along those ancient channels of trade, this
goal also clearly reinforces China's BRI story.

Control over media and the dominant narratives that are expressed
via television, internet, and radio are also clearly a crucial component of
soft power. Since 2018, China has created television and radio programming for a foreign audience under its Voice of China (a name clearly
redolent of Voice of America, the US-owned radio broadcasting service
that has been a staple of US soft power for foreign audiences since the
mid-twentieth century). The Voice of China includes the China Global
Television Network and China Radio International, which broadcast in
over forty languages, offering an alternative to Western media outlets
that elevates the voices of the global South. The main organ of Chinese

state news, too, the Xinhua News Agency, now has over 170 Chinese overseas bureaus. Cold War news-based information operations aside, such efforts remain challenging, both in terms of audience building and offering local news. Relationships between local journalists and Chinese leads remain difficult, both in terms of content production and workplace hierarchy.[70]

China's move into far more self-conscious and assertive institutional-order building over the past decade has some parallels with the development of international order following World War II. The key difference, however, is that today's existing order is deeply rooted. In the past, wars among the Great Powers have been the harbinger of epochal international change, whereby destruction is followed by reconstruction, generally under the auspices of a new hegemonic power. But China's path has, so far, been different. Although it has worked within the institutions of the existing order, advocating for their reform, China is also, with the BRI, constructing the building blocks of an alternative order within the interstices and forgotten places of the current system, across a temporal horizon that stretches over decades. China's bid for a new world order is a long-term play, and its eventual direction is far from clear.

CHAPTER FIVE

International Order

China's Search for a Place in the World

I N JULY 2021, ON the centenary of the founding of the Chinese Communist Party, President Xi Jinping made a landmark speech in Beijing during which he predicted "bright prospects for the rejuvenation of the Chinese nation."[1] As Xi looked out onto a Tiananmen Square bedecked with red flags, and over a sea of faces arranged in a broad crescent across the vast hundred-acre site, he probably felt some satisfaction in knowing that he was firmly ensconced in power, and would continue to have the opportunity to reshape China's orientation to the world. The military flyovers, patriotic songs in honor of the party, and other displays of loyalty and strength evoked the kind of power wielded by Chinese emperors past, to which Xi's style of leadership is now often compared.

It had been almost eight full years since he announced the BRI in Astana, Kazakhstan, and as he spoke, President Xi stressed the core aims for CCP rule in the twenty-first century: to deepen the bond between party and people; to continue to direct the insights of Marxist thought toward Chinese development and the ongoing Chinese social revolution that defines the foundation of the CCP's legitimacy; to further develop a socialism with distinctive "Chinese characteristics" (he stressed China's unique path to modernization here); to view contemporary China within the wider arc of five thousand years of Chinese history; and to create an

understanding of international order in which the party would be instrumental in shaping a shared future for what he called the "human community," offering to use China's "new achievements in development to
provide the world with new opportunities."

As Xi painted this picture of China's domestic and international future, he stood at Tiananmen's "gate of heavenly peace," which might
itself be seen as a portal between past and present. Although today it is
the symbolic center for the CCP, containing great monuments to the
revolution as well as the Great Hall of the People, which hosts the CCP's
political congresses, it was once the main gateway to the imperial Forbidden City, the great palace complex constructed by the Yongle emperor of the mighty fifteenth-century Ming dynasty.

The heart of Beijing has been the center of political power in China
since the twelfth century. Occupying the site of a two-millennia-old
northern border garrison town, by the footings of a section of the Great
Wall that separated China from the Mongolian plateau, Beijing is the last
of a series of Chinese imperial capital cities built across the millennia.
The twelfth-century Jin dynasty made the site its capital. Although it was
burned to the ground by Genghis Khan in 1215, it was rebuilt by his
grandson, Kublai Khan, as the great capital of Mongol China, the symbolic center of the largest contiguous land empire in history that in the
thirteenth and fourteenth centuries dominated Eurasia from eastern
Europe to the Sea of Japan. Reaching a population of between two and
three million, Beijing was for centuries the largest city in the world until
it was finally overtaken by London during the Industrial Revolution.
Connected to a vast empire by China's canal system, its grand palaces,
walls, bridges, gardens, and six great gates were arranged in symbolic
symmetry around a north-south axis that hinged on the person of the
emperor. Beijing was built in the likeness of past Chinese imperial capitals such as Chang'an, for when the imperial capital moved, as it had done
many times in Chinese history, so too did the center of the universe.

As with all cities, the imperial Chinese capital expressed its underlying social logics in material form. The core of the city, from which cosmic and earthly authority emanated outward, was the imperial palace and
bureaucratic and administrative complex. The Ming dynasty created on
earth a mirror of the cosmos with a series of miniature walled cities, each
nested within the next, and a walled enclosure at the center called the
Forbidden City.[2] There the emperor was shielded from the scrutiny of

the common people, and imperial administration was conducted from the symbolic center of the world.

Beijing, and previous iterations of the Chinese capital city through the ages, then, were built on the blueprint of what the architectural historian Spiro Kostof has called a political diagram; one that drew inspiration from Chinese cosmology and society.[3] The earth was envisaged as a stable cube, with the heavens expanding around it. The capital city represented this cosmology in its series of nested rectangles, oriented to the four compass points, in the center of which lay the imperial core, around the personage of the emperor. The city was not just a cosmological representation, but also a representation of social hierarchy and earthly authority.

Contemporary Beijing retains its historic center, and when Xi delivered his speech, he was standing within the symbolic core of a newly assertive China. The Chinese Communist Party today has inherited both the administrative complex of the old city, as well as the long-standing tradition in China of authoritarian and centralized rule occurring out of public view. For the contemporary Chinese state, for all its modern trappings, is also successor to thousands of years of imperial bureaucracy, dating back to the Han dynasty that first unified and centralized China under one rule 2,500 years ago. The story of the Han, which reappeared throughout Chinese imperial history as an example of how to administer such a vast civilization efficiently, is employed even today to glorify and legitimate the one-party authoritarian political system. According to Xi Jinping, political centrality and authority once again reverberate outward from an axis centered on the wisdom of a Chinese leader, one who is strongly influenced by models from the imperial past.

Political commentators and historians tend to ascribe political agency to state capitals as a kind of shorthand for government, diplomacy, and power. Beijing or Washington "acts," as if power and agency are neatly contained within the heart of state government, and projected outward, by decree, from its buildings and institutions. But this is true only to an extent. In this book we have highlighted how power and agency are diffused throughout the material structures of society: the layouts of cities; the disposition of technologies; the arrangement of districts, buildings, parks and squares; the patterns and materials of connecting infrastructures. These material infrastructures are multi-scalar, straddling the local, the regional, the national, and the transnational. As they are shaped, built, and assembled, the dominant ideas, ideologies, and power relations that led to their development are inscribed in space, thus both giving them a durability they could not otherwise attain, and augmenting their reach. This process is what makes the BRI, and Belt and Road Cities, so central to China's attempts to materialize and stabilize its long-term vision for an alternative international order.

But if material infrastructure and urbanization are at the core of this ambition, the power and agencies that shape material infrastructure are multi-directional. Agencies from the past have left deep legacies that any new vision must contend with. There is no blank canvas, but instead deep, durable, path-dependent legacies, in the forms of existing cities inherited from earlier forms of society, in the connections between these cities, and in the very structures of thought that define and delimit political order, such as those that carved out the modern territorial state system from the bedrock of the past.

Here we consider the competing visions that are vying to shape how China will use its growing power and influence to order itself and the world around it. How does the return of older Chinese ideas about the relationship between domestic and international order, such as the renewed focus on *tianxia* and Confucian political philosophy more broadly, find resonance today, and play into China's strategic thinking? How do these ideas fit with the continued, perhaps even renewed, influence of Marxism in China, with its own focus on the continuing evolution of world capitalism? Standing behind these questions is another, deeper question, one that stretches far back into ancient history: how does China's rise feed into the ever-shifting pattern of relations between Great Powers, cities, and world order? And how does China's growing power fit into the unique conditions of the twenty-first century?

China and the Question of World Order

As we have stressed, the concept of the BRI is neither entirely new, having longer precedents in Chinese policy circles, where there has long been talk about westward expansion and peripheral diplomacy, nor is it a creation of President Xi, despite his laying claim to it.[4] But after Xi consolidated his power at the 20th National Congress of the CCP in October 2022—by effectively eliminating rival factions from the Politburo, packing the Standing Committee with loyalists, and guaranteeing himself an unprecedented third five-year term—the Chinese Dream, and the BRI, have become central narratives sculpting China's relationship to international order today.

Like all national narratives, the Chinese Dream looks selectively to the past in order to support a particular vision of the future.[5] China's historical relationship to the outside world across millennia of imperial dynasties is one core influence, as are ideas from Chinese culture like Confucian notions of harmony, relationality, reciprocity, and moral leadership. Marxism, too, is a factor; the Chinese Communist Party is continuing to negotiate its relationship with the surviving fragments of Marxist thought from which it once drew its legitimacy and animating purpose, and connect those to its future trajectory, which must contend with many Marxian theoretical concerns: the continued evolution of capitalism, the nature of technological transformation, and the relationship of human society to its environment.[6] All of these influences are shaping ideas about China's position and orientation in the world, as well as the *material* expression of those ideas, in the urban and infrastructural forms that China is building and influencing.

As discussed earlier, Chinese ideas about world order have the potential to diverge quite radically from the contemporary Westphalian order that has comprised the core of the international system over the past four centuries, and certainly since the post–World War II era, when it was extended to include former colonial states and given a broad institutional framework via the United Nations and other multilateral institutions. The growth of Chinese power, in other words, is set to challenge an international system where the rules have been set in place by other powers. As many have perceived, there is a disturbing historical echo here: the late nineteenth-century rise of German power, in a world already parceled up into European empires and spheres of influence.[7]

But a unified German nation was a product of the nineteenth century. China, as much a civilization as a state, has over two millennia of history as a unified political entity—a very long pre-Westphalian past.[8] And although China has actually been a staunch supporter in recent decades of the foundation stones of the Westphalian international order— sovereignty, hard territorial boundaries, non-intervention, the role of the United Nations—there are distinct signs that its priorities are beginning to shift (particularly in the face of a series of "liberal" interventions by Western powers in the post–Cold War era). China's gaze has become increasingly transnational, and its reach is one that now stretches well beyond its own borders.[9]

World order can be a nebulous term, quickly invoked and yet hard to pin down. The simplicity of the phrase is deceptive. But understanding the dilemmas surrounding China's rise, and the emergence and meaning of the Belt and Road City, requires an appreciation of its complex meanings.

After a lifetime of thought and practice in international diplomacy, Henry Kissinger argues that, at its broadest, world order may describe the concept held by a civilization about the nature of just arrangements and distributions of power applicable to the entire world.[10] Thus, the notion of world order encompasses attempts to identify the very broadest ordering principles of political life.

In practice, however, such a world order has never existed. Such a definition would always be contested by the diverse cultures and civilizations of the world. No civilization has been powerful enough to capture the hearts and minds of all peoples. The closest we have today to a form of world order is, indeed, that founded on the generally accepted principle of the norm of territorial state sovereignty—the Westphalian settlement.

In the absence of a shared value system to order political life at the international or world scale, and in the absence of a world government—a structural condition that scholars of international relations call "international anarchy"—we find order elsewhere. For although international anarchy lacks an orderer, it does not lack order, stability, or regularity. Territory, national independence, sovereignty, non-interference, and the setting up of common institutions with which to regulate interaction and expectations, like the United Nations, has allowed states to form an "international society," aimed at peaceful coexistence. Indeed, Hedley Bull famously brought together these realities in his 1979 book by naming such a condition the "anarchical society."[11]

Despite the absence, then, of shared universal values, the world has found a level of stability and peaceful coexistence by embracing the very minimalist shared norms and legitimate practices built on the foundations of the Westphalian settlement. Even so, underlying this thin social layer, fundamental questions of power remain.[12] And the balance of power never rests for long. It shifts across time, and significant changes in its composition, such as the rise of China, are never far from the surface. When power is in balance, we tend to see periods of relative stability. The Concert of Europe that followed the Napoleonic Wars of the nineteenth century, or the Cold War of the twentieth century, although not without conflict, were periods of relative stability. But when the balance of power shifts, as existing powers decline or new powers emerge, periods of instability, conflict, and breakdown in international order occur: the unification of Germany in 1871, for example, created a big recalibration of the balance of power that was a contributory factor in two world wars.

What this means, for thinkers such as Bull, is that international society is a historical construct, as well as a historical achievement. The international society we have today represents the values of a particular time and place in history. It is not static: the norms, rules, and principles underpinning international society change across time.[13] Some of its more recent developments have pushed in the direction of the collective governance of global problems such as climate change, with the UN Sustainable Development Goals and Paris Climate Accords, for example, becoming part of that normative structure. Although far from optimal, because of the significant elements of competition within the system, these are examples of the emergence of new norms, values, and goals around which expectations of appropriate behavior by states and their citizens can converge.

It is this form of international society, with its nascent attempts to engage with global-scale governance issues, that China's engagement with international order may destabilize as it grows in power. For China under Xi is drawing ever clearer dividing lines between its own values and approach and those of the West.

There has been a lot of thought devoted to improving the ability of contemporary international society to generate shared problem-solving and effective global governance around collective issues like climate change, health, or the global economic system.[14] But it has become increasingly apparent that the transnational scale of such problems is at odds with the very structure of international society. In the absence of an effective world or transnational authority, and in a world where states pursue competing national interests, the management of global challenges has become a major structural problem.

What the advent of the BRI reveals is that China has ambitions to construct the footings for an alternative governance system, and, potentially, an Afro-Eurasian international society, that might have very different characteristics than the current Westphalian system, which is built upon the demarcation of national spaces, and clear national borders. Indeed, what some of the developments that we have charted in this book describe is an attempt to build not so much a world order, as a walled order. Alongside the BRI, as we have seen, are alternative forms of international institutions, urban forms, and technological systems that diverge radically from those that have characterized the recent liberal order. China's attempts to build an alternative internet, within which alternative values, meanings, and principles are projected, speak to the material basis of this kind of logic of partition. In this example, the Chinese regime is trying to balance its own fear of openness, and of foreign influence and ideas, with a need to go out into the world, to be open to the flows of the global economy and its resources and markets. Whether this balancing act is possible in the long term remains to be seen.

China has framed the BRI as offering the prospect of peaceful international transformation via economic development. The Chinese have repeatedly made the case that the BRI is about peaceful co-development, and have claimed, somewhat disingenuously, given that there have been some periods in Chinese history where the empire had expanded aggressively into new territories, that it does not have a history of conquest beyond its borders. China's ascendency to Great Power status, however, and its capacity to generate new forms of international order, may well offer a way for peaceful transition—a new pathway out of the Thucydides Trap. It is possible that, within such an alternative form of regional international society, alternative forms of transnational governance may arise, perhaps without some of the roadblocks that have hampered efforts at global governance in the Westphalian order. If recent forms of global governance have been ineffective under the "anarchical" international society, an alternative pattern of ordering may be seen as attractive to some—especially those within the international system that don't share liberal values (see Chapter 4).

It remains, however, to be seen how attractive this alternative vision will be to other states and their peoples. The rush to take up the offer of BRI financing is one thing, especially given the huge gap in infrastructure development funding in Asia. The acceptance of Chinese values and moral leadership is quite another, as we saw earlier in the discussion of China's stubbornly low soft-power rankings. How attractive will the kind of ideas underpinning China's coalescing vision be? How easy will it be to enroll other states into a China-dominated international society? How far will other states go in wanting to emulate the characteristics of Chinese society, culture, and urban form within their own lands? And to what extent does accepting Chinese models of urbanism and technological systems start other states and societies, perhaps unwittingly, down a developmental path that will incorporate such values into their cities and connective infrastructures, and so shape their populations' lives, freedoms, and even the ideas available to them?

To get a clearer picture of what is at stake here, we must look to the rise to power of Xi Jinping, a mere decade ago, and the ideas and forces that have shaped the BRI as a component of a wider strategy for Chinese transformation of the international order.

The Rise of Xi Jinping and China's New Direction

Xi Jinping became China's president in 2013. Almost a decade later, there is speculation that he may become the first Chinese leader since Mao Zedong to take the title of chairman. His rise to power has brought with it a dramatic new direction in Chinese foreign relations. In less than a decade, his leadership has overseen the refinement and acceleration of a long-term grand strategy to reshape China's position in the world. Xi's consolidation of power has placed him at the heart of the Chinese Communist Party, and solidified his cult of personality. *Xi Jinping's Thought on Socialism with Chinese Characteristics for a New Era* has been enshrined in the constitution, and is now given equal status with the thought of Mao Zedong. In 2018 the National People's Congress amended the Chinese Constitution in order to lift the term limit on the presidency, opening the way for the 2022 National Congress of the CCP to endorse another five years, quite possibly more, of Xi's leadership, and bringing to a close the collective leadership that had characterized the Reform Period.

Before Xi's ascent to the pinnacle of Chinese political power, in the post-Mao Reform Period led by Deng Xiaoping, China's policy was characterized by the slogan "hide our capacities and bide our time." During this period, China focused on peaceful economic development, taking advantage of globalization, but being careful not to draw opposition by pressing for any change in the international order that had supported China's supercharged development. Growing steadily within the existing international order, drawing strength from the global economy over time, even if its institutional architecture was crafted by foreign powers; such a strategy was designed to promote domestic stability and provide the foundations for future Chinese power, while avoiding balancing or containment policies from geopolitical competitors that might otherwise be alarmed by Chinese size and weight.

Under Xi, much of the Reform Period liberalization of Chinese politics and society has been decisively rolled back. The "hide and bide" strategy has been replaced with a far more outward looking and assertive stance. Domestically, power has been not just recentralized, but also concentrated in the person of President Xi himself. Xi has crafted a narrative that associates decentralization and liberalization with corruption, using Maoist-style "anti-corruption" political campaigns and "self-criticism" sessions to push back decentralization. Xi has also put the brakes on domestic market liberalization, and envisages a careful calibration of the relationship between state and markets going forward. Xi does not reject globalization, as he made clear in his speech at the World Economic Forum at Davos in 2017.[15] But it is apparent that he envisages a very different form of globalization than the neoliberal global economy crafted over the past four decades by leading Western states. There is talk of globalization with Chinese characteristics, but as yet, there has been no clear articulation of what this might mean in practice.

Until the COVID-19 pandemic, Xi's gaze spanned the globe. Even now, despite the increasing emphasis on self-reliance and a dual-circulation economy, Xi's vision for the future will be achieved by throwing off the shackles of the compliant and quiet foreign policy of his immediate predecessors, and more assertively reclaiming China's position of leadership. This shift has caused alarm in the region and beyond, as have China's territorial claims, land reclamation, and militarization in the South China Sea, which began in 2014, soon after Xi took power. But despite tensions over disputed islands and territorial waters, as well as the outstanding issue of Taiwan, both of which have captured the headlines and attention of many analysts, it is Xi's flagship foreign-policy initiative, the BRI, that is the far more profound development.

When Xi rose to power in 2013, China was experiencing a raft of external and internal pressures. Despite the economic successes of the Reform Period, China's growth had been slowing, and the 2008 financial crisis had generated further problems, marking the end of the upswing of US-led liberal globalization, from which China had drawn much momentum. Hastening China's search for alternatives were instability in the broader international environment, including a deteriorating relationship with the United States under the Trump administration, as well as the sense that the United States—and by extension, the international order that it had crafted and led—was in an accelerating period of decline.

Domestically, too, Xi was exercised by the CCP's legitimacy problem. A party formed on the principles of a Marxian critique of capitalism, and on the promise of ushering in a socialist society, now found itself embracing rampaging capitalism and presiding over a highly unequal distribution of wealth. Neither the party nor the people seemed to have much faith in Marxist principles or ideas anymore. In many of his presidential speeches, Xi has described a reading of history in which regimes crumble from within because the ideological core that gave them purpose has been abandoned.[16] This danger is clearly on his mind as he seeks to reinvigorate the CCP with new sources of legitimacy and purpose.

The CCP had always based its claim to legitimate power on its ability to lead the country to a more prosperous future, and to provide for the needs of its people. The loss of the basis of this narrative has been seen by Xi as a form of weakness. Accordingly, there seems to be an attempt under way now to revamp the historical narrative of the CCP—by reconnecting it with its socialist purpose, and by linking its modern history with the much longer run of Chinese history. The idea is to combine "socialism with Chinese characteristics" with past glories of the centrally administered imperial Middle Kingdom, which was the moral leader of a wider international order. The CCP is, then, reframed not as a revolutionary force sweeping away the past, as it was in the Maoist period, but as the legitimate heir to thousands of years of the administration of the Chinese state, and playing a central role in a Sino-centric international order.

How successful this uneasy ideological marriage of modernity and pre-modern history will be, time will tell. Part of the return to an emphasis on the traditional past under Xi has been an attempt to reincorporate some of the Confucian elements of Chinese political culture. An emphasis on virtue in government and public office underpins the anti-corruption and self-criticism campaigns that have focused on both the political class and the wider society. These moves have sought to address the general perception that the CCP had become a vehicle for personal advancement rather than the transformation of society, while at the same time leaving the one-party system and Xi's own sources of authority intact; a tactic borrowed straight from the Maoist playbook. The overall thrust has been to reshape the relationship of the CCP to the Chinese people, and to reinvigorate its legitimacy. This feeds into the Chinese Dream, which has long been linked to the ultimate goal of "national rejuvenation," and which Xi seems determined to fulfill. At the same time, the anti-corruption campaign has been a very effective political tool against political opponents, rival factions, and alternative positions, allowing Xi to purge rivals and to entrench his own personal power and rule.

   The Chinese Dream, as characterized under Xi, represents both a vision for this rejuvenation of the Chinese nation (a familiar trope in many
previous periods, too), as well as a set of concrete markers to show its
success. The first of these markers, the achievement of a more prosperous society, was realized by a doubling of per capita GDP between 2010
and 2020. Another, the construction of a capable military, continues
apace. The overall message presented in this narrative is of a CCP meeting the social welfare needs of its people, and standing up for its people's
interests abroad. The Chinese Dream, then, is a collective dream quite
unlike the American Dream, which emphasizes individual and personal
attainment. Indeed, Xi's time in office has been distinguished by a clear
rejection of "foreign values" as a danger to China, particularly those liberal ideas that had grown popular in the Reform Period.[17]
   At the same time, another pressure facing China at the beginning of
Xi's tenure, and one of the oldest concerns of Marxist thought, was the unstable and crisis-prone nature of capitalism. Growth had slowed in the late
Reform Period under the premiership of Hu Jintao, and China's vast reserves of accumulated capital had presented a series of problems for China
in the late Reform Period. The dropoff from an average of 10 percent annual growth across the Reform Period to around 6 percent in recent years
reflects both the growing maturity of the Chinese economy and a series of
long-term, structural economic challenges that the development of the BRI
is designed to help solve. After decades of growth, the sources of new labor
have now dried up, and rural to urban migration has slowed to a trickle.
Wage demands have risen, placing China in the classic middle-income trap:
labor is increasingly uncompetitive, but manufacturing is not yet sophisticated enough to reach the higher-value market niches. China has also accumulated vast reservoirs of savings that need to be put to productive use:
aggregate domestic savings is a huge 50 percent of total national income.[18]
Although there had been significant investment in its own domestic infrastructure, surplus capital on this scale would inevitably require new avenues
of investment abroad. The way in which China has focused on developing
its own urban spaces and infrastructures is a classic "spatial-fix" to the over-
accumulation of capital—putting it to productive use in long-term fixed
capital investments, and along the way rebalancing the historic gap in
China between the highly urbanized east and the vast open spaces of the
west.[19] The phenomenon of "ghost cities," the building of infrastructure in
anticipation of future need, is perhaps the most extreme version of this tendency. The BRI opens up a new outlet for this huge reservoir of capital.

But perhaps the key catalyst for the embrace of a new outward-looking economic strategy for China was the 2008 global financial crisis. One of the ways in which China had invested its surplus was in the US bond market—locking the two countries into an economic relationship so symbiotic (China saved, America consumed) that historian Niall Ferguson coined the term "Chimerica" to describe it. The 2008 crash, the perception of regulatory and policy failure in the West, and the general loss of confidence in the US-led model of heavily financialized market economies that accompanied it, has fed into Chinese attempts to decouple and to forge a new path. In addition, the role of Chinese policy and stimulus packages in helping to reboot the world economy after the crisis has emboldened the Chinese leadership to use their growing economic strength in new ways.

So in a period of time so short that the world has yet to come to terms with the ambition and evolving reality, the Xi Jinping administration has reshaped the trajectory of China, harnessing its growing economic might and military strength to reorient the Chinese state, both at home and abroad. In domestic politics, Xi has recharged the CCP's mission in relation to society, as well as recrafted its historical narrative. He has reshaped the party and political institutions to ensconce his own personal political power, jettisoning the collective system of rule that had characterized the Reform Period.

Xi has also made a radical course correction to the way that China and others perceive its place and purpose in the world. A more assertive, aggressive, and purposive China has emerged—reflected, perhaps, in the popular idea of "wolf warrior" diplomacy, which draws on a source in popular culture that depicts China as combating aggressive enemies abroad. A turn to nationalism, including some ugly symptoms of a racist xenophobia, has been in evidence. A narrative of China standing up in the world, particularly after a "century of humiliation," is being accentuated.[20] Increasingly bellicose diplomacy—such as the almost comical level of hostility seen at the 2021 US-China summit in Anchorage—has led to a deterioration in relations with many states.

But in addition to the image of a China that refuses to be pushed around, there is also the image of China as benefactor and leader, shaping and directing a wider "community of common destiny" for those who want to join it. China is projecting itself, not entirely without foundation, but also not entirely accurately either, as a civilizational state that does not have a tendency to colonize or invade others. Via the BRI,

China seeks to materialize a grand strategy that would reshape the international order not via war, but via trade and development, offering the prospect that the epochal historical transformation currently under way might avoid fueling a hegemonic war of succession like those experienced in earlier times.

Foundations for a Chinese-Led International Society

China's last imperial dynasty collapsed in 1911–1912. Just as at many points in China's long history, the end of the Qing dynasty was followed by an ignominious period of collapse and fragmentation. This time it took the form of warlordism, social breakdown, and, later, occupation and civil war, which were caught up with the wider maelstrom of World War II. The CCP's ultimate victory over Chiang Kai-shek's Nationalists in 1949 set China on a new path, but a no less tumultuous one, as the events of the second half of the twentieth century would prove. Today Xi is trying to help rebuild and reinvigorate both the CCP and Chinese society, by reuniting China's present with agreeable aspects of its past. Whether this is achievable in the long run is an open question.

China's disorienting experience of the past two centuries, and its reemergence in the very different international order of today, have given it a difficult puzzle to solve. As Henry Kissinger has argued, China has no historical precedent for playing the role of equal among other states.[21] Over the past two millennia, in those historical experiences that it likes to recall, China has led some form of hierarchically organized regional international system. Although the post-Mao policy direction since 1976 has been one of ever greater participation in the Westphalian order and its institutions, China has always retained a sense that the rules of the game were set by others. Despite assertions to the contrary, this is the real meaning of the "hide and bide" approach—a sense that China would eventually be able to reassert its natural weight on the international stage. Under Xi Jinping, there appears to be confidence that this moment has now arrived. But the problem remains that China once ruled at the apex of a hierarchical international society, whereas today it stands as a state that is, nominally at least, the equal of others. The Chinese Dream involves hierarchy; the current reality is sovereign equality. And the strength of contemporary nationalism in the region will make it difficult to enroll others into the Chinese Dream. How can these puzzles be reconciled?

As China seeks to redefine its place in the world, it is becoming apparent, especially via the implementation of the BRI, that the hazy vision of world order that it is articulating is actually neither a reversion to different models of Chinese imperial order, nor a renewed version of the Maoist emphasis on world revolution, nor the Westphalian status quo. It is something new, something struggling to be born. Although it incorporates elements of all these historical legacies, if any stable form emerges it will be a fundamentally novel response to the challenges of the twenty-first century. As China draws on these elements of the past, applying them in new ways to the environment in which it finds itself, the process of accommodation will also transform China and its self-perception. No Chinese imperial dynasty ever had the reach and scope of the BRI, or a wider concept of Eurasia. No former Chinese polity engaged with new visions of transnational space in the ways that China does in today's world of digital communications, vast urban corridors, and new virtual spaces. Just as one cannot step into the same river twice, so the way in which China blends past, present, and future will be something new in the annals of history.

Having celebrated the centenary of its founding in 2021, those at the helm of the CCP today seem to want to emphasize its continuity with millennia of Chinese centralized rule, rather than its origins as a force for world revolution. Indeed, the CCP is an offshoot of modernity that is now being integrated into a much longer historical narrative in the search to legitimate its rule over one-sixth of the world's population. Principles drawn from China's 2,500-year Confucian heritage are being woven into this narrative, despite having been an anathema in the Mao era, when the impulse was to attack and denigrate the past. In many respects, the CCP, as a form of concentrated elite power—and despite originally being a kind of Leninist state with a Politburo and Central Committee—fits into these ancient Chinese traditions of centralized power, legalism, and bureaucracy. Centralized power and elite leadership, with a focus on the personality and morality of the leader and his advisers, has always been the rule in China, where there are no indigenous traditions of bottom-up democratic participation.[22]

Although the CCP originated as one of several nationalist parties that vied for power after the collapse of the Qing dynasty, its socialist mission and Marxian influences contain strong elements of internationalism. As China rises in power, as the CCP seeks to shore up domestic legitimacy for the future, and as liberal internationalism appears to be in retreat around the world, the Chinese are beginning to extol internationally the decision-making and leadership virtues of centralized rule. Indeed, the CCP believes implicitly in the supremacy of its socialist system over Western-style liberal democracy.[23] The CCP as a leader in international development, and as a purveyor of new norms within an emerging Sino-centric international society, could then, in theory, fit in with the original revolutionary goals and ambitions of international socialism. The current regime appears to have decided that this historical moment, if seized decisively, could drive a transformation of international order—with the CCP at the vanguard.

The Xi regime consistently stresses both the centrality of Chinese power and China's cultural and moral superiority. In doing so it invokes the ancient Chinese concept of *tianxia* (all under heaven), the Confucian ethics of the ancient Zhou dynasty (1046–256 BCE), and the historical achievements of the Han (206 BCE–220 CE), Ming (1368–1644), and Qing (1644–1912) empires, which are often cited to illustrate the majesty and superiority of Chinese civilization and to offer exemplars of alternative, Sino-centric international orders.

Indeed, there has long been a recognition that Chinese understandings of international order might give us very different ideas than those undergirding the Westphalian system.[24] The recent focus on indigenous Chinese philosophical and political traditions by Chinese intellectuals signals that China's influence is growing once again.[25] There is now a vibrant Chinese School of International Relations, which has been consolidating over the past two decades, and from which various strands of thought have emerged that engage with older ideas and principles drawn from China's long political history. Several of its thinkers have utilized concepts such as *tianxia*, tributary and hierarchical systems of international society, ideas around Confucian ethics and moral international leadership, and harmony and coevolution among state systems, to develop insights into past, present, and future international politics.[26]

The relationship between Chinese thinking on world order and international relations for most of the twentieth century had been heavily influenced by Western traditions and ideas. Marxism informs the rationale of the CCP, of course, while more recently, Chinese scholars of international relations have been heavily influenced by Realist thinking. Realism focuses on the hard facts of survival in an often dangerous and competitive international system, where there is no higher authority than the state to provide security from invasion or destruction; states are on their own, and must watch carefully for changes in the balance of power, for both threats and opportunities.[27] Perhaps the dominant school of international theory, especially in the United States, Realist thinking has tended to dominate in China too. Yan Xuetong of Tsinghua University, for instance, studied in the United States in his early career with Realist masters such as Kenneth Waltz. But, as we will see, Yan has taken those Realist ideas from the Western context and reexamined them in light of ancient Chinese political theory and history. A group of thinkers around Yan, who also have the ear of the foreign-policy-making community, as well as others within a broader Chinese School of International Relations, have been beginning to marry this new thinking about the international system, drawing on Chinese thought and history, to China's growing power and influence on the world stage.[28]

Theories and scholarship about the nature of international politics are naturally influenced by the configuration of power in successive historical moments. This has been the case with Western theories of international relations in the twentieth century, when its great debates and controversies responded to, and shaped, the tumultuous history of that century—including the failure of the League of Nations to prevent world war, the superpower struggles of the Cold War, and the nature of US hegemonic power after the Cold War ended. So it will be for China as it rediscovers the responsibilities and interests associated with Great Power status. Its vast size, economic strength, growing strategic capabilities, as well as its long and rich civilizational history, make this an inevitability. The question for Chinese scholars, leaders, and policymakers will be whether the Chinese can develop and implement new ideas about international order that go on to influence other states and peoples around the world, as the United States, the Soviet Union, or European powers have in the past; and, indeed, as past iterations of imperial China have done in epochs gone by.[29] Today Chinese scholars are considering questions such as how China, as a rising power, might be peacefully integrated into the international community; what conditions might allow for a peaceful rise; what China's evolving responsibilities as a Great Power with aspirations to leadership are; and what alternative structures for international society Chinese values and concepts might lead to.[30]

The Chinese School of International Relations, then, refers loosely to a set of complementary and coevolving concepts, theories, and arguments— drawn from the uniquely Chinese perspective—that challenge the canon of Western-dominated international theory in a variety of ways.[31] Close connections and interactions between Chinese academics and scholars of the Chinese School and policymakers mean that these ideas can and do influence the direction of Chinese strategic thinking. In fact, many of these ideas mesh quite nicely with the material and infrastructural foundations being laid down with BRI projects, so that these ideas may have shaped, and continue to influence, the grand strategic thinking behind the BRI, while the BRI lays the footings to extend new ideas about international society across space and through time, giving them the durability they would need to make a difference in the world.

For example, the contemporary Chinese philosopher Zhao Tingyang has provided a framework for thinking of *tianxia* as inspiration for a model of universal governance.[32] Zhao argues that *tianxia* can offer a superior set of ideas for a more inclusive and harmonious world order to those that we currently have—ideas that stress an ontology of coexistence rather than endless competition between states; harmony and coevolution rather than endless shifts in the balance of power. *Tianxia* is a larger unit of analysis than the state, and so can perhaps point to a world of global governance beyond Westphalia, one that can expand to meet the unique transnational global governance challenges of the twenty-first century. For Zhao, an embrace of *tianxia* thinking can be both a scholarly and political project.

According to this perspective, *tianxia* describes a type of international society organized around a core state and deriving moral leadership from that state. In theory this state could be any state—although clearly the implication is that it has been in the past, and should be again, China. From the central state emanates the moral ideology and guiding principles that the surrounding states are guided by. Traditionally the Chinese emperor had the "mandate of heaven," and so—when acting in morally proper ways—could provide a conduit between cosmic harmony and the earthly realm. Such cosmic wisdom would then be universally accepted and a stable moral international community would be built. The power exercised by the central state in this framework is thus not primarily material, but normative—that of a moral exemplar and benevolent hegemon binding others to it in an evolving community of common destiny—the very image contained in the Chinese Dream. It is an ideal to be aspired to, even if perhaps never fully attainable in practice. Given that presumably such a harmonious international order would only truly be realized under Chinese leadership, some critics have suggested that this is merely philosophical cover for the renewal of the Chinese imperial hierarchical systems of the past.[33]

Today China argues that its imperial history was largely characterized by benevolence—and that it has never had a history of aggressive colonial expansion. But this is a fairly selective interpretation. The Ming dynasty (1368–1644) carved out a tributary system that included modern Korea, Japan, and Mongolia. The Qing (Manchu) dynasty (1644–1912) was aggressively expansionist, creating a sweeping Eurasian land empire, settling colonists in the Khanates of eastern Turkestan, extending authority into Tibet and Bhutan, and imposing tributary status on other territories such as Burma (now Myanmar). As the historian Odd Arne Westad points out, if we really want to look to history for the origins of the contemporary Chinese state, it is the "restless empire" of the Qing period that is most relevant.[34] Regardless of the question of benevolence, these are inherently hierarchically ordered international systems—and, indeed, much of the history of East Asia features such systems. Some have argued, in fact, that China has found it hard to reconcile itself with modernity precisely because it has always conceived of itself as the center of the world, and has struggled to accommodate other understandings.[35]

The spatial imaginary of international order at work in much of Chinese history, then, from the Chinese perspective, is one of concentric circles in which China sits at the center, a benign moral and civilizational exemplar to the rest of the world. The majesty of China's cultural soft power, and economic and technological magnificence, were thought to be enough to awe other states and peoples into deference and tribute. But if historical Chinese emperors were believed to be in possession of the "mandate of heaven," from which their wisdom and benevolence radiated out to more peripheral peoples, it is less clear today where the CCP's and Xi's mandate come from. The current framing is one in which China offers financial, technological, and developmental leadership to states that need it. With such largesse comes not just a reformation of transnational space and urban morphology, but also a new position at the center of a growing web of influence, ties, and planetary urbanism.

This is a *relational* system, some have argued, that offers a very different understanding of international order than that derived from the intellectual foundations of Westphalia, which is far more contractual and based on legal equality, and on bounded notions of space and temporality. It is within this understanding of international order as a constantly evolving relational network that ancient Confucian ideas have begun to find their way back into contemporary debates about China's orientation to the world. Indeed, as the balance of power shifts away from the

West, it should be no surprise that we see alternative understandings of
international order come to the fore, given the relation between power
and knowledge.³⁶ Some of the concepts and ideas that emerge will, no
doubt, seem alien to established ways of thinking about international
politics. But with the rise of Chinese power, and the growing power of
other non-Western states in the international system, there is an imperative to engage in unfamiliar ways of thinking through ways of ordering
political, social, and economic life.

In particular, the Confucian understanding of social relations as a coevolving web of reciprocal obligations relies on the Chinese concepts of
guanxi and *gong sheng*. *Guanxi* expands on the logic of relationality outlined above. In such a system, actors, such as states, only ever act in relation to others, relations are always in process, and the web of relations is
ontologically prior to, and more important than, the individual actors.³⁷
Guanxi moves us beyond the familiar Westphalian model of international
society and international security that stresses the sovereign independence
of equals. It refers to a coevolving network of asymmetrical, yet volitional,
relationships, established by the practice of exchanging favors between
members who are bound by reciprocal obligations, assurance, and mutual-
ity.³⁸ Members within this network of relations give, receive, and repay.
Over time these members become increasingly enmeshed within a complex and enduring set of customary norms and behaviors that regulate
their interaction and cement their place in the network. The asymmetrical
element inherent to the system places one power at the moral center of
the dynamic and evolving web of relations, a power guided by Confucian
principles of benevolence, wisdom, and priority: China as the guide of a
constantly evolving and enduring community of common destiny. These
are the kind of dynamics that we see forming along with the BRI as it
facilitates Chinese construction of transport infrastructures, urban development via economic corridors, digital connectivity, and financial architectures across Afro-Eurasia; a new and parallel relational system taking
shape in the interstices of the existing international order.

These kinds of ideas offer new perspectives on power and governance. Instead of a balance of power, we may have a "balance of relationships," moving toward the achievement of reciprocity and harmony—a
crucial consideration in Chinese ideas about government and gover-
nance.³⁹ This notion of harmony is fairly alien to Western international
thought, and some doubt if it can be expressed within the existing
intellectual framework of Western international relations.⁴⁰ But it has

implications for the understanding of how international security might be achieved: through a correctly harmonized balance of relationships. Highlighting again the link between the exploration of these traditional concepts and ideas and the policy community, the China Institute of Contemporary International Relations, a think tank linked to the Ministry of State Security, has sketched the outline of a new global security initiative (GSI), aimed at "world peace" and "tranquillity," that appears to rest on some of these influences. The document outlining the new concept (which is big on ambition for international order, but short on details), says that it represents

> not only a continuation and development of China's fine traditional culture and wisdom and an integration and innovation of international security thinking with Chinese characteristics, but also the sublation and transcendence of Western security theory . . . [and] a strong response to the main security threats of today's world.[41]

President Xi has thrown his weight behind the GSI, which is apparently "a concrete manifestation of *Xi Jinping's Thought on Diplomacy* and [his] global security outlook." At a recent virtual presentation for the annual Boao Forum for Asia in 2022, Xi noted its promise of "indivisible security" as a response to the many pressing security concerns that the world faces, including the continuing global pandemic, the spiraling food and energy crises unleashed by Russia's invasion of Ukraine, and continuing conflict in the Middle East and Africa.[42] Whether China can step up to the role of providing international security as a public good is a question that will be answered in the next decades.

A related and similar take on relational theory that has emerged from the Chinese School is *gong sheng*, or symbiotic theory.[43] Symbiotic theory speaks to the issue of difference that underpins much conflict in international relations and international history. It recognizes the inherent pluralism and diversity that exists within the world, in its multiple cultures, value systems, and civilizations. It accepts difference as a fact—and seeks a world that takes the acceptance of difference as a starting point. The coming together of such differences can, in the right conditions, lead to mutual learning and appreciation, co-development and coevolution. Again, harmony and balance are key, as is the shift to an understanding of international society as a coevolving whole, which some Chinese scholars believe offers a way to get beyond Westphalian dynamics of conflict.

Another major strand of thinking coming out of the Chinese School is inspired by Yan Xuetong and others at Tsinghua University.[44] This approach focuses on Great Power *leadership* as a core element of international transformation. In particular, it asks what benevolent and moral leadership might look like, and how it might provide authority and legitimacy to aspiring Great Powers. As noted earlier, Yan was educated in the Western tenets of Realism, and he maintains some of that hardedged focus on Great Power politics. But he has delved deeply into Chinese history—the ancient, pre-Qin, Warring States period (475–221 BCE) looms large in his historical exegesis—in order to extract lessons for how we think about the role of political leadership in affecting the balance of power and moments of power transition. Yan's reading of history leads him to believe that when a dominant or hegemonic state within a system yields to its rising challenger, the quality and content of the rising state's leadership are what is key, exceeding that of the declining power it replaces. This has come to be termed "moral realism." According to this view, moral concepts—such as fairness, justice, civility, and wisdom—become crucial variables in the struggle for influence and power, and are critical to shaping the evolving normative content of international order.[45]

Drawing on these Confucian ideals, China offers a metaphor of kinship and leadership to the peoples of Eurasia. But the concepts of *guanxi* and *symbiosis* refer to a constantly evolving system in which the identity of the components, *including the Chinese state*, changes over time. This means that China's own identity, despite its centrality in the web of relationships, must also evolve, as it engages with others and listens to their needs. This openness to others, which China is tentatively moving toward with the BRI, is both the promise and the risk of its international engagement. In its attempt to recraft international order, and in its engagement with global processes, it may well open up to forces that challenge its own understanding of itself, its own stability and sense of purpose in the world.

As an inscription of an evolving Chinese-led international society in space, the Belt and Road City is also evolving and in flux, trying to find its form as it contends with multiple contradictory impulses, influences, and forces. It is, of course, possible that it may never find a stable form, and that the Chinese Dream will fail to take shape and instead dissipate, as dreams often do. If the Chinese Dream does not take shape, it will be because China was unable to realize itself as a hegemonic power with a coherent project and purpose—much as the Soviet Union ultimately failed because it was unable to resolve its internal contradictions and divergent impulses.

This instability is complicated by the ambivalent identity of the CCP in the twenty-first century. That is, the CCP, despite its tight grip on power, and its ability to ride out the various challenges thrown at it in the past hundred years, is itself today composed of some highly contradictory and unstable ideological elements. With ninety million members, the CCP is the world's largest political party, in control of the world's most populous country. Yet it has always struggled to work out its purpose. A putatively communist political party, it now presides over a dynamic capitalist economy. Such foundational contradictions inevitably lead to a search for legitimacy. Can such an unstable mix ever articulate a convincing vision for international order, and a stable urban form with which to imprint that vision?

During the Reform Period, China's supercharged economic growth allowed the CCP to ride on the wave of rising living standards, and to paper over the ideological rupture that had taken place. While the country experienced an astonishing economic boom—with per capita GDP since 1980 increasing 75-fold, and annual growth rates consistently 8 percent or more—such questions were put on hold.[46] Millions were lifted out of poverty after decades of stagnation.

But now, as the economy has matured, and begun to slow down, questions have again arisen over how the CCP can justify its iron rule. What does the CCP stand for? How can it relate to the world outside of China? Can its model be a sustainable and attractive basis for shaping an international order? It is here, in the difficult search for answers to such questions, that the attraction of the past is most evident. As we noted earlier, the party-state model of today is not so far out of line with two millennia of centralized, bureaucratic, and authoritarian rule in China— and some argue that it is the only appropriate governance model for a civilizational state of China's size. Many authoritarian regimes across Eurasia also find appealing the tight centralized control of the Chinese model. At the same time, the Western liberal democratic models are suffering their own crises of legitimacy and confidence.

The abandonment of Marxism in the Reform Period left the "communist" element of the CCP open to question. China today is a country

whose cities are being reshaped by rampant capitalism into unequal cita-
dels of consumption, where places like Shanghai or Guangzhou have
come to resemble some of the Global Cities of the West. Trade unions, a
core feature of most socialist societies, are now repressed in China; civil
society has been curtailed; power is increasingly centralized; and the collective leadership of the Reform Period, which was designed to limit the
ability of a powerful individual to make mistakes, has been rolled back.
At home, Xi's regime has tightened control and closed down venues and
spaces for critical thought, a practice that is only likely to intensify after
Xi's consolidation of power in 2022. Perennial fears for the integrity of
the homeland have also led to crackdowns in Xinjiang and Hong Kong,
and the future of Taiwan remains a dangerous flashpoint.

Perhaps the newest and most important development in state control
over the population has been the capacity for surveillance offered by new
technologies embedded in the urban fabric. The application of these new
surveillance tools, as well as the collection, storage, and processing of
data, now leave little outside the pervasive eye of the state. Monitoring of
personal communication devices; social-credit scoring systems that re-
ward and punish certain behaviors; biometric surveillance, such as facial
and gait recognition and, potentially, DNA markers—all extend possibilities for deep and pervasive control over populations, of which the city of
Kashgar today stands as nightmarish exemplar. The response to the
COVID-19 pandemic, when digital tools developed by the state pene-
trated even further into people's lives so as to monitor the progress of
the virus, has accelerated these trends. The incorporation of such technical tools into the very fabric of Belt and Road urban forms, inside and
outside of China, via the construction of Smart Cities, offers new possibilities for controlling and monitoring billions of people across the Afro-
Eurasian space, potentially projecting the power and preferences of
forms of society whose values become embedded in these technological
systems. A CCP-crafted form of *tianxia*, a techno-totalitarian center for
an evolving web of relations defining a new form of international control
society, may well be finding its conditions of possibility in the nexus of
the present moment, as a new socio-technical model and urban form
fuses from the disparate components of the CCP's tumultuous historical
experience.

Yet, as we have seen, the BRI is not a unidirectional project, imposed
by China on others, but, for now at least, an open system. Many other
powerful agencies go into shaping its form. Some of these are the agencies

of other states. But there are also other forces and logics, not least the dynamics of globalized capitalism, which is itself a system of even greater extent, in which state actors are now embedded. Having embraced global capitalism and opened up its society to it, China now is subject to its wild fluctuations and demands, its insatiable logics.

As with all states that embrace global capitalism, tensions have arisen between the territorial logics of a bounded state, even one as large as China, and the fundamentally transnational logics of capital. As we discussed in the Introduction, this tension was one of the drivers behind the emergence of the Global City: an urban and infrastructural form that came to facilitate, extend, and express a new form of deregulated, neoliberal, globalized capitalism. Neil Brenner calls the process by which states generate new urban spaces that can enlarge the capitalist market "state-rescaling." In this process, the state is used as a vehicle to both generate and encourage an enlarged sphere for transnational capitalism, as a way to bridge the scalar gap between national territory and transnational circuits of value, and so to facilitate a new round of capitalist accumulation that can overcome the spatial constraints and limits of the old system.

Just as the Great Powers in the past have confronted this problem, so now does China.[47] As we noted, a key problem that China faced after the decades of extraordinary growth was its immense surfeit of capital. This over-accumulation is a historical pattern; China is the latest, perhaps the largest, in a string of Great Powers to face it.[48] In the past the problem has been solved, at least for a time, by what David Harvey has called the spatial fix: using spates of urban development and infrastructure construction to soak up excess capital.[49] These building sprees can take place domestically: think of Roosevelt's New Deal and the reconstruction of America in the postwar period, or Hausmann's reconstruction of Paris in the eighteenth century. Across China, and, indeed, beyond its borders, we can see the remnants of "ghost cities"—infrastructure developed to soak up capital awaiting a population that never came—often with functioning roads, infrastructure, public spaces, sometimes even skyscrapers, but without residents. Consider the cities of Tianducheng, two hours west of Shanghai, built as a tasteless miniature simulacrum of Paris; or Ordos, in Inner Mongolia, built to house 300,000 people, but eerily unpopulated. Such spatial fixes can also happen in territories outside of the home state: think of how French imperialism reshaped North Africa, or the British transformed India.

China, as a new capitalist power, potentially the largest ever yet seen, seems to be conforming to this historical pattern by pursuing the possibilities for transnational expansion offered by the BRI. What is driving these transnational developments is not just what China wants, but also the demands of capital accumulation. That is, when we think about China's struggles to articulate a new global identity, and its strategy for creating a new international order that can transcend the limits of national boundaries in a world of global flows, the demands placed on it by capitalism are just as important as the geostrategic factors. China's gaze is transnational not simply because it is seeking to recapitulate the glories of empires past, but because it is itself caught up in the empire of capital.[50]

The BRI does not conform to the earlier models of European imperialism as a spatial fix. It is, perhaps, a far more subtle strategy, albeit one that does seek to place China at the center of global economic flows. Neither, however, can we fit the BRI neatly into the concentric circle worldview that characterized the imperial dynasties of China past. As the BRI is currently portrayed in official maps, the imaginary is neither one of Westphalian borders, nor the concentric circles of *tianxia*. Instead the BRI is primarily portrayed as a network of cities connected by infrastructure—with the BRI becoming the core mechanism being used to redesign an international order not via conquest, but by *reshaping the nature of space*. That is, by cutting across borders and boundaries, projecting influence, and bending transnational corridors toward China's growing center of gravity as the terminus of a multitude of tendrils and networks of global value, the BRI reflects a novel way to think about the spatiality of international order, one that transgresses Westphalian boundaries.[51] With it, China offers a new way to match the economic scale of global capital to the political scale, just as, from the 1970s on, Western powers have experimented with Global Cities as the mechanism to solve this problem.[52]

The urban and infrastructural initiatives represented by existing and planned BRI corridors do not signal a desire to appropriate or annex territory, but they do fundamentally transform the spatial relations of the Chinese state to those territories touched and reshaped to greater or lesser degree by the BRI—via investment, influence over technological systems, and the ways in which urban forms are always socially shaped by the values of the dominant society of the day. We must watch the emerging form of BRI urbanism to see what it reveals about the nature and

durability of any Chinese-led international society, for as we have argued, any new form of international society and political order must be
expressed via a new type of city and transnational urban spatial form.
China's experiment with transnational urbanism and governance, whatever its eventual result, will express itself in cities across Eurasia, just as
urban forms have been shaped by Great Powers in the past. The Belt and
Road City will be the barometer of China's attempt to recraft international order. In its evolving forms we will be able to see its success, or its
failure.

Conclusion

THE BELT AND ROAD INITIATIVE is the centerpiece of China's long-term ambition to return to a role of international leadership. Its advent in 2013 marked a distinct shift in Chinese foreign policy, ending a period of peaceful economic development within the parameters of the existing international order, and signaling China's growing confidence in its power to shape the international environment to reflect its own interests and values. It is clear now that China seeks to challenge and transform the current international order across multiple arenas, and through diverse mechanisms and instruments.

As a new grand strategy for connectivity across Afro-Eurasia, the Belt and Road Initiative sits at the core of all of these efforts, with material infrastructure operating as an instrument of geopolitics. There can be no new infrastructure order, however, without urban effects and urban inputs. Enabling flows and exchanges of food, water, consumer goods, data, energy, and people between places alters, intentionally or unintentionally, the places where people work, consume, live, and transit. For the majority of the world, those places are cities. For significant portions of Africa and Asia, rapidly changing and expanding cities, funded and built through an alliance with the BRI, are transforming the very nature of what urban life looks like and means.

The scope of the BRI comes closer to a new vision for globalization than any offered by other global powers, and in that vision, infrastructure and urban systems are intertwined. And so in Vientiane, a terminus of the China–Laos Railway alters the urban fabric with new design—that supposedly speaks to friendship—while also displacing urban residents. In Gwadar City, a port grows without the urban ecosystem—water, healthcare, education institutions—to support its employees. And in Nairobi, the data privacy of city residents is tangled with access to infrastructure for intra-city commutes. To be sure, China is not unique in influencing global urban spaces. The aid or development programs of the United States, Japan, the Netherlands, Denmark, the United Kingdom, South Korea, the European Union, and many other national and international bodies continue to do so, as do the private-sector firms of those countries. But China is unique in its global vision that connects the urban dots. By placing itself at the core of a developing web of flows and exchanges, one embodied by durable technological and urban infrastructures, China is laying the foundations for a new form of international society—one in which Chinese influence, norms, values, and interests can be projected beyond its borders.

This is not to say that the BRI is some kind of master plan guaranteed to reorder the world. International politics is far too big and complicated for that to be the case. Just as in the climate-change space adaptation can deliver maladaptation, so too can foreign-policy implementation lead to unexpected results. The local environment has a say, in a way, in the construction of international order itself. But in its cause and effect, the BRI is more subtle and long-term than even a maximalist foreign policy or exercise in cause and effect. It is an order-building project that could only be envisaged by a civilizational state the size of China, and an administration like the CCP that can strategize decades ahead and with the entire world in mind. The projects of the BRI, despite their seeming ad hoc nature, should not be viewed as simply China's accumulation of various strategic assets, as is often the case when approached via a military lens. Nor should they be dismissed as crude attempts at debt diplomacy—the acquisition of a Sri Lankan port here, or a Cameroonian subsea-internet-cable link there—as states default on their loans. Although there are elements of truth in these perspectives, the BRI is something more grand in scope and ambition. It is, in many ways, an appreciation that international order has, as its basis, a set of material foundations, and a recognition that international systems have historically been built on the technological and infrastructural components of their day.

In recognizing this, China reminds us of an important truth about geopolitics—one that scholars of international relations have forgotten in recent debates about the nature of international transformation: that the ability to design, implement, and maintain infrastructure is a core aspect of being a Great Power in the international system, and a way to shape and reshape international systems and international order. China is combining its rise and bid for international leadership with an attempt to reshape the material foundations and productive capacities of billions of people, and the large technical systems to lock them into particular patterns, influenced from the Chinese core. Moreover, those infrastructures run through, and their material manifestations appear within, the cities and urban spaces where people live and work. Historically this has been a unique property of Great Power states—the ability, in those rare moments of transformation, to mold material and urban life in ways that reflect their interests and values. In this sense, China is now following in a long historical lineage.

International order is not easy to grasp, let alone see. The UN Security Council, where power is named and seats assigned, operates with a politics hidden from plain sight. But one of the ways in which this process of domestic and international order-making becomes visible to us is in the forms that cities take, and in the ways in which they are connected. In examining the ways in which Chinese state power, finance, firms, technologies, and developmental models are shaping and connecting both its own cities, and cities across Eurasia and parts of Africa, via the BRI, we hope to have opened a conversation about how this relationship between the rise of a new Great Power, urbanization, and international systemic transformation is playing out today.

As we have seen, Belt and Road Cities are already beginning to take on a set of recognizable features, even within all of their diversity—just as Global Cities, tied to the conjuncture of US hegemony, a liberal world economy, and a new form of urbanization, had their distinctive features. It remains possible, however, that for all its size, and growing strength and influence, China's increasingly ambitious reach may exceed its grasp. It may be that it fails to realize its vision of an Afro-Eurasia, or indeed a global system, connected to a core of Chinese leadership. It may be that China ultimately fails to produce *durable* urban spaces that inscribe its values and its model in space. Cities, whether the shrinking cities of the global North or the rapidly expanding informal urban areas of the global South, are complex systems that defy the simple projection and application of power. And it may be that the Chinese Dream, along with its Belt and Road Cities, will be swept away on history's capricious tides. Already,

China's vaulting ambitions are beginning to draw opposition, sometimes from the very states and peoples it has sought to enroll. Already, China's plans for future BRI investment have had to be tightened in the light of economic slowdown at home and abroad, and the continuing effects of COVID-19 and Russia's war in Ukraine. Already peer competitors, such as the United States and the European Union, are looking at the decade in which China has stolen a march on them in shaping infrastructure geopolitics, and are developing their own responses for the next decade. We are entering a new decade of infrastructural geopolitics, and a battle for influence throughout the global South is about to begin in earnest.

For these reasons—structural weakness, bottom-up resistance, and Great Power competition—the idea of a grand master plan imposed by Beijing policymakers on immense swaths of the world, as is sometimes imagined, should be set aside. It is unlikely that most readers will visit Kotokuraba Market in Cape Coast, Ghana, to shop at the market stalls. But those stalls, envisioned by Chinese designers from afar, have been refashioned in local traditions and to fit local goods. As China attempts to reshape the international order, the spaces it seeks to shape are themselves being refashioned by local pressures and contexts. Not unlike urban spaces, the significance of the BRI as a mechanism by which international order may be reshaped is to be found in its creation of an open-ended roster of *components* that have the potential to reorient from within the existing structures, patterns, and relationships of international politics. New market squares, industrial parks, ports, dams, railways, cities, pipelines, cables, satellites, data centers, buildings, connections, technologies, institutions—these are the material elements that have been inserted into existing systems, structures, and flows, with the capacity to redirect them, to forge new relations, to attract away from existing trajectories, to cut new pathways. Such components are like depth charges dropped into existing arrangements, with disruptive effects. Or, to use a metaphor from the science of complex systems, they are like attractors, pushing the dynamic systems of economy and society into new trajectories, and away from their established orbits. Rather than a top-down blueprint for a new Sino-centric world, the creation of so many new components, inserted into so many different regions and countries, represents an unpredictable set of material interventions, with the potential to attract and shape self-organizing processes—like the economic agglomeration and clustering so long associated with urban development.

Whether Chinese policymakers see these interventions in this way is beside the point: the ultimate effect of inserting these new components into existing systems is likely to be a significant reshaping of social and economic life, as new activities coalesce around them, and as flows of energy, matter, and information are attracted to them. When viewed in this way, the seemingly uncoordinated and patchwork nature of the BRI project—which mostly relies on bilateral relations and shifting political alliances—is not a weakness for China, but a source of strength, making the BRI a more adaptable, self-organizing, and open-ended long-term intervention. It has allowed China to build the potential foundations for a diverging form of international order, and prize open new channels of connectivity skewed toward China's center of gravity, without raising much alarm. Indeed, this past decade may come to be seen by the United States as the one in which its hegemonic grip on international order was allowed to slip, and the battle to shape the international order lost.

China has used the past decade of the BRI project to build up a number of key advantages that will be difficult to overturn now that they are in place. The economic corridors of the BRI are already having a significant effect on the shape and nature of the global economy, and the global urban hierarchy, as we have seen. Highway construction, rail investment, and new and upgraded ports have begun to impact supply chains and logistics, generating a world in which more and more roads lead to China, and in which more and more states become tied into China's emerging form of transnational state capitalism. The Digital Silk Road, and the huge and sometimes pioneering efforts to build out new digital infrastructure and architectures in the developing world, are likely to leave a lasting legacy, because, as we have seen, these technologies offer an alternative system, imbued with very different values than those that underpin the US-dominated internet of the 1990s onward. These alternative pathways and architectures offer far greater control of information flows, and furnish authoritarian regimes with both greater control over their populations, via new surveillance technologies, and greater insulation from content produced outside of the system. For China, this monumental effort offers two great advantages—less dependency on Western digital infrastructure, but also more dependency on its own digital infrastructure for those that choose to partner with China. In summarizing the staggering achievement of China's efforts to build out this new technical infrastructure, Jonathan Hillman writes that "collectively the new routes outline a China-centric global infrastructure that did not exist a decade ago."[1] As we have seen, these efforts have been accompanied by a push to gain greater diplomatic influence within the United Nations and other international institutions; other examples include China's successful attempts to link its "ecological civilization" concept with the United Nations' sustainable development goals, and its creation of alternative international organizations like the Asian Infrastructure Investment Bank.

Over the past few years, there has been a dawning realization in the West that a fight is on for geopolitical influence via infrastructure provision. Some have talked about a widespread "infrastructure turn," or a coming "infrastructure scramble," as Great Powers seek to influence the developmental patterns of the global South. As this reality has begun to take root in the minds of policymakers in the United States and the European Union, various early attempts have been made to counter China's BRI. In 2019, the White House administration took a step in this direction with the $60 billion International Development Finance Cooperation aimed at lower- and middle-income countries. The Blue Dot Network, an infrastructure alliance between the United States, Japan, and Australia, provides an alternative to the BRI, with higher standards than many BRI projects. Japan has also developed important recent infrastructure initiatives. And although the European Union has been slower to respond to a Chinese strategy that reaches deep into its member territories, it too seems to be waking up to the fact that a new gravitational force is pulling Eurasia eastward, and so has offered its own series of new strategies outlined for Africa and India, and its Global Gateway initiative. These fledgling efforts at a coordinated response produced the Build Back Better World initiative, announced at the 2021 G7 Summit in Cornwall. Aimed at coordinated investment in low- and middle-income countries, it was a clear attempt to respond to China's influence in the global South. A year later, at the G7 summit in June 2022, this collaboration was rebranded as the Partnership for Global Infrastructure and Investment. Only now, it seems, with a growing focus on infrastructure at home and abroad, has the United States begun to fully grasp the scale of the challenge ahead, with a new agenda-setting vision seen in the 2022 Inflation Reduction Act—an act that, despite its name, is focused on infrastructure and climate change, at home and abroad, with around $370 billion slated for energy transition programs— and the 2022 National Security Strategy's robust characterization of the threats posed by China. These responses signal a shift from the neoliberal model of the past four decades to one in which major states are playing a more central and interventionist role in economic and infrastructural planning. They represent a return of the type of large-scale infrastructure planning not seen since right after World War II, and the apogee of Keynesian-style state intervention. But the hour is likely later than many policymakers have thought.

Many have characterized the BRI and the West's responses as the opening moves in a new Cold War between the West and China's emerging system. One notable trend playing into this idea is that China appears to be gathering around itself a core group of states, including Russia, Iran, and Pakistan, that both share its dissatisfaction and general ambitions toward revising the existing international order and are deeply imbricated in the BRI's evolution. China is building a potential bloc of like-minded authoritarian and anti-liberal revisionist states, and integrating them into its own economic system and political sphere of influence.

The BRI, then, may eventually be the catalyst for the splintering of international order, and the emergence of two rival geopolitical and geoeconomic blocs, each with their own technological and infrastructural foundations. If this came to pass, the current international society would be divided into two distinctive international societies, each with its own material and technological basis, and economic and political models. The power of digital connectivity, and of control over digital networks, could shape what the vast populations of such systems get to see and how they think. And the ways in which the transition to net zero is led within these rival blocs, and within the cities that form their bedrock, could lead to radically different outcomes for billions.

Changes to economies, social relations, and the material world of cities are, by their very nature, destabilizing. They offer revolution in their own right, bringing into tension concepts once compatible: rights and progress; wealth and well-being. President Xi recognized this in 2017, when he opened his watershed Davos speech with a literary reference as well as a theory of history. "It was the best of times, it was the worst of times," explained the Chinese president, who placed the famous line in the context of socioeconomic tumult rather than political revolution— "These are the words used by the English writer Charles Dickens to describe the world after the Industrial Revolution"—then went on: "Today, we also live in a world of contradictions." He spoke of the American-led international order and the globalization of the early twenty-first century. But he could equally have been discussing the BRI.

Despite China's desire to appear as a benevolent international leader, as a Great Power leading a society of states and a community of common destiny forward into the Chinese Dream of a better twenty-first century, this all sits uncomfortably alongside the emergence of a technological basis for a totalitarian surveillance state at home, elements of which have been exported abroad along the BRI. China still needs to work out its balance between freedom and security, openness to the world and control of its population, growth and self-reliance, globalization and a decoupling of the economy, the balance between innovation and creativity within a political system that increasingly brooks no dissent, in a country where the president's new third term appears to end the stability offered by four decades of collective leadership.

Even if some of these contradictions are ideological or philosophical, they will, and must, manifest themselves in urban spaces. Hong Kong has tragically proven the greatest testing ground for China's ability to project authoritarian control on areas where it was once anathema, but it is unlikely to be the last. Ambitions for authoritarian domestic control have traditionally vied with the vitality, creativity, and tumult of urban spaces, long considered to be crucibles of freedom, as we have seen in the Color Revolutions, which were rooted in the urban spaces of Tbilisi, Kyiv, and even Beirut, among others, and those of the Arab Spring, which were centered in cities like Tunis, Cairo, Benghazi, and Misrata.

Perhaps most pressing for the world writ large, and for every city, remains the question of whether new visions for international society can be implemented in ways that will not push ecosystems beyond breaking points. Development without trade-offs is a difficult dance, and it may be that the cities of BRI corridors can have connectivity, but with it will come increased flooding, typhoons, drought, and other environmental impacts from climate change. China's emergent role in the mid-2010s as the "eco-veto player" derived from the size of both its consumer market and its pollutant- and energy-heavy manufacturing industries. If, as climate scientists continue to demonstrate, future industrial production and consumption will be essential for determining the planet's future, China's centrality remains clear. But we might go even further. Those consumption patterns, as well as manufacturing supply chains, are increasingly linked to the wider world through new, transnational infrastructure systems like the BRI. China's influence on global infrastructure and urban spaces, then, further fixes China at the center of the contest over who will shape the future of both urban environments and our shared global one.

But while the BRI maps more precisely over the systems theory of leading climate scientists, its implementation in practice has yet to demonstrate the commitment needed to limit warming to the ambitions of the Paris Agreement. It seems, then, that neither the West nor China are offering a vision of the future that precludes an ever-increasing arrival of climatic impact drivers in cities and urban spaces. For while the Global City offered the hope of growth, and delivered that hope only alongside wider inequality and heightened emissions, the Belt and Road Cities offer the hope of development, and may succeed in delivering it locally— but that development may also be accompanied by unprecedented tumult and instability wherever we may live.

How will China reconcile all of these conflicting forces and impulses? Only the next decades will tell. But the outcome matters enormously, because how it navigates these issues will shape both the international system and the cities in which billions will live. China's growing weight in world affairs—the gravitational pull of its economy, society, and culture on those states, cities, and peoples around it—is altering the very structures of international society that many have taken for granted in recent decades. The BRI is urbanism as grand strategy: an attempt to make the Chinese Dream manifest in concrete and steel. It is a set of mechanisms to mold, shape, and channel the futures of many billions of people in ways that reflect China's values and interests—even if those values and interests are themselves yet to be fully worked out and articulated. It is an urban world and an international order under construction.

Notes

Introduction

1. Apostolopoulou, "Novel Geographical Research Agenda," 386–393.
2. IPCC, *Climate Change, 2022: Impacts, Adaptation, and Vulnerability*, technical summary TS.C.5.4, cross-chapter paper 2.
3. IPCC, *Climate Change, 2014*, chapter 12.
4. US White House, "New National Security Strategy."
5. US White House, "National Security Strategy: October 2022," 12.
6. Zipp, *Manhattan Projects*.
7. US White House, "Remarks by President Biden."
8. US White House, "Memorandum on the Partnership."
9. Sassen, *Global City*.
10. Castells, *Rise of the Network Society*.
11. Amen, *Cities and Global Governance*; Acuto, *Global Cities*; Bouteligier, *Cities, Networks, and Global Environmental Governance*; Curtis, *Global Cities and Global Order*; Ljungkvist, *Global City 2.0*.
12. Curtis and Acuto, "Foreign Policy of Cities," 8–17.
13. Kostof, *City Shaped*; Lynch, *Image of the City*; DeLanda, *New Philosophy of Society*.
14. Robinson, *Ordinary Cities*.
15. Lefebvre, *Production of Space*.
16. Kennedy, *Rise and Fall*.
17. For a selection of the key works that have had an influence on our approach to bringing together the social and material components of international order, see Deleuze and Guattari, *Thousand Plateaus*; Latour, *We Have Never Been Modern*; DeLanda, *Intensive Science and Virtual Philosophy*; DeLanda, *New Philosophy of Society*; Hirst, *Space and Power*; Harvey, *Limits to Capital*; Easterling, *Extrastatecraft*; MacKenzie and Wajcman, *Social Shaping of Technology*; and Acuto and Curtis, *Reassembling International Theory*.

18. Many of our most celebrated theories of international relations offer attempts to think about international order with the greater part of its mass missing. For a selection of international relations texts that have had a big influence on the discipline, yet fail to consider the importance of material infrastructures in the way that we do here, see Wendt, *Social Theory of International Politics;* Hurrell, *On Global Order;* and Waltz, *Theory of International Politics.* For a practitioner's account with a similar lacuna, see Kissinger, *World Order.*

19. Part of why the importance of material infrastructure has been rendered invisible in international relations can be found in the historiography of the discipline, in particular, long years of nation-state-centrism, which obscured the transnational nature of many key infrastructures, and the recent disciplinary hegemony of social constructivism, which has not been attuned to the significance of material objects, but has instead focused on the ideational components of world order. The sheer scale of human-built socio-technical systems in the twenty-first century, however, and their increasingly apparent entanglement with the rhythms of the natural world, demand that the apparatus with which international-relations scholarship apprehends its own universe be refocused. Some crucial resources with which to do this have emerged in the "new materialism" literature in recent years: new ways to conceptualize the relationship between material, technological, and ideational components of social formations. Some of these kinds of arguments can be found in Coole and Frost, *New Materialisms;* Connolly, *Facing the Planetary;* Bennett, *Vibrant Matter;* and Salter, *Making Things International.* Bruno Latour, in particular, in his *Reassembling the Social,* argued that it is the construction and maintenance of a fragile meshwork of both material and ideational elements that hold society in place, and make it stable. Ideas, or institutions, such as sovereignty or territory, or narratives of historical destiny, shape our political imaginations. But they do not endure unless they are inscribed in material forms such as cities and infrastructures.

20. Burdett, *Shaping Cities.*

21. Mayer and Acuto, "Global Governance," 660–683.

22. Khanna, *Connectography,* xxiii.

23. Bratton, *The Stack.*

24. Indeed, insight into the inherent materiality of international orders is lacking in dominant ways of conceptualizing international society, such as in the English School of international relations, which relies on tracing the ideational and normative components of international order, but misses the material components that hold them in place. For an overview of the English School and its core concept of International Society, see Buzan, *Introduction to the English School.*

25. For a discussion of the nature of abstract diagrams, see Deleuze and Guattari, *Thousand Plateaus;* DeLanda, *Intensive Science and Virtual Philosophy;* and DeLanda, *New Philosophy of Society.*

26. Mayer and Acuto, "Global Governance."
27. Bull, *Anarchical Society.*

Chapter One. Ties of Silk and Steel

1. Ministry of Foreign Affairs of the People's Republic of China, "President Xi Jinping Addresses the Opening Ceremony."
2. Ponzini, *Transnational Architecture and Urbanism,* 216.
3. OECD, *Belt and Road Initiative.*
4. The BRI is, in fact, the second attempt to render the concept into English, with the first, "One Belt, One Road," proving a little too obscure for Western audiences.
5. Maçães, *Belt and Road.*
6. "Silk Roads" is a broad term that describes a vast network of enduring trade routes and cultural and intellectual interactions connecting cities, lands, and peoples from across Afro-Eurasia by land, sea, and river, from around 200 BCE to 1400 CE. The term Silk Roads is itself a relatively modern one, attributed to the German geographer Ferdinand von Richthofen in the 1870s, as he sought to describe the networks of exchange that spread out from westward expansion of Han dynasty China (206 BCE—220 CE). Silk was only one of the multitudes of commodities and materials traded across the vast Eurasian landmass. Precious metals, ceramics, glass, spices, fruit, fur, slaves, and horses flowed along these interweaving conduits, as did cultural exchange, knowledge, new ideas, languages, religions, music, and stories—as well as disease, armies, and violence. See Whitfield, *Silk Roads,* 15.
7. Ibid.
8. Scott, *Against the Grain.*
9. Frankopan, *New Silk Roads,* xvii.
10. Jacobs, *Cities and the Wealth of Nations*; Polèse, *Wealth and Poverty of Regions.*
11. Hall, *Cities in Civilization.*
12. Latour, *Reassembling the Social.*
13. Lefebvre, *Production of Space.*
14. Kostof, *City Shaped.*
15. Soja, *Postmetropolis*; Yates, *Real Estate and Global Urban History.*
16. Sassen, *Global City*; Curtis, *Global Cities and Global Order.*
17. Gibbon, *Decline and Fall.*
18. Crowley and Pavitt, *Cold War Modern.*
19. The Westphalian international order so familiar today is, in fact, an unusual configuration, one that had its origins in a very specific time and place, the Europe of the seventeenth century. Named after the Peace of Westphalia in 1648, one of a series of treaties that ended the Thirty Years' War, this form of international order was originally designed by European diplomats in order to provide the basis for peaceful coexistence between the patchwork of warring princedoms that had torn Europe apart over differences in

religious belief for decades. Its solution—sovereign independence, territorial integrity, non-interference, and the rejection of universal authority—has come, over the intervening centuries, via mechanisms of imperialism and emulation, to also define the basis of our contemporary globe-spanning international order. Relatively peaceful coexistence in a world of competing values and belief systems and political systems is today predicated on many of those same institutions and diplomatic practices. And so, the Westphalian settlement, crafted so long ago, has also become the basis of international order today; a framework that allows for multiple and diverse forms of political life to exist within the universally accepted framework of state independence. It has provided a basis for relatively peaceful coexistence between states that share similar outward-facing political forms, but may have various governmental structures, political cultures, and belief systems.

20. Buzan and Little, *International Systems*; Maier, *Among Empires*.
21. Watson, *Evolution of International Society*.
22. Ikenberry, *World Safe for Democracy*.
23. Daalder and Lindsay, *Empty Throne*.
24. Kupchan, *No One's World*.
25. Immerwahr, *How to Hide an Empire*.
26. Mitchell, *Carbon Democracy*.
27. Burdett, *Shaping Cities*.
28. Kwak, *World of Homeowners*, 10, 15, 25.
29. Winner, "Do Artifacts Have Politics?"
30. Easterling, *Extrastatecraft*.
31. Mayer, "Return of History," 1217–1235.
32. Du, *Shenzhen Experiment*.
33. Morton, *Hyperobjects*.
34. There is a vast literature on the emergence of the Global City (sometimes termed the "World City" in earlier literature linked explicitly to Immanuel Wallerstein's Marxian World Systems Theory: see Wallerstein, *Modern World-System*, vol. 3). For some of the key milestones in the historiography of the Global City literature, see Friedmann, "World City Hypothesis," 69–83; Sassen, *Global City*; Soja, *Postmetropolis*; Taylor, *World City Network*; Brenner, *New State Spaces*; Castells, *Rise of the Network Society*; Massey, *World City*; Brenner and Keil, *Global Cities Reader*.
35. Gordon and Ljungkvist, "Theorizing the Globally Engaged City," 58–82.
36. Graham and Marvin, *Splintering Urbanism*.
37. Graham, *Vertical*.
38. Bobbitt, *Shield of Achilles*.
39. Lefebvre, *Production of Space*.
40. IPCC, *Climate Change*, 2021.
41. Bazaz et al., *Summary for Urban Policymakers*, 13.
42. Tooze, *Shutdown*.

43. Lovell, *Opium Wars*.

44. Jacques, *When China Rules the World*.

45. For a recent forensic account of Chinese strategic thought over the past three decades, see Doshi, *Long Game*. Chinese-language sources analyzed by Doshi include CCP documents; speeches; memoirs of important political figures, generals, and diplomats; analysis from CCP foreign-policy institutions and think tanks; government white papers; and addresses to foreign audiences.

46. The literature on Chinese grand strategy, or, in alternative interpretations, its absence, is considerable. Unlike Doshi there are those who consider that China has no comprehensive grand strategy, and no particular plan to displace the United States regionally or globally. Such arguments tend to view China's policies as aimed primarily at domestic stability and development, a vast enough challenge for a country of China's size, which, when added to its internal factionalism and the complexity of its domestic politics, make the formulation of a coherent grand strategy problematic; see Jisi, "China's Search." But there is a growing weight of books and articles arguing that China's strategy does indeed now aim to revise the existing framework of international order, and that China is no longer willing to accept playing a subordinate role to US hegemony, either regional or globally; examples here include Pillsbury, *Hundred-Year Marathon*; Goldstein, *Rising to the Challenge*; Goldstein, "China's Grand Strategy"; and Friedberg, *Contest for Supremacy*. What is certainly true is that China's current ambitions, as signaled by its signature foreign-policy moves such as the BRI, are leading to the biggest reassessment in a generation of China policy by the United States and Europe.

47. Wang, *China Reconnects*.

48. Ferdinand, "Westward Ho," 941–957.

49. Lacher, *Beyond Globalization*; Lee, *Global China*.

50. Arrighi, *Long Twentieth Century*.

51. Wallerstein, *Modern World-System*, vol. 3.

52. Kennedy, *Made in China 2025*.

53. Harvey, *Limits to Capital*.

54. Jessop and Sum, "Geopolitics," 474–478.

55. Silver, "Corridor Urbanism"; Wiig and Silver, "Turbulent Presents, Precarious Futures," 912–923; Apostolopoulou, "Tracing the Links," 831–858; Liu et al., "Spatio-Temporal Evolution," 919–936.

56. Demissie, "Special Economic Zones."

57. Pantucci and Petersen, *Sinostan*.

58. UN Development Programme and Swiss Agency for Development Cooperation, *Development Advocate*.

59. Chen, "Globalisation Redux," 35–58.

60. Brunnermeier, Doshi, and James, "Beijing's Bismarckian Ghosts," 161–176.

61. Liao, "Out of the Bretton Woods."

62. Nordin, *China's International Relations.*
63. Allison, *Destined for War.*

Chapter Two. Infrastructure

1. The ships in which Columbus sailed to the Americas later in the same century were around sixty-five feet long.
2. Keay, *China.*
3. Osterhammel, *Transformation.*
4. Shen and Chan, "Comparative Study," 32.
5. Asia Development Bank, "Meeting Asia's Infrastructure Development Needs."
6. Coker, *Rise of the Civilizational State.*
7. MacKenzie and Wajcman, *Social Shaping of Technology.*
8. Anand, Gupta, and Appel, *Promise of Infrastructure.*
9. Bennett, *Vibrant Matter.*
10. Foucault, *Archaeology of Knowledge*; Hirst, *Space and Power.*
11. Lall and Lebrand, "Who Wins, Who Loses?"
12. Mayer and Zhang, "Theorizing China-World Integration," 1–30.
13. As mentioned earlier, the national logistics network that China is helping to build across Pakistan represents a longer-term plan that can help bring this about, as do the new freight railways connecting China to multiple points across Eurasia. See Maçães, *Belt and Road*, 83–100.
14. Jacobs, *Cities and the Wealth of Nations.*
15. Chen, "Globalisation Redux," 35–58; Smith, "World Urban Hierarchy," 45–55.
16. World Bank, "Belt and Road Economics."
17. Silver, "Corridor Urbanism."
18. Barry, "Technological Zones," 239–253.
19. Silver, "Corridor Urbanism."
20. Freymann, *One Belt One Road.*
21. Latour, "Technology Is Society Made Durable," 103–131.
22. Hillman, *Emperor's New Road*, 86.
23. Ibid., 8.
24. Ibid., 44.
25. Chen, "Europe's Freight Infrastructure."
26. Hillman, *Emperor's New Road*, 92.
27. Maçães, *Belt and Road*, 63.
28. Miller, *China's Asian Dream*, 163–165; Cobbett and Mason, "Djiboutian Sovereignty," 1767–1784.
29. Doshi, *Long Game*, 206–207.
30. Maçães, *Belt and Road*, 63.
31. Ferrari and Tei, "Effects of BRI Strategy," 14.
32. Freymann, *One Belt One Road*, 161–188.

33. Ferrari and Tei, "Effects of BRI Strategy."

34. Muchira, "China Pushes."

35. Freymann, *One Belt One Road*, 132–133.

36. Hillman, *Emperor's New Road*.

37. Sitas et al., "Platform Politics and Silicon Savannahs."

38. Bratton, *The Stack*.

39. Castells, *Rise of the Network Society*.

40. Turner, *Democratic Surround*.

41. Zuboff, *Age of Surveillance Capitalism*.

42. Hillman, *Digital Silk Road*.

43. Zuckerman, "Can Russia Really Disconnect?"

44. Hillman, *Digital Silk Road*, 14.

45. Pollio, Cirolia, and Pieterse, "Infrastructure Financing."

46. Huawei, Building Digital Guinea homepage.

47. Kelkar, "From Silk Threads to Fiber Optics."

48. Page and Taylor, "America's Undersea Battle."

49. "Pacific Data Cable Not Safe."

50. Halegoua, *Smart Cities*.

51. Mozer, Xiao, and Liu, "An Invisible Cage."

52. Hillman, *Digital Silk Road*, 125.

53. Kurlantzick, "China's Digital Silk Road Initiative."

54. Boer, Cantley-Smith, and Qin, "Introduction," 121–129.

55. Yan, *Leadership and the Rise of Great Powers*.

56. Wang-Kaeding, "What Does Xi Jinping's New Phrase 'Ecological Civiliza-
    tion' Mean?"

57. Moore, *China's Next Act*, 74.

58. Shepherd, "China's Belt and Road."

59. Moore, *China's Next Act*, 72.

60. Shepherd, "China Pours Money."

61. BNP Paribas, "China Megatrends."

62. Boyle, "China's Zero Carbon Pledge."

63. IPCC, *Climate Change, 2022: Impacts, Adaptation and Vulnerability*, chapter
    6.3.2.

64. Boer, Cantley-Smith, and Qin, "Introduction."

65. Hanson, "Ecological Civilization."

66. Peng and Deng, "Research on the Sustainable Development Process of
    Low-Carbon Pilot Cities," 2382–2403.

67. Williams, *China's Urban Revolution*.

68. Downie, "Powering the Globe."

69. Cornell, "Energy Governance and China's Bid for Global Grid Integra-
    tion."

70. Patterson, "Why an Asian Super Grid Is a Political Fantasy."

71. Liu, *Global Energy Interconnection*.

Chapter Three. Urban Spaces

1. UN General Assembly. Resolution 70/1, "Transforming Our World"; UN General Assembly. Resolution 71/256, "New Urban Agenda."
2. Latin America is an important exception.
3. Wetherell, *Foundations;* Kelly and Lu, *Critical Landscape Planning,* 73, 88; Dwyer, "They Will Not Automatically Benefit."
4. Phelps, *Urban Planning Imagination,* 166.
5. Cody, *Exporting American Architecture,* 89.
6. Ibid., 95.
7. Ponzini, *Transnational Architecture and Urbanism,* 3.
8. Phelps, *Urban Planning Imagination,* 7.
9. For a slightly different example of city typologies, see IPCC, *Climate Change, 2022: Mitigation of Climate Change,* chapter 8; Becker and Klaus, "(In)Visible Policy."
10. Stanek, *Architecture in Global Socialism,* 75.
11. Golubev, *Things of Life,* 3, 11.
12. Scott, *Against the Grain.*
13. Therborn, *Cities of Power.*
14. Barrett, *Rome Is Burning.*
15. Simone, *Improvised Lives,* 128.
16. Ibid.
17. Quoted in Soja, *Postmodern Geographies,* 21.
18. Moyn, *Last Utopia,* 88.
19. Moyn, *Not Enough,* 44.
20. Maier, *Once Within Borders,* 268.
21. Tutino, "Power, Marginality, and Participation," 86.
22. Ibid., 87.
23. Wetherell, *Foundations,* 3.
24. Ibid., 41.
25. Ibid., 83.
26. Ibid., 77.
27. Cupers, *Social Project,* xii.
28. Ibid., 4.
29. Therborn, *Cities of Power,* 9.
30. Castillo, *Cold War on the Homefront;* Kanigel, *Eyes on the Street,* chapters 7–8.
31. MacCarthy, *Gropius,* 417.
32. Castillo, *Cold War on the Homefront;* Kwak, *World of Homeowners.*
33. Zipp, *Manhattan Projects,* 36.
34. Ibid., 178.
35. Cohen, *Saving America's Cities,* 37–38.
36. Ibid., 42.
37. Ibid., 36.
38. Zubovich, *Moscow Monumental,* 17–18.

39. Hatherley, *Landscapes of Communism*, 18.
40. Fitzpatrick, *Everyday Stalinism*, 42.
41. Link, *Forging Global Fordism*; Zubovich, *Moscow Monumental*.
42. Zubovich, *Moscow Monumental*, 1.
43. Ibid., 3.
44. Ibid., 5.
45. Hatherley, *Landscapes of Communism*, 22.
46. Zubovich, *Moscow Monumental*, chapter 8.
47. Golubev, *Things of Life*, 92.
48. Lee, *Think Tank Aesthetics*; Wellerstein, "36-Hour War."
49. Kanigel, *Eyes on the Street*, 104–109.
50. Castillo, *Cold War on the Homefront*, xxi–xxii.
51. Ibid.
52. Campanella, *Concrete Dragon*, 99.
53. Wu, *Remaking Beijing*, 9.
54. Therborn, *Cities of Power*, 265; Wu, *Remaking Beijing*, 22.
55. Campanella, *Concrete Dragon*, 107; Therborn, *Cities of Power*, 268.
56. Coalition for Urban Transitions, *Accelerating China's Urban Transition*, 76.
57. *Hukou* is the system of household registration in China that identifies a person as the permanent resident of a particular area.
58. Huang, *Capitalism with Chinese Characteristics*.
59. Ren, *Urban China*, 8.
60. Wu and Gaubatz, *Chinese City*, 1–7.
61. Ibid., 346.
62. World Resources Institute, *Accelerating Building Decarbonization*, 51.
63. World Bank and the Development Research Center of the State Council, China, *Urban China*, figure 0.1, 5.
64. Campanella, *Concrete Dragon*, 14.
65. Ibid., 15.
66. Coalition for Urban Transitions, *Accelerating China's Urban Transition*, 13.
67. World Bank and the Development Research Center of the State Council, China, *Urban China*, part 2, 81.
68. Koleski, *13th Five-Year Plan*.
69. Ibid., chapter 34, section 1.
70. World Resources Institute, *Accelerating Building Decarbonization*, 54.
71. Ibid., table 12, 57.
72. Li and Shapiro, *China Goes Green*, 61–62.
73. World Resources Institute, *Fewer Emissions, Better Life*.
74. Phelps, *Urban Planning Imagination*, 64.
75. Center for Security and Emerging Technology, "Outline of the People's Republic of China 14th Five-Year Plan."
76. Ibid., article 29, section 2.
77. Ibid., article 29, section 1.
78. Campanella, *Concrete Dragon*, 36.

79. Du, *Shenzhen Experiment*, 75, 190.
80. Ibid., 29.
81. Phelps, *Urban Planning Imagination*, 162.
82. Du, *Shenzhen Experiment*, 60.
83. Ibid., 32.
84. Wu, "Proximity," 773.
85. Ibid., 779.
86. Ibid., 783.
87. Vogel, "Foreword," xiii.
88. Du, *Shenzhen Experiment*, 309.
89. Ibid., 23.
90. Ibid., 311. See also O'Donnell, Wong, and Bach, "Introduction," 3.
91. O'Donnell, "Heroes of the Special Zone," 59.
92. Greenspan, *Shanghai Future*, 23.
93. Li and Shapiro, *China Goes Green*, 43.
94. Greenspan, *Shanghai Future*, 46.
95. Chow, *Changing Chinese Cities*, 56.
96. Ibid., 64.
97. Liu, Horn-Phathanothai, and Zhang, "5 Ways China's Cities Can Drive Equitable and Sustainable Urbanization."
98. Center for Security and Emerging Technology, "Outline of the People's Republic of China 14th Five-Year Plan," article 32, section 3.
99. Chen, "A (Long) Tale."
100. Ibid., 12–13. On regional development of the northeast, west, and center, and their connectivity, see also Fei, "Worlding Developmentalism."
101. Chen, "Europe's Freight Infrastructure"; Chen, "Reconnecting Eurasia," 13.
102. Chen, "Reconnecting Eurasia," 6–7.
103. Quoted in ibid., 7.
104. Ibid., 16.
105. See Hirst, *Space and Power*, 42.
106. Chen, "Reconnecting Eurasia," 17.
107. Phelps, *Urban Planning Imagination*, 7.
108. Asante and Helbrecht, "Urban Dimension"; Asante, "Urban Governance."
109. China Aiddata.org, "China Eximbank."
110. Keeton, "Case Study."
111. Croese, "State-led Housing Delivery," 82, 90.
112. Keeton, "Case Study," 344.
113. Noorloos and Avianto, "New Towns, Old Places," 396–398.
114. Keeton, "Case Study," 336.
115. Croese, "State-led Housing Delivery," 94.
116. Keeton, "Case Study," 335.
117. Iftikhar et al., "Institutional and Urban Design."
118. Gwadar Development Authority, "Masterplan 2050."

119. Zhang, "Gwadar Port and Free Zone."

120. Rafiq, "Gwadar's Real Estate Market."

121. "Gwadar Protest Comes to an End."

122. Chen, "A (Long) Tale."

123. DiCarlo, "Boten Special Economic Zone/Boten Beautiful Land."

124. Babiker et al., "What the Latest Science on Climate Change Mitigation Means," figure 1.

125. DiCarlo, "Boten Special Economic Zone/Boten Beautiful Land."

126. Chen, "Corridor-ising Impact."

127. CIMB Asean Research Institute/LSE Ideas, *China's Belt and Road Initiative.*

128. Thanabouasy, "Laos-China Railway."

129. Jianhua and Mixayboua, "World Insights."

130. Chen, "Corridor-ising Impact."

131. UN Habitat, *World Cities Report 2022*, table A.1, 330.

132. Ibid., table B.3, 348.

133. Prak, "Phnom Penh–Sihanoukville Expressway."

134. Long, "Capital-S'ville Expressway."

135. Bo and Loughlin, "Overlapping Agendas," 87.

136. Ibid., 90.

137. Ibid., 92.

138. Ibid.

139. Inclusive Design International, "Sihanoukville Special Economic Zone."

140. Loughlin and Grimsditch, "How Local Political Economy Dynamics Are Shaping the Belt and Road Initiative."

141. Ibid., 2343.

142. Ibid., 2345.

143. Meng and Nyantakyi, "Local Skill Development," 6, figure 1.

144. Economic Community of West African States, "ECOWAS Signs MOU with China."

145. Amaresh, "China's Stadium Diplomacy."

146. Pollio, Cirolia, and Pieterse, "Infrastructure Financing."

147. Tarrósy and Vörös, "China and Ethiopia, Part 1."

148. Adelekan et al., *What the Latest Science on Impacts, Adaptation and Vulnerability Means.*

149. IPCC, *Climate Change, 2022: Impacts, Adaptation, and Vulnerability*, box 8.5; box 8.6; 9.9.4; 9.9.5; 10.4.6.2; 12.5.7.

150. Lamson-Hall, "How They Do It In Ethiopia."

151. Tarrosy and Vörös, "China and Ethiopia, Part 2."

152. Brautigam, Bhalaki, Deron, and Wang, "How Africa Borrows from China."

153. Styan, "Doraleh Multipurpose Port (I)."

154. Ibid.; also Djibouti Ports and Free Zone Authority, homepage.

155. See Djibouti Business District, homepage.

156. Quayson, *Oxford Street, Accra*, 17.

Chapter Four. Tools of Influence

1. Associated Press, "Text of the Roosevelt Message."
2. Waltz, *Theory of International Politics;* Mearsheimer, *Tragedy of Great Power Politics.*
3. Carr, *Twenty Years' Crisis.*
4. Ruggie, "International Regimes," 379–415.
5. Gallagher and Kozul-Wright, *Case for a New Bretton Woods.*
6. Liao, "Out of the Bretton Woods."
7. Naughton, "China's Global Economic Interactions," 113–136.
8. Herrero, "What Is Behind China's Dual Circulation Strategy?"
9. Shambaugh, *China and the World,* 346.
10. Naughton, "China's Global Economic Interactions," 130.
11. UNCTAD, *New Centre of Gravity.*
12. Maçães, *Belt and Road,* 55.
13. Economy, *World According to China,* 30.
14. Beeson, "Geoeconomics with Chinese Characteristics," 240–256.
15. Naughton and Tsai, *State Capitalism;* Kurlantzick, *State Capitalism.*
16. Bremmer, *End of the Free Market.*
17. Strange, *States and Markets.*
18. Polanyi, *Great Transformation.*
19. Nölke, "International Financial Regulation."
20. Petry, "Same Same, but Different."
21. Drezner and McNamara, "International Political Economy"; Germain, "Financial Order and World Politics," 669–687.
22. Naughton and Tsai, *State Capitalism,* McNally, "Political Economic Logic of RMB Internationalization," 704–723.
23. Heilmann, "Regulatory Innovation."
24. Maçães, *Belt and Road,* 48–56.
25. Wahid, Mumtaz, Kowalewski, and Adil, "Post-Spillover Effects."
26. Petry, "Beyond Ports, Roads and Railways."
27. Armijo and Katada, "Theorizing."
28. Petry, "Beyond Ports, Roads and Railways," 25.
29. Summers, "Structural Power."
30. Cendrowski, "China's Global 500 Companies."
31. Brenner, *New Urban Spaces.*
32. Government of Pakistan, Ministry of Planning Development and Reform, *Long-Term Plan.*
33. Smith, "World Urban Hierarchy."
34. Chen, "Globalisation Redux."
35. Silver, "Corridor Urbanism"; Wiig and Silver, "Turbulent Presents."
36. Barry, "Technological Zones."
37. Economy, *World According to China,* 200.
38. Easterling, *Extrastatecraft.*

39. Baldwin, *Great Convergence.*
40. Knight, "China Wants to Shape."
41. Maçães, *Belt and Road,* 75–104.
42. Asian Infrastructure Investment Bank, homepage.
43. Doshi, *Long Game,* 115–224.
44. Wahba, "Integrating Infrastructure"; Tian, "China Willing."
45. Economy, *World According to China,* 52–54.
46. Doshi, *Long Game,* 225–230.
47. Brady, *China as a Polar Great Power.*
48. Curtis and Acuto, "Foreign Policy of Cities." See also Klaus, "State of City Diplomacy"; Klaus, "Subnational Diplomacy Evolves."
49. Coalition for Urban Transitions, *Seizing China's Urban Opportunity,* 12.
50. Tillu et al., "Accelerating China's Urban Transition," 12.
51. Ibid., 21.
52. Acuto, Morissette, Chan, and Leffel, *"City Diplomacy" and Twinning.*
53. Acuto, "Give Cities a Seat," 611–613.
54. G7 Germany, Ministerial Meeting on Sustainable Urban Development, "Communiqué."
55. Klaus, "Invited to the Party."
56. Acuto, Morissette, Chan, and Leffel, *"City Diplomacy" and Twinning.*
57. Custer et al., "Ties That Bind."
58. Mierzejewski, "Role of Guangdong and Guangzhou's Subnational Diplomacy," 99–119.
59. Quoted from a report in the authors' possession. For more on the C40 program, see China Energy Program, International Energy Analysis, Berkeley Lab, https://international.lbl.gov/china-energy-program.
60. Metropolis, "Agreement of Scientific and Educational Cooperation."
61. Nye, *Soft Power.*
62. Repnikova, *Chinese Soft Power,* 57.
63. Economy, *World According to China,* 43.
64. Breslin, "China's Global Cultural Interactions," 138–142.
65. Economy, *World According to China,* 58–60.
66. Soft Power 30, homepage.
67. Times Higher Education, World University Rankings, 2021.
68. Breslin, "China's Global Cultural Interactions," 149.
69. Economy, *World According to China,* 45.
70. Repnikova, *Chinese Soft Power,* 27.

Chapter Five. International Order

1. Xinhua. "Speech by Xi Jinping."
2. Whitfield, *Cities of the World,* 41.
3. Kostof, *City Shaped.*
4. Doshi, *Long Game.*

5. Mayer, "Return of History."
6. Marx and Engels, *Capital.*
7. Brunnermeier et al., "Beijing's Bismarckian Ghosts."
8. Coker, *Rise of the Civilizational State.*
9. Ferdinand, "Westward Ho," 941–957.
10. Kissinger, *World Order.*
11. Bull, *Anarchical Society.*
12. Donnelly, "Sovereign Inequalities and Hierarchy."
13. Watson, *Evolution of International Society.*
14. Hurrell, *On Global Order.*
15. World Economic Forum, "China's Xi Jinping Defends Globalization."
16. Economy, *Third Revolution*, 42.
17. Ibid., 37.
18. Naughton, "China's Global Economic Interactions," 116.
19. Chen, "Globalisation Redux."
20. Gries, "Nationalism," 63–84.
21. Kissinger, *On China.*
22. Wang, *China Reconnects*; Sterckx, *Chinese Thought.*
23. Doshi, *Long Game.*
24. Nordin, *China's International Relations.*
25. Callahan, "Chinese Visions," 749–761; Perdue, "Tenacious Tributary System," 1002–1014.
26. Ren, "Grown from Within," 386–412; Yaqing, "Development of International Relations Theory," 185–201; Zhang, *Chinese Hegemony*; Yan, Bell, Sun, and Ryden, *Ancient Chinese Thought.*
27. Waltz, *Theory of International Politics*; Mearsheimer, *Tragedy of Great Power Politics*; Morgenthau, *Politics among Nations.*
28. Cunningham-Cross and Callahan, "Ancient Chinese Power," 349–374.
29. Cox, "Social Forces," 126–155; Cox, *Production, Power, and World Order.*
30. Ren, "Grown from Within," 395.
31. Ling, *Dao of World Politics.*
32. Zhao, "Rethinking Empire," 29–41.
33. Callahan, "Chinese Visions."
34. Westad, *Restless Empire*; see also Westad, "Legacies," 25–36.
35. Babones, "Taking China Seriously."
36. Qin, *Relational Theory.*
37. In this sense, there are clear parallels with some recent thought on relationality in international theorizing in the West. A good example can be found in Jackson and Nexon, "Relations before States," 291–332.
38. Kavalski, "Guanxi," 397–420.
39. Sterckx, *Chinese Thought*; Shih, *China and International Theory*; Shih and Huang, "Balance."
40. Ren, "Grown from Within," 404.
41. Center for Strategic and International Studies, "Deep Comprehension."

42. Eguegu, "Will China's 'Global Security Initiative' Catch On?"
43. Ren, "Grown from Within," 405–407.
44. Yan, "International Leadership and Norm Evolution," 233–264; Yan, Bell, Sun, and Ryden, *Ancient Chinese Thought*; Yan, "Political Leadership and Power Redistribution," 1–26; Yan, *Leadership*; Xu and Sun, "Tsinghua Approach."
45. There are today some parallels and crossovers between Chinese School scholars, with their focus on historical and classical scholarship, sensitivity to international change, and the evolution of international norms and structures, and the thinkers of the "English School" of International Relations, which has had some recent influence in Chinese academic circles: see Ren, "Grown from Within," 391. Many core English School texts, such as Bull, *Anarchical Society*; Watson, *Evolution of International Society*; and Buzan and Little, *International Systems*, have been translated into Chinese, and have helped to show that there is a strong and vibrant tradition outside of US international relations scholarship. There are clear overlaps here with the English School's focus on how norms evolve through state interaction over time, and constitute successive versions of international society.
46. Lucas, "China Rewrites History."
47. Braudel, *Civilization and Capitalism*.
48. Arrighi, *Long Twentieth Century*; Arrighi, *Adam Smith in Beijing*.
49. Harvey, *Limits to Capital*.
50. Rosenberg, *Empire of Civil Society*; Li, *China*.
51. Mayer and Zhang, "Theorizing China-World Integration."
52. Curtis, *Global Cities and Global Order*.

Conclusion

1. Hillman, *Digital Silk Road*, 150.

Bibliography

Acuto, Michele. "Give Cities a Seat at the Top Table." *Nature* 537, no. 7622 (2016).

———. *Global Cities, Governance, and Diplomacy: The Urban Link.* Abingdon, UK: Routledge, 2013.

Acuto, Michele, and Simon Curtis. *Reassembling International Theory: Assemblage Thinking and International Relations.* London: Palgrave Macmillan, 2014.

Acuto, Michele, Mika Morissette, Dan Chan, and Benjamin Leffel. *"City Diplomacy" and Twinning: Lessons from the UK, China, and Globally.* London: UK Government Office for Science, 2016. https://assets.publishing.service.gov. uk/government/uploads/system/uploads/attachment_data/file/545780/ gs-16-13-future-of-cities-diplomacy-uk-china-twinning.pdf.

Adelekan, Ibidun, et al. *What the Latest Science on Impacts, Adaptation and Vulnerability Means for Cities and Urban Areas.* Vol. 2. Summary for Urban Policymakers, 2022. https://supforclimate.com/sup-volume-2/.

Allison, Graham. *Destined for War: Can America and China Escape Thucydides's Trap?* Boston: Houghton Mifflin Harcourt, 2017.

Amaresh, Preethi. "China's Stadium Diplomacy: All That Glitters Is Not Gold." *The Diplomatist* (November 2020).

Amen, Mark. *Cities and Global Governance: New Sites for International Relations.* Farnham, UK: Ashgate, 2011.

Anand, Nikhil, Akhil Gupta, and Hannah Appel. *The Promise of Infrastructure.* Durham, NC: Duke University Press, 2018.

Apostolopoulou, Elia. "A Novel Geographical Research Agenda on Silk Road Urbanisation." *Geographical Journal* 187 (2021): 386–393.

———. "Tracing the Links between Infrastructure-Led Development, Urban Transformation, and Inequality in China's Belt and Road Initiative." *Antipode* 53 (2021): 831–858.

Armijo, Leslie Elliott, and Saori N. Katada. "Theorizing the Financial Statecraft of Emerging Powers." *New Political Economy* 20 (2015): 42–62.

Arrighi, Giovanni. *Adam Smith in Beijing: Lineages of the Twenty-First Century.* London: Verso, 2007.

——. *The Long Twentieth Century: Money, Power, and the Origins of Our Times.* London: Verso, 1994.

Asante, Lewis Abedi. "Urban Governance in Ghana: The Participation of Traders in the Redevelopment of Kotokuraba Market in Cape Coast." *African Geographical Review* 39, no. 4 (2020).

Asante, Lewis Abedi, and Ilse Helbrecht. "The Urban Dimension of Chinese Infrastructure Finance in Africa: A Case of the Kotokuraba Market Project, Cape Coast, Ghana." *Journal of Urban Affairs* 42, no. 8 (2020).

Asia Development Bank. "Meeting Asia's Infrastructure Development Needs." February 2017. https://www.adb.org/publications/asia-infrastructure-needs.

Asian Infrastructure Investment Bank. Homepage: https://www.aiib.org/en/index.

Associated Press. "The Text of the Roosevelt Message on Bretton Woods Financial Proposals." *New York Times*, February 13, 1945.

Babiker, Mustafa, et al. "What the Latest Science on Climate Change Mitigation Means for Cities and Urban Areas." Vol. 1. *Summary for Urban Policymakers*, 2022. https://supforclimate.com/wp-content/uploads/2022/11/SUPVol3_15 Nov-reduced.pdf.

Babones, Salvatore. "Taking China Seriously: Relationality, *Tianxia*, and the 'Chinese School' of International Relations." *Politics* (September 26, 2017).

Baldwin, Richard. *The Great Convergence: Information Technology and the New Globalization.* Cambridge, MA: Harvard University Press, 2019.

Barrett, Anthony A. *Rome Is Burning: Nero and the Fire That Ended a Dynasty.* Princeton, NJ: Princeton University Press, 2020.

Barry, Andrew. "Technological Zones." *European Journal of Social Theory* 9 (2006): 239–253.

Bazaz, Amir, et al. *Summary for Urban Policymakers: What the IPCC Special Report on 1.5°C Means for Cities.* Summary for Urban Policymakers. December 2018. doi: https://doi.org/10.24943/SCPM.2018.

Becker, Daniel Levin, and Ian Klaus. "(In)Visible Policy." *Arcade: The Humanities in the World* (2021). https://shc.stanford.edu/arcade/interventions/invisible-policy.

Bednar, Jenna, and Mariano-Florentino Cuéllar. "The Fractured Superpower." *Foreign Affairs* (September/October 2022).

Beeson, Mark. "Geoeconomics with Chinese Characteristics: The BRI and China's Evolving Grand Strategy." *Economic and Political Studies* 6 (2018): 240–256.

Bennett, Jane. *Vibrant Matter: A Political Ecology of Things.* Durham, NC: Duke University Press, 2010.

BNP Paribas. "China Megatrends: Belt and Road Initiative Brings Green Opportunities and Challenges." https://www.investmentofficer.nl/analyse/document/15287.

Bo, Mark, and Neil Loughlin. "Overlapping Agendas on the Belt and Road: The Case of the Sihanoukville Special Economic Zone." *Global China Pulse* 1, no. 1 (2022): 87.

Bobbitt, Philip. *The Shield of Achilles: War, Peace, and the Course of History*. London: Allen Lane, 2002.

Boer, Ben, Rowena Cantley-Smith, and Tianbao Qin. "Introduction to the Special Issue on Ecological Civilization and Environmental Governance." *Chinese Journal of Environmental Law* 4 (2020): 121–129.

Bouteligier, Sofie. *Cities, Networks, and Global Environmental Governance: Spaces of Innovation, Places of Leadership*. New York: Routledge, 2013.

Boyle, Louise. "China's Zero Carbon Pledge: What Does It Mean for the Global Climate Change Fight?" *The Independent* (July 24, 2020).

Brady, Anne-Marie. *China as a Polar Great Power*. Cambridge, UK: Cambridge University Press, 2017.

Bratton, Benjamin. *The Stack: On Software and Sovereignty*. Cambridge, MA: MIT Press, 2015.

Braudel, Fernand. *Civilization and Capitalism, 15th–18th Century*. 3 vols. Berkeley: University of California Press, 1992.

Brautigam, Deborah, Vijay Bhalaki, Laure Deron, and Yinxuan Wang. "How Africa Borrows from China: And Why Mombasa Port Is Not Collateral for Kenya's Standard Gauge Railway." Working paper no. 2022/52, China Africa Research Initiative, School of Advanced International Studies, Johns Hopkins University, 2022.

Bremmer, Ian. *The End of the Free Market: Who Wins the War between States and Corporations?* New York: Portfolio, 2010.

Brenner, Neil. *New State Spaces: Urban Governance and the Rescaling of Statehood*. Oxford, UK: Oxford University Press, 2004.

———. *New Urban Spaces: Urban Theory and the Scale Question*. New York: Oxford University Press, 2019.

Brenner, Neil, and Roger Keil. *The Global Cities Reader*. London: Routledge, 2006.

Breslin, Shaun. "China's Global Cultural Interactions." In David Shambaugh, ed., *China and the World*. New York: Oxford University Press, 2020.

Brunnermeier, Markus, Rush Doshi, and Harold James. "Beijing's Bismarckian Ghosts: How Great Powers Compete Economically." *Washington Quarterly* 41 (2018): 161–176.

Bull, Hedley. *The Anarchical Society: A Study of Order in World Politics*. 3rd ed. Basingstoke, UK: Palgrave, 2002.

Burdett, Richard. *Shaping Cities in an Urban Age*. London: Phaidon, 2018.

Buzan, Barry. *An Introduction to the English School of International Relations: The Societal Approach*. Cambridge, UK: Polity, 2014.

Buzan, Barry, and Richard Little. *International Systems in World History: Remaking the Study of International Relations*. Oxford, UK: Oxford University Press, 2000.

Callahan, William. "China's 'Asia Dream': The Belt and Road Initiative and the New Regional Order." *Asian Journal of Comparative Politics* 1 (2016): 226–243.

———. "Chinese Visions of World Order: Post-Hegemonic or a New Hegemony?" *International Studies Review* 10 (2008): 749–761.

Campanella, Thomas J. *The Concrete Dragon: China's Urban Revolution and What It Means for the World.* New York: Princeton Architectural Press, 2008.

Carr, Edward Hallett. *The Twenty Years' Crisis, 1919–1939: An Introduction to the Study of International Relations.* 2nd ed. Basingstoke, UK: Palgrave, 2001.

Castells, Manuel. *The Rise of the Network Society.* Malden, MA: Blackwell, 1996.

Castillo, Greg. *Cold War on the Homefront.* Minneapolis: University of Minnesota Press, 2010.

Cendrowski, Scott. "China's Global 500 Companies Are Bigger Than Ever—and Mostly State-Owned." *Fortune* (June 2015).

Center for Security and Emerging Technology. "Outline of the People's Republic of China 14th Five-Year Plan for National Economic and Social Development and Long-Range Objectives for 2035." Translation. May 2021. https://cset.georgetown.edu/publication/china-14th-five-year-plan.

Center for Strategic and International Studies. "Deep Comprehension of the Global Security Initiative: Coordinating Our Own Security and Common Security." May 9, 2022. https://interpret.csis.org/translations/deep-compre hension-of-the-global-security-initiative-coordinating-our-own-security-and-common-security/.

Chen, Xiangming. "Corridor-ising Impact along the Belt and Road: Is the Newly Operational China-Laos Railway a Game-Changer?" *World Financial Review* (February 22, 2022).

———. "Europe's Freight Infrastructure vs. Russia's War in Ukraine." Report, Chicago Council on Global Affairs, October 13, 2022. https://globalaffairs. org/research/report/eurasias-freight-infrastructure-vs-russias-war-ukraine.

———. "Globalisation Redux: Can China's Inside-Out Strategy Catalyse Economic Development and Integration across Its Asian Borderlands and Beyond?" *Cambridge Journal of Regions, Economy, and Society* 11 (2018): 35–58.

———. "A (Long) Tale of Two Leaders: Charting the Spatial and Sectoral Roles of the West and China in Shaping Past, Present, and Future Economic Globalization(s)." *New Global Studies* (September 2022).

———. "Reconnecting Eurasia: A New Logistics State, the China-Europe Freight Train, and the Resurging Ancient City of Xi'an." *Eurasian Geography and Economics* 64, no. 1 (2021).

China Aiddata.org. "China Eximbank Provides RMB 200 Million Government Concessional Loan for Cape Coast Kotokuraba Market Project. https:// china.aiddata.org/projects/30087.

Chow, Renee Y. *Changing Chinese Cities: The Potentials of Field Urbanism.* Honolulu: University of Hawai'i Press, 2015.

CIMB Asean Research Institute/LSE Ideas. *China's Belt and Road Initiative (BRI) and Southeast Asia*. October 2018. https://www.lse.ac.uk/ideas/Assets/Documents/reports/LSE-IDEAS-China-SEA-BRI.pdf.

Coalition for Urban Transitions. *Accelerating China's Urban Transition: Priority Actions for High-Quality Growth and Enhancing Leadership for Carbon Neutrality*. March 23, 2021. https://urbantransitions.global/wp-content/uploads/2021/03/Accelerating_Chinas_Urban_Transition_EN_WEB.pdf.

———. *Seizing China's Urban Opportunity: Cities at the Heart of the 14th Five-Year Plan and a National Vision for Net-Zero Emissions*. March 6, 2021. https://urbantransitions.global/wp-content/uploads/2021/03/Seizing_Chinas_Urban_Opportunity_ENG_FINAL.pdf.

Cobbett, Elizabeth, and Ra Mason. "Djiboutian Sovereignty: Worlding Global Security Networks." *International Affairs* 97 (2021): 1767–1784.

Cody, Jeffrey. *Exporting American Architecture, 1870–2000*. New York: Routledge, 2003.

Cohen, Lizabeth. *Saving America's Cities: Ed Logue and the Struggle to Renew Urban America in the Suburban Age*. New York: Farrar, Straus, and Giroux, 2019.

Coker, Christopher. *The Rise of the Civilizational State*. Cambridge, UK: Polity, 2019.

Connolly, William. *Facing the Planetary: Entangled Humanism and the Politics of Swarming*. Durham, NC: Duke University Press, 2017.

Coole, Diana, and Samantha Frost. *New Materialisms: Ontology, Agency, and Politics*. Durham, NC: Duke University Press, 2010.

Cornell, Phillip. "Energy Governance and China's Bid for Global Grid Integration." *Atlantic Council* (May 30, 2019).

Cox, Robert. *Production, Power, and World Order: Social Forces in the Making of History*. New York: Columbia University Press, 1987.

———. "Social Forces, States and World Orders: Beyond International Relations Theory." *Millennium* 10 (1981): 126–155.

Croese, Sylvia. "State-led Housing Delivery as an Instrument of Developmental Patrimonialism: The Case of Post-War Angola." *African Affairs* 116, no. 462 (January 2017): 80–100.

Crowley, David, and Jane Pavitt. *Cold War Modern: Design, 1945–1970*. London: V&A Publishing, 2008.

Cunningham-Cross, Linsay, and William A. Callahan. "Ancient Chinese Power, Modern Chinese Thought." *Chinese Journal of International Politics* 4 (2011): 349–374.

Cupers, Kenny. *The Social Project: Housing in Postwar France*. Minneapolis: University of Minnesota Press, 2014.

Curtis, Simon. *Global Cities and Global Order*. Oxford, UK: Oxford University Press, 2016.

Curtis, Simon, and Michele Acuto. "The Foreign Policy of Cities." *RUSI Journal* 163 (2018): 8–17.

Custer, Samantha, et al. "Ties That Bind: Quantifying China's Public Diplomacy and Its 'Good Neighbor' Effect." Policy report for AidData at William & Mary (June 27, 2018). https://www.aiddata.org/publications/ties-that-bind.

Daalder, Ivo, and James Lindsay. *The Empty Throne: America's Abdication of Global Leadership.* New York: PublicAffairs, 2018.

DeLanda, Manuel. *Intensive Science and Virtual Philosophy.* London: Continuum, 2002.

———. *A New Philosophy of Society: Assemblage Theory and Social Complexity.* London: Continuum, 2006.

Deleuze, Gilles, and Felix Guattari. *A Thousand Plateaus: Capitalism and Schizophrenia.* London: Athlone, 1987.

Demissie, Alexander. "Special Economic Zones: Integrating African Countries in China's Belt and Road Initiative." In Maximilian Mayer, ed., *Rethinking the Silk-Road.* New York: Springer, 2017.

DiCarlo, Jessica. "Boten Special Economic Zone/Boten Beautiful Land." People's Map of Global China Project, April 1, 2022. https://thepeoplesmap.net/project/boten-special-economic-zone-boten-beautiful-land/.

Djibouti Business District. Homepage: http://dpfza.gov.dj/Djibouti-Business-District.

Djibouti Ports and Free Zone Authority. Homepage: http://dpfza.gov.dj/.

Donnelly, Jack. "Sovereign Inequalities and Hierarchy in Anarchy: American Power and International Society." *European Journal of International Relations* 12 (2006): 139–170.

Doshi, Rush. *The Long Game: China's Grand Strategy to Displace American Order.* New York: Oxford University Press, 2021.

Downie, Edmund. "Powering the Globe: Lessons from Southeast Asia for China's Global Energy Interconnection Initiative." Columbia SIPA Center on Global Energy Policy, Belt and Road Initiative Series, April 23, 2020. https://www.energypolicy.columbia.edu/publications/powering-globe-lessons-southeast-asia-china-s-global-energy-interconnection-initiative.

Drache, Daniel, A. T. Kingsmith, and Duan Qi. *One Road, Many Dreams: China's Bold Plan to Remake the Global Economy.* London: Bloomsbury, 2019.

Drezner, Daniel W., and Kathleen R. McNamara. "International Political Economy, Global Financial Orders, and the 2008 Financial Crisis." *Perspectives on Politics* 11 (2013): 155–166.

Du, Juan. *The Shenzhen Experiment: The Story of China's Instant City.* Cambridge, MA: Harvard University Press, 2020.

Dwyer, Michael B. "'They Will Not Automatically Benefit': The Politics of Infrastructure Development in Laos's Northern Economic Corridor." *Political Geography* 78 (April 2020).

Easterling, Keller. *Extrastatecraft: The Power of Infrastructure Space.* London: Verso, 2014.

Economic Community of West African States. "ECOWAS Signs MOU with China for the Construction of the New ECOWAS Commission Headquarters." Press release, ECOWAS, March 14, 2018.

Economy, Elizabeth. *The Third Revolution: Xi Jinping and the New Chinese State.* New York: Oxford University Press, 2018.

———. *The World According to China.* Medford, MA: Polity Press, 2021.

Eguegu, Ovigwe. "Will China's 'Global Security Initiative' Catch On?" *The Diplomat* (May 8, 2022). https://thediplomat.com/2022/06/will-chinas-global-security-initiative-catch-on/.

Fei, Ding. "Worlding Developmentalism: China's Economic Zones within and beyond Its Border." *Journal of International Development* 29, no. 6 (2017).

Feigenbaum, Evan. "China and the World." *Foreign Affairs* 96, no. 1 (January/February 2017).

———. "The New Asia Order." *Foreign Affairs* (February 2, 2015).

Ferdinand, Peter. "Westward Ho—the China Dream and 'One Belt, One Road': Chinese Foreign Policy under Xi Jinping." *International Affairs* 92 (2016): 941–957.

Ferrari, Claudio, and Alessio Tei. "Effects of BRI Strategy on Mediterranean Shipping Transport." *Journal of Shipping and Trade* 5 (2020): 14.

Fitzpatrick, Sheila. *Everyday Stalinism.* Oxford, UK: Oxford University Press, 1999.

Foucault, Michel. *The Archaeology of Knowledge.* New York: Pantheon, 1972.

Frankopan, Peter. *The New Silk Roads: The Present and Future of the World.* New York: Alfred A. Knopf, 2019.

———. *The Silk Roads: A New History of the World.* New York: Alfred A. Knopf, 2016.

Freymann, Eyck. *One Belt One Road: Chinese Power Meets the World.* Cambridge, MA: Harvard University Asia Center, 2021.

Friedberg, Aaron. *A Contest for Supremacy: China, America, and the Struggle for Mastery in Asia.* New York: W.W. Norton, 2011.

Friedmann, John. "The World City Hypothesis." *Development and Change* 17 (1986): 69–83.

G7 Germany, Ministerial Meeting on Sustainable Urban Development. "Communiqué." September 13, 2022. https://www.bmwsb.bund.de/SharedDocs/downloads/Webs/BMWSB/DE/veroeffentlichungen/termine/communique-g7.pdf?__blob=publicationFile&v=3.

Gallagher, Kevin, and Richard Kozul-Wright. *The Case for a New Bretton Woods.* Cambridge, UK: Polity, 2022.

Germain, Randall. "Financial Order and World Politics: Crisis, Change and Continuity." *International Affairs* 85 (2009): 669–687.

Gibbon, Edward. *The Decline and Fall of the Roman Empire.* New York: Modern Library, 1983.

Goldstein, Avery. "China's Grand Strategy under Xi Jinping: Reassurance, Reform, and Resistance." *International Security* 45 (2020): 164–201.

———. *Rising to the Challenge: China's Grand Strategy and International Security.* Stanford, CA: Stanford University Press, 2005.

Golubev, Alexey. *The Things of Life: Materiality in Late Soviet Russia.* New York: Cornell University Press, 2020.

Gordon, David J., and Kristin Ljungkvist. "Theorizing the Globally Engaged City in World Politics." *European Journal of International Relations* 28 (2022): 58–82.

Governa, Francesca, and Angelo Sampieri. "Urbanisation Processes and New Towns in Contemporary China: A Critical Understanding from a Decentred View." *Urban Studies Journal Limited* 57, 2 (February 2020): 366–382.

Government of Pakistan, Ministry of Planning Development and Reform. *Long-Term Plan for China-Pakistan Economic Corridor (2017–2030)*. https://www.pc.gov.pk/uploads/cpec/LTP.pdf.

Graham, Stephen. *Vertical: The City from Satellites to Bunkers*. London: Verso, 2016.

Graham, Stephen, and Simon Marvin. *Splintering Urbanism: Networked Infrastructures, Technological Mobilities and the Urban Condition*. London: Routledge, 2001.

Greenspan, Anna. *Shanghai Future: Modernity Remade*. New York: Oxford University Press, 2014.

Gries, Peter. "Nationalism, Social Influences, and Chinese Foreign Policy." Pp. 63–84 in David L. Shambaugh, ed., *China and the World*. New York: Oxford University Press, 2020.

Gwadar Development Authority. "Masterplan 2050." https://www.gda.gov.pk/masterplan/.

"Gwadar Protest Comes to an End after 32 Days." *The News* (December 16, 2021). https://www.thenews.com.pk/latest/917269-gwadar-protest-comes-to-an-end-after-32-days.

Halegoua, Germaine. *Smart Cities*. Cambridge, MA: MIT Press, 2020.

Hall, Peter. *Cities in Civilization: Culture, Innovation, and Urban Order*. London: Weidenfield, 1998.

Hanson, Arthur. "Ecological Civilization in the People's Republic of China: Values, Action, and Future Needs." *Asian Development Bank East Asia Working Papers Series* (December 2019). https://www.adb.org/publications/ecological-civilization-values-action-future-needs.

Harvey, David. *The Limits to Capital*. Chicago: University of Chicago Press, 1982.

Hatherley, Owen. *Landscapes of Communism: A History through Buildings*. New York: New Press, 2016.

Heilmann, Sebastian. "Regulatory Innovation by Leninist Means: Communist Party Supervision in China's Financial Industry." *China Quarterly* 181 (2005): 1–21.

Herrero, Alicia García. "What Is Behind China's Dual Circulation Strategy?" *China Leadership Monitor* (September 1, 2021).

Hillman, Jonathan. *The Digital Silk Road: China's Quest to Wire the World and Win the Future*. New York: Harper Business, 2021.

———. *The Emperor's New Road: How China's New Silk Road Is Remaking the World*. New Haven: Yale University Press, 2020.

Hirst, Paul. *Space and Power: Politics, War and Architecture*. Cambridge, UK: Polity, 2005.

Ho, Selina. "Infrastructure and Chinese Power." *International Affairs* 96 (2020): 1461–1485.

Hu, Biliang. "Belt and Road Initiative: Five Years On. Implementation and Reflection." *Global Journal of Emerging Market Economies* 11 (2019): 1–10.

Huang, Yasheng. *Capitalism with Chinese Characteristics: Entrepreneurship and the State*. Cambridge, UK: Cambridge University Press, 2008.

Huawei. Building Digital Guinea Homepage: https://www.huawei.com/en/facts/ voices-of-huawei/guinea_backbone_network.

Hurrell, Andrew. *On Global Order: Power, Values, and the Constitution of International Society*. Oxford, UK: Oxford University Press, 2007.

Iftikhar, Muhammad Naveed, et al. "Institutional and Urban Design of Gwadar City." Report C-37422-PAK-1, International Growth Centre, May 2019. https://www.researchgate.net/publication/335060441_The_institutional_ and_urban_design_of_Gwadar_City.

Ikenberry, John. *A World Safe for Democracy: Liberal Internationalism and the Crises of Global Order*. New Haven: Yale University Press, 2020.

Immerwahr, Daniel. *How to Hide an Empire: A History of the Greater United States*. New York: Farrar, Straus, and Giroux, 2019.

Inclusive Design International. "Sihanoukville Special Economic Zone." The People's Map of Global China (March 31, 2021). https://thepeoplesmap. net/project/sihanoukville-special-economic-zone/.

Intergovernmental Panel on Climate Change (IPCC). *Climate Change, 2014: Mitigation of Climate Change*. Contribution of Working Group III to the *Fifth Assessment Report of the Intergovernmental Panel on Climate Change*, ed. O. Edenhofer et al. Cambridge, UK: Cambridge University Press, 2014.

———. *Climate Change, 2021: The Physical Science Basis*. Contribution of Working Group I to the *Sixth Assessment Report of the Intergovernmental Panel on Climate Change*, ed. V. Masson-Delmotte et al. Cambridge, UK: Cambridge University Press, 2021.

———. *Climate Change, 2022: Impacts, Adaptation, and Vulnerability*. Contribution of Working Group II to the *Sixth Assessment Report of the Intergovernmental Panel on Climate Change*, ed. H.-O. Pörtner et al. Cambridge, UK: Cambridge University Press, 2022.

———. *Climate Change, 2022: Mitigation of Climate Change*. Contribution of Working Group III to the *Sixth Assessment Report of the Intergovernmental Panel on Climate Change*, ed. R. Shukla et al. Cambridge, UK: Cambridge University Press, 2022.

Jackson, Peter, and Daniel Nexon. "Relations before States: Substance, Process and the Study of World Politics." *European Journal of International Relations* 5 (1999): 291–332.

Jacobs, Jane. *Cities and the Wealth of Nations: Principles of Economic Life*. New York: Random House, 1985.

Jacques, Martin. *When China Rules the World: The End of the Western World and the Birth of a New Global Order*. London: Penguin, 2012.

Jessop, Bob, and Sum Ngai-Ling. "Geopolitics: Putting Geopolitics in Its Place in Cultural Political Economy." *Environment and Planning A: Economy and Space* 50 (2018): 474–478.

Jianhua, Zhang, and Chanthaphaphone Mixayboua. "World Insights: China, Laos Cooperate in Building Low-Carbon Demonstration Zone." Xinhuanet.com, April 26, 2021. http://xinhuanet.com/english/2021-04/26/c_13990 7400.htm.

Jisi, Wang. "China's Search for a Grand Strategy: A Rising Power Finds Its Way." *Foreign Affairs* (March/April 2011).

Jones, Lee, and Jinghan Zeng. "Understanding China's 'Belt and Road Initiative': Beyond 'Grand Strategy' to a State Transformation Analysis." *Third World Quarterly* 40 (2019): 1415–1439.

Kanigel, Robert. *Eyes on the Street: The Life of Jane Jacobs.* New York: Knopf, 2016.

Kavalski, Emilian. "Guanxi; or, What Is the Chinese for Relational Theory of World Politics." *International Relations of the Asia-Pacific* 18 (2018): 397–420.

Keay, John. *China: A History.* London: Harper, 2008.

Keeton, Rachel. "Case Study: Kilamba, Angola." In Rachel Keeton and Michelle Provoost, eds., *To Build a City in Africa: A History and Manual.* Rotterdam: Nai010 Publishers, 2019.

Kelkar, Keshav. "From Silk Threads to Fiber Optics: The Rise of China's Digital Silk Road." *Observer Foundation* (August 8, 2018).

Kelly, Ashley Scott, and Xiaoxuan Lu. *Critical Landscape Planning during the Belt and Road Initiative.* Singapore: Springer, 2021.

Kennedy, Paul. *The Rise and Fall of the Great Powers: Economic Change and Military Conflict from 1500 to 2000.* New York: Random House, 1987.

Kennedy, Scott. *Made in China 2025.* Center for Strategic and International Studies online, June 1, 2015, https://www.csis.org/analysis/made-china-2025.

Khanna, Parag. *Connectography: Mapping the Future of Global Civilization.* New York: Random House, 2016.

Kissinger, Henry. *On China.* New York: Penguin, 2011.

———. *World Order.* New York: Penguin, 2014.

Klanten, Robert, and Elli Stuhler. *Beauty and the East.* Berlin: Gestalten, 2021.

Klaus, Ian. "Invited to the Party: International Organizations Evolve in an Urban World." Chicago Council on Global Affairs, October 29, 2018. https://globalaffairs.org/research/report/invited-party-international-organi zations-evolve-urban-world.

———. "The State of City Diplomacy." *Urbanisation* 5, no. 1 (2020).

———. "Subnational Diplomacy Evolves: From Urban Arenas to City Partners." *Columbia Journal of International Affairs* 74, no. 1 (2022).

Klaus, Ian, and Russ Springer. "The United Nations: Local Authorities in Four Frameworks." *Penn: Current Research on Sustainable Urbanization* (February 2018). https://penniur.upenn.edu/uploads/media/Klaus.pdf.

Knight, Will. "China Wants to Shape the Global Future of Artificial Intelligence." *MIT Technology Review* (March 2018).

Koleski, Katherine. *The 13th Five-Year Plan*. US-China Economic and Security Review Commission. February 14, 2017. https://www.uscc.gov/sites/default/files/Research/The%2013th%20Five-Year%20Plan_Final_2.14.17_Updated%20(002).pdf.

Kostof, Spiro. *The City Shaped: Urban Patterns and Meanings through History*. London: Thames and Hudson, 1991.

Kupchan, Charles. *No One's World: The West, the Rising Rest, and the Coming Global Turn*. New York: Oxford University Press, 2012.

Kurlantzick, Joshua. "China's Digital Silk Road Initiative: A Boon for Developing Countries or a Danger to Freedom?" *Diplomat* (September 17, 2020).

———. *State Capitalism: How the Return of Statism Is Transforming the World*. New York: Oxford University Press, 2016.

Kwak, Nancy. *A World of Homeowners: American Power and the Politics of Housing Aid*. Chicago: University of Chicago Press, 2015.

Lacher, Hannes. *Beyond Globalization: Capitalism, Territoriality, and the International Relations of Modernity*. London: Routledge, 2006.

Lall, Somik V., and Mathilde Lebrand. World Bank Policy Research Paper 8806, "Who Wins, Who Loses? Understanding the Spatially Differentiated Effects of the Belt and Road Initiative." April 8, 2019. https://documents.worldbank.org/en/publication/documents-reports/documentdetail/292161554727963020/who-wins-who-loses-understanding-the-spatially-differentiated-effects-of-the-belt-and-road-initiative.

Lamson-Hall, Patrick. "How They Do It in Ethiopia: Making Room for Urban Expansion." Marron Institute, New York University, September 22, 2020. https://marroninstitute.nyu.edu/blog/how-they-do-it-in-ethiopia-making-room-for-urban-expansion.

Latour, Bruno. *Reassembling the Social: An Introduction to Actor-Network-Theory*. Oxford, UK: Oxford University Press, 2005.

———. "Technology Is Society Made Durable." *Sociological Review* 38 (1990): 103–131.

———. *We Have Never Been Modern*. Cambridge, MA: Harvard University Press, 1993.

Lee, Ching Kwan. *Global China*. Cambridge, UK: Cambridge University Press, 2022.

———. The Specter of Global China: Politics, Labor, and Foreign Investment in Africa. Chicago: University of Chicago Press, 2017.

Lee, Pamela. *Think Tank Aesthetics: Midcentury Modernism, the Cold War, and the Neoliberal Present*. Cambridge, MA: MIT Press, 2020.

Lefebvre, Henri. *The Production of Space*. Oxford, UK: Blackwell, 1991.

Li, Minqi. *China and the Twenty-First-Century Crisis*. London: Pluto Press, 2016.

Li, Yifei, and Judith Shapiro. *China Goes Green: Coercive Environmentalism for a Troubled Planet*. Cambridge, UK: Polity, 2020.

Li, Yuan, and Markus Taube, eds. *How China's Silk Road Initiative Is Changing the Global Economic Landscape.* London: Routledge, 2021.

Liao, Rebecca. "Out of the Bretton Woods: How the AIIB Is Different." *Foreign Affairs* (July 27, 2015).

Ling, Lily. *The Dao of World Politics: Towards a Post-Westphalian, Worldist International Relations.* London: Routledge, 2014.

Link, Stefan. *Forging Global Fordism: Nazi Germany, Soviet Russia, and the Contest over the Industrial Order.* Princeton, NJ: Princeton University Press, 2020.

Liu, Daizong, Leo Horn-Phathanothai, and Daiyang Zhang. "5 Ways China's Cities Can Drive Equitable and Sustainable Urbanization." World Resources Institute, December 17, 2021. https://www.wri.org/insights/china-five-year-plan-equitable-sustainable-urbanization.

Liu, Haimeng, et al. "Spatio-Temporal Evolution of Population and Urbanization in the Countries along the Belt and Road, 1950–2050." *Journal of Geographical Sciences* 28 (2018): 919–936.

Liu, Zhenya. *Global Energy Interconnection.* Amsterdam: Elsevier/AP, 2015.

Ljungkvist, Kristin. *The Global City 2.0: From Strategic Site to Global Actor.* New York: Routledge, 2016.

Long, Kimmarita. "Capital-S'ville Expressway Sees Increase in Traffic." *Phnom Penh Post*, October 18, 2022. https://www.phnompenhpost.com/national/capital-sville-expressway-sees-increase-traffic.

Loughlin, Neil, and Mark Grimsditch. "How Local Political Economy Dynamics Are Shaping the Belt and Road Initiative." *Third World Quarterly* 42, no. 10 (2021): 2334–2352.

Lovell, Julia. *The Opium Wars: Drugs, Dreams, and the Making of Modern China.* New York: Abrams, 2014.

Lucas, Edward. "China Rewrites History in Its Drive to Reshape the World Order." *The Times.* (July 2, 2021). https://www.thetimes.co.uk/article/china-rewrites-history-in-its-drive-to-reshape-the-world-order-hkfzk8bfk.

Lynch, Kevin. *The Image of the City.* Cambridge, MA: Harvard-MIT Joint Center for Urban Studies, 1960.

Maçães, Bruno. *Belt and Road: A Chinese World Order.* London: Hurst & Company, 2018.

———. *The Dawn of Eurasia: On the Trail of the New World Order.* New Haven: Yale University Press, 2018.

MacCarthy, Fiona. *Gropius: The Man Who Built the Bauhaus.* Cambridge, MA: Belknap Press of Harvard University Press.

MacKenzie, Donald A., and Judy Wajcman. *The Social Shaping of Technology.* 2nd ed. Buckingham, UK: Open University Press, 1999.

Maier, Charles. *Among Empires.* Cambridge, MA: Harvard University Press, 2006.

———. *Once within Borders: Territories of Power, Wealth, and Belonging since 1500.* Cambridge, MA: Harvard University Press, 2017.

Marx, Karl, and Friedrich Engels. *Capital: A Critique of Political Economy*. New York: International Publishers, 1967.

Massey, Doreen. *World City*. Cambridge, UK: Polity, 2007.

Mayer, Maximilian, ed. *Rethinking the Silk-Road: China's Belt and Road Initiative and Emerging Eurasian Relations*. New York: Springer 2017.

———. "The Return of History and China's Historical Statecraft." *International Affairs* 94 (2018): 1217–1235.

Mayer, Maximilian, and Michele Acuto. "The Global Governance of Large Technical Systems." *Millennium* 43 (2015): 660–683.

Mayer, Maximilian, and Xin Zhang. "Theorizing China-World Integration: Sociospatial Reconfigurations and the Modern Silk Roads." *Review of International Political Economy* (2020): 1–30.

McNally, Christopher A. "The Political Economic Logic of RMB Internationalization: A Study in Sino-Capitalism." *International Politics* 52 (2015): 704–723.

Mearsheimer, John. *The Tragedy of Great Power Politics*. New York: Norton, 2001.

Meng, Qingwei, and Eugene Bempong Nyantakyi. "Local Skill Development from China's Engagement in Africa: Comparative Evidence from the Construction Sector in Ghana." Working paper no. 2019/22, China Africa Research Initiative, School of Advanced International Studies, Johns Hopkins University, 2022.

Metropolis. "An Agreement of Scientific and Educational Cooperation Celebrating One of the Biggest International Gateway Hubs in China." December 27, 2019. https://www.metropolis.org/news/agreement-scientific-and-educational-cooperation-celebrating-one-biggest-international-gateway.

Mierzejewski, Dominik. "The Role of Guangdong and Guangzhou's Subnational Diplomacy in China's Belt and Road Initiative." *China: An International Journal* 18, no. 2 (2020): 99–119.

Miller, Tom. *China's Asian Dream: Empire Building along the New Silk Road*. London: Zed Books, 2017.

Ministry of Foreign Affairs of the People's Republic of China. "President Xi Jinping Addresses the Opening Ceremony of the 14th Meeting of the Conference of the Contracting Parties to the Ramsar Convention on Wetlands." November 5, 2022. https://www.mfa.gov.cn/eng/zxxx_662805/202211/t20221105_10801007.html.

Mitchell, Timothy. *Carbon Democracy: Political Power in the Age of Oil*. London: Verso, 2011.

Moore, Jason. *Capitalism in the Web of Life: Ecology and the Accumulation of Capital*. New York: Verso, 2015.

Moore, Scott. *China's Next Act: How Sustainability and Technology Are Reshaping China's Rise and the World's Future*. New York: Oxford University Press, 2022.

Morgenthau, Hans. *Politics among Nations: The Struggle for Power and Peace*. New York: Alfred A. Knopf, 1948.

Morton, Timothy. *Hyperobjects: Philosophy and Ecology after the End of the World*. Minneapolis: University of Minnesota Press, 2013.

Moyn, Samuel. *The Last Utopia: Human Rights in History*. Cambridge, MA: Belknap Press of Harvard University Press, 2010.

———. *Not Enough: Human Rights in an Unequal World*. Cambridge, MA: Harvard University Press, 2018.

Mozer, Paul, Muyi Xiao, and John Liu. " 'An Invisible Cage': How China Is Policing the Future." *New York Times* (June 25, 2022).

Muchira, Nhiraini. "China Pushes for Implementation of Tanzania's Bagamoyo Port." *Maritime Executive* (April 29, 2022). https://maritime-executive.com/article/china-pushing-for-implementation-of-tanzania-s-bagamoyo-port.

Munn, Luke. "Red Territory: Forging Infrastructural Power." *Territory, Politics, Governance* 11, no. 1 (2023).

Murgia, Madhumita, and Anna Gross. "Inside China's Controversial Mission to Reinvent the Internet." *Financial Times* (March 27, 2020).

Naughton, Barry. "China's Global Economic Interactions." Pp. 113–136 in David L. Shambaugh, ed., *China and the World*. New York: Oxford University Press, 2020.

Naughton, Barry, and Kellee Tsai. *State Capitalism, Institutional Adaptation, and the Chinese Miracle*. New York: Cambridge University Press, 2015.

Nölke, Andreas. "International Financial Regulation and Domestic Coalitions in State-Permeated Capitalism: China and Global Banking Rules." *International Politics* 52 (2015).

Noorloos, Femke van, and Diky Avianto. "New Towns, Old Places: Four Lessons from Konza Techno City, Kenya. " Pp. 396–398 in Rachel Keeton and Michelle Provoost, eds., *To Build a City in Africa: A History and Manual*. Rotterdam: Naio10 Publishers, 2019.

Nordin, Astrid. *China's International Relations and Harmonious World: Time, Space and Multiplicity in World Politics*. London: Routledge, 2016.

———. "Futures beyond 'the West'? Autoimmunity in China's Harmonious World." *Review of International Studies* 42 (2016).

Nye, Joseph S., Jr. *Soft Power: The Means to Success in World Politics*. New York: PublicAffairs, 2004.

O'Donnell, Mary Ann. "Heroes of the Special Zone: Modeling Reform and Its Limits." In Mary Ann O'Donnell, Winnie Wong, and Jonathan Bach, eds., *Learning from Shenzhen: China's Post-Mao Experiment from Special Zone to Model City*. Chicago: University of Chicago Press, 2017.

O'Donnell, Mary Ann, Winnie Wong, and Jonathan Bach. "Introduction: Experiments, Exceptions, and Extensions." In O'Donnell, Wong, and Bach, eds., *Learning from Shenzhen: China's Post-Mao Experiment from Special Zone to Model City*. Chicago: University of Chicago Press, 2017.

Organization for Economic Cooperation and Development (OECD). *The Belt and Road Initiative in the Global Trade, Investment and Finance Landscape*. Paris:

OECD Publishing, 2018. https://www.oecd.org/finance/Chinas-Belt-and-Road-Initiative-in-the-global-trade-investment-and-finance-landscape.pdf.

Osterhammel, Jürgen. *The Transformation of the World: A Global History of the Nineteenth Century*. Vol. 15: *America in the World*. Princeton, NJ: Princeton University Press, 2014.

"Pacific Data Cable Not Safe from China if Hong Kong Included, Says US." *The Guardian* (June 18, 2020). https://www.theguardian.com/technology/2020/jun/18/pacific-data-cable-not-safe-from-china-if-hong-kong-included-says-us.

Page, Jeremy, and Rob Taylor. "America's Undersea Battle with China for Control of the Global Internet." *Wall Street Journal* (February 12, 2017).

Pan, Chengxin, and Emilian Kavalski. *China's Rise and Rethinking International Relations Theory*. Bristol, UK: Bristol University Press, 2022.

Pantucci, Raffaello, and Alexandros Petersen. *Sinostan: China's Inadvertent Empire*. Oxford, UK: Oxford University Press, 2022.

Patterson, Walt. "Why an Asian Super Grid Is a Political Fantasy." *China Dialogue* (June 2, 2016). https://chinadialogue.net/en/energy/8973-why-an-asian-super-grid-is-a-political-fantasy.

Peng, Tao, and Hongwei Deng. "Research on the Sustainable Development Process of Low-Carbon Pilot Cities: The Case Study of Guiyang, a Low-Carbon Pilot City in South-West China." *Environment, Development and Sustainability* 23 (2021): 2382–2403.

Perdue, Peter. "The Tenacious Tributary System." *Journal of Contemporary China* 24 (2015): 1002–1014.

Petry, Johannes. "Beyond Ports, Roads and Railways: Chinese Economic State-craft, the Belt and Road Initiative, and the Politics of Financial Infrastructures." *European Journal of International Relations* (2022). https://journals.sagepub.com/doi/pdf/10.1177/13540661221126615.

———. "Same Same, but Different: Varieties of Capital Markets, Chinese State Capitalism and the Global Financial Order." *Competition & Change* 25 (2020): 605–630.

Phelps, Nicholas A. *The Urban Planning Imagination: A Critical International Introduction*. Cambridge, UK: Polity, 2021.

Pillsbury, Michael. *The Hundred-Year Marathon: China's Secret Strategy to Replace America as the Global Superpower*. New York: Henry Holt, 2015.

Polanyi, Karl. *The Great Transformation: The Political and Economic Origins of Our Time*. Boston: Beacon Press, 1957.

Polèse, Mario. *The Wealth and Poverty of Regions: Why Cities Matter*. Chicago: University of Chicago Press, 2009.

Pollio, A., L. R. Cirolia, and E. Pieterse. "Infrastructure Financing in Africa: Overview, Research Gaps, and Urban Research Agenda." Cape Town: African Centre for Cities & Alfred Herrhausen Gesellschaft, 2022. https://www.researchgate.net/publication/360939114_Infrastructure_Financing_in_Africa_Overview_Research_Gaps_and_Urban_Research_Agenda.

Ponzini, Davide. *Transnational Architecture and Urbanism: Rethinking How Cities Plan, Transform and Learn.* London: Routledge, 2020.

Prak, Sek. "Phnom Penh–Sihanoukville Expressway Opens to the Public." *Phnom Penh Post*, October 1, 2022. https://www.phnompenhpost.com/national/phnom-penh-sihanoukville-expressway-opens-public.

Qin, Yaqing. "Continuity through Change: Background Knowledge and China's International Strategy." *Chinese Journal of International Politics* 7 (2014): 285–314.

———. *A Relational Theory of World Politics.* New York: Cambridge University Press, 2018.

———. "Why Is There No Chinese International Relations Theory?" *International Relations of the Asia-Pacific* 7 (2007): 313–340.

Quayson, Ato. *Oxford Street, Accra: City Life and the Itineraries of Transformation.* Durham, NC: Duke University Press, 2014.

Rafiq, Arif. "Gwadar's Real Estate Market Picks Up." *CPEC Wire* (May 7, 2018).

Ren, Xiao. "Grown from Within: Building a Chinese School of International Relations." *Pacific Review* 33 (2020): 386–412.

Ren, Xuefei. *Urban China.* Cambridge, UK: Polity, 2013.

Repnikova, Maria. *Chinese Soft Power.* Cambridge, UK: Cambridge University Press, 2022.

Robinson, Jennifer. *Ordinary Cities: Between Modernity and Development.* London: Routledge, 2006.

Rosenberg, Justin. *The Empire of Civil Society: A Critique of the Realist Theory of International Relations.* London: Verso, 1994.

Ruggie, John Gerard. "International Regimes, Transactions, and Change: Embedded Liberalism in the Postwar Economic Order." *International Organization* 36 (1982): 379–415.

Salter, Mark. *Making Things International.* Minneapolis: University of Minnesota Press, 2016.

Sassen, Saskia. *The Global City: New York, London, Tokyo.* Princeton, NJ: Princeton University Press, 1991.

Scott, James C. *Against the Grain: A Deep History of the Earliest States.* New Haven: Yale University Press, 2017.

Shambaugh, David. *China and the World.* New York: Oxford University Press, 2020.

Shen, Simon, and Wilson Chan. "A Comparative Study of the Belt and Road Initiative and the Marshall Plan." *Palgrave Communications* 4 (2018): 32.

Shepherd, Christian. "China Pours Money into Green Belt and Road Projects." *Financial Times* (January 26, 2021).

———. "China's Belt and Road Urged to Take Green Route." *Financial Times* (June 5, 2022).

Shih, Chih-yu. *China and International Theory: The Balance of Relationships.* London: Routledge, 2019.

Shih, Chih-yu, and Chiung-chi Huang. "Balance of Relationship and the Chinese School of IR." In Yongjin Zhang and Teng-Chi Chang, eds., *Constructing a Chinese School of International Relations: Ongoing Debates and Sociological Realities*. London: Routledge, 2016.

Silver, Jonathan. "Corridor Urbanism." In Michele Lancione and Colin McFarlane, *Global Urbanism: Knowledge, Power, and the City*. Abingdon, UK: Routledge, 2021.

Simone, AbdouMaliq. *Improvised Lives: Rhythms of Endurance in an Urban South*. Cambridge, UK: Polity, 2019.

Sintusingha, Sidh, et al., eds. *International Perspectives on the Belt and Road Initiative: A Bottom-up Approach*. New York: Taylor & Francis, 2021.

Sitas, Rike, et al. "Platform Politics and Silicon Savannahs: The Rise of On-Demand Logistics and Mobility in Nairobi and Kigali." Report 19582621, African Centre for Cities, University of Cape Town, 2022. doi: 10.25375/uct.19582621.

Smith, David A. "The World Urban Hierarchy: Implications for Cities, Top to Bottom." *Brown Journal of World Affairs* 11 (2005): 45–55.

Soft Power 30. Homepage: https://softpower30.com.

Soja, Edward W. *Postmetropolis: Critical Studies of Cities and Regions*. Oxford, UK: Blackwell, 2000.

———. *Postmodern Geographies: The Reassertion of Space in Critical Social Theory*. London: Verso, 1989.

Stanek, Łukasz. *Architecture in Global Socialism: Eastern Europe, West Africa, and the Middle East in the Cold War*. Princeton, NJ: Princeton University Press, 2020.

Sterckx, Roel. *Chinese Thought: From Confucius to Cook Ding*. London: Pelican, 2019.

Strange, Susan. *States and Markets*. London: Pinter, 1988.

Styan, David. "China's Maritime Silk Road and Small States: Lessons from the Case of Djibouti." *Journal of Contemporary China* 29 (2020): 191–206.

———. "Doraleh Multipurpose Port (I)." The People's Map of Global China (March 4, 2021). https://thepeoplesmap.net/project/doraleh-multipurpose-port-phase-i/.

Summers, Tim. "China's 'New Silk Roads': Sub-National Regions and Networks of Global Political Economy." *Third World Quarterly* 37 (2016): 1628–1643.

———. "Structural Power and the Financing of the Belt and Road Initiative." *Eurasian Geography and Economics* 61 (2020): 146–151.

Tarrosy, Istvan, and Zoltán Vörös. "China and Ethiopia, Part 1: the Light Railway System." *The Diplomat* (February 13, 2018).

———. "China and Ethiopia, Part 2: The Addis Ababa–Djibouti Railway." *The Diplomat* (February 22, 2018).

Taylor, Peter J. *World City Network: A Global Urban Analysis*. London: Routledge, 2004.

Thanabouasy, Phayboune. "Laos-China Railway May Not be Completed on Schedule." *Laotian Times* (November 30, 2020).

Therborn, Göran. *Cities of Power: The Urban, the National, the Popular, the Global.* London: Verso, 2017.

Tian, Y. L. "China Willing to Work with Build Back World Initiative." Reuters (February 2022). https://www.reuters.com/world/china/china-willing-work-with-us-build-back-better-world-initiative-2022-02-28/.

Tillu, Jasmine, et al. "Accelerating China's Urban Transition Priority Actions for High-Quality Growth and Enhancing Leadership for Carbon Neutrality." Coalition for Urban Transitions (March 23, 2021). https://urbantransitions. global/wp-content/uploads/2021/03/Accelerating_Chinas_Urban_Transition_ EN_WEB.pdf.

Times Higher Education. World University Rankings, 2021. https://www. timeshighereducation.com/search?search=world%20university%20rankings %202021.

Tooze, Adam. *Shutdown: How Covid Shook the World's Economy.* New York: Viking, 2021.

Turner, Fred. *The Democratic Surround.* Chicago: University of Chicago Press, 2006.

Tutino, John. "Power, Marginality, and Participation in Mexico City, 1870–2000." In John Tutino and Martin V. Melosi, eds., *New World Cities: Challenges of Urbanization and Globalization in the Americas.* Chapel Hill: University of North Carolina Press, 2019.

UN Conference on Trade and Development (UNCTAD). *A New Centre of Gravity: The Regional Comprehensive Economic Partnership and Its Effects.* Geneva: UNCTAD, December 15, 2021. https://unctad.org/system/files/official-document/ditcinf2021d5_en_0.pdf.

UN Development Programme and Swiss Agency for Development Cooperation. *Development Advocate: Pakistan—Sustainable Urbanization* 5, no. 4 (December 2018).

UN General Assembly. Resolution 70/1, "Transforming Our World: The 2030 Agenda for Sustainable Development." A/RES/70/1, 25 September 2015. undocs.org/A/RES/70/1.

UN General Assembly. Resolution 71/256. "New Urban Agenda." A/RES/ 71/256, 23 December 2016. undocs.org/A/RES/71/256.

UN Habitat. *World Cities Report 2022: Envisaging the Future of Cities.* https:// unhabitat.org/wcr.

US White House. "Memorandum on the Partnership for Global Infrastructure and Investment." June 26, 2022. https://www.whitehouse.gov/briefing-room/ presidential-actions/2022/06/26/memorandum-on-the-partnership-for-global-infrastructure-and-investment.

———. "National Security Strategy: October 2022." October 12, 2022. https:// www.whitehouse.gov/wp-content/uploads/2022/10/Biden-Harris-Adminis trations-National-Security-Strategy-10.2022.pdf.

———. "A New National Security Strategy for a New Era." December 18, 2017. https://trumpwhitehouse.archives.gov/articles/new-national-security-strat egy-new-era.

———. "Remarks by President Biden before the 76th Session of the UN General Assembly." September 21, 2021. https://www.whitehouse.gov/briefing-room/speeches-remarks/2021/09/21/remarks-by-president-biden-before-the-76th-session-of-the-united-nations-general-assembly.

Vogel, Ezra. "Foreword." In Mary Ann O'Donnell, Winnie Wong, and Jonathan Bach, eds., *Learning from Shenzhen: China's Post-Mao Experiment from Special Zone to Model City.* Chicago: University of Chicago Press, 2017.

Wahba, Sadek. "Integrating Infrastructure in US Domestic & Foreign Policy: Lessons from China." The Wilson Center (September 2021). https://www.wilsoncenter.org/sites/default/files/media/uploads/documents/Integrating%20Infrastructure%20in%20US%20Domestic%20and%20Foreign%20Policy%20%20Full%20Report.pdf.

Wahid, Abdul, et al. "Post-Spillover Effects of China's Integration on Pakistan Stock Exchange." *Strategic Change* 30 (2021): 581–588.

Walker, Rob. *Inside/Outside: International Relations as Political Theory.* Cambridge, UK: Cambridge University Press, 1993.

Wallerstein, Immanuel. *The Modern World-System: The Second Era of the Great Expansion of the Capitalist World-Economy, 1730–1840s.* Vol. 3. San Diego: Academic Press, 1989.

Waltz, Kenneth. *Theory of International Politics.* Reading, MA: Addison-Wesley, 1979.

Wang, Gungwu. *China Reconnects: Joining a Deep-Rooted Past to a New World Order.* Hackensack, NJ: World Scientific, 2019.

Wang, Jisi. "China's Search for a Grand Strategy: A Rising Great Power Finds Its Way." *Foreign Affairs* (March/April 2011).

Wang-Kaeding, Heidi. "What Does Xi Jinping's New Phrase 'Ecological Civilization' Mean?" *Diplomat* (March 6, 2018).

Watson, Adam. *The Evolution of International Society: A Comparative Historical Analysis.* London: Routledge, 1992.

Wellerstein, Alex. "The 36-Hour War: *Life Magazine,* 1945." Restricted Data: The Nuclear Secrecy Blog, April 5, 2013. https://blog.nuclearsecrecy.com/2013/04/05/the-36-hour-war-life-magazine-1945.

Wendt, Alexander. *Social Theory of International Politics.* Cambridge, UK: Cambridge University Press, 1999.

Westad, Odd Arne. "Legacies of the Past." Pp. 25–36 in David L. Shambaugh, ed., *China and the World.* New York: Oxford University Press, 2020.

———. *Restless Empire: China and the World since 1750.* New York: Basic Books, 2012.

Wetherell, Sam. *Foundations: How the Built Environment Made Twentieth-Century Britain.* Princeton, NJ: Princeton University, 2020.

Whitfield, Peter. *Cities of the World: A History in Maps.* Berkeley: University of California Press, 2005.

Whitfield, Susan. *The Silk Roads: Peoples, Cultures, Landscapes.* London: Thames and Hudson, 2019.

Wiig, Alan, and Jonathan Silver. "Turbulent Presents, Precarious Futures: Urbanization and the Deployment of Global Infrastructure." *Regional Studies* 53 (2019): 912–923.

Williams, Austin. *China's Urban Revolution: Understanding Chinese Eco-Cities.* London: Bloomsbury, 2018.

Winner, Langdon. "Do Artifacts Have Politics?" In Donald A. MacKenzie and Judy Wajcman, eds., *The Social Shaping of Technology.* 2nd ed. Buckingham, UK: Open University Press, 1999.

World Bank. "Belt and Road Economics: Opportunities and Risks of Transport Corridors." June 18, 2019. https://www.worldbank.org/en/topic/regional-integration/publication/belt-and-road-economics-opportunities-and-risks-of-transport-corridors.

World Bank and the Development Research Center of the State Council, China. *Urban China: Toward Efficient, Inclusive, and Sustainable Urbanization.* Washington, DC: World Bank, 2014.

World Economic Forum. "China's Xi Jinping Defends Globalization from the Davos Stage." January 27, 2017. https://www.weforum.org/agenda/2017/01/chinas-xi-jinping-defends-globalization-from-the-davos-stage.

World Resources Institute. *Accelerating Building Decarbonization: Eight Attainable Policy Pathways to Net Zero Carbon Buildings for All.* World Resources Institute, 2019. https://www.wri.org/research/accelerating-building-decarbonization-eight-attainable-policy-pathways-net-zero-carbon.

———. *Fewer Emissions, Better Life: Beijing Low Emission Zone Final Report.* World Resources Institute, 2018. https://wrirosscities.org/research/publication/fewer-emissions-better-life-beijing-low-emission-zone-final-report.

Wu Hung. *Remaking Beijing: Tiananmen Square and the Creation of a Political Space.* Chicago: University of Chicago Press, 2005.

Wu, Weiping. "Proximity and Complementarity in Hong Kong-Shenzhen Industrialization." *Asian Survey* 37, no. 8 (1997): 771–793.

Wu, Weiping, and Piper Gaubatz. *The Chinese City.* Abingdon, UK: Routledge, 2013.

Xinhua. "Speech by Xi Jinping at a Ceremony Marking the Centenary of the CCP." July 1, 2021. http://www.xinhuanet.com/english/special/2021-07/01/c_1310038244.htm.

Xu, J., and X. Sun. "The Tsinghua Approach and the Future Direction of Chinese International Relations." In Yongjin Zhang and Teng-chi Chang, eds., *Constructing a Chinese School of International Relations: Ongoing Debates and Sociological Realities.* London: Routledge, 2016.

Yan, Xuetong. "International Leadership and Norm Evolution." *Chinese Journal of International Politics* 4 (2011): 233–264.

———. *Leadership and the Rise of Great Powers.* Princeton, NJ: Princeton University Press, 2019.

———. "Political Leadership and Power Redistribution." *Chinese Journal of International Politics* 9 (2016): 1–26.

Yan, Xuetong, et al. *Ancient Chinese Thought, Modern Chinese Power.* Princeton, NJ: Princeton University Press, 2011.

Yaqing, Qin. "Development of International Relations Theory in China." *International Studies* 46 (2009): 185–201.

Yates, Alexia. *Real Estate and Global Urban History.* Cambridge, UK: Cambridge University Press, 2021.

Zarakol, Ayşe. *Before the West: The Rise and Fall of Eastern World Orders.* Cambridge, UK: Cambridge University Press, 2022.

———. *Hierarchies in World Politics.* New York: Cambridge University Press, 2017.

Zhang, Feng. *Chinese Hegemony: Grand Strategy and International Institutions in East Asian History.* Stanford, CA: Stanford University Press, 2015.

———. "The Tsinghua Approach and the Inception of Chinese Theories of International Relations." *Chinese Journal of International Politics* 5 (2011): 73–102.

Zhang, Hong. "Gwadar Port and Free Zone." The People's Map of Global China project, October 2021. https://thepeoplesmap.net/project/gwadar-port-and-free-zone/.

Zhao, Tingyang. "All-under-Heaven and Methodological Relationalism: An Old Story and New World Peace." In Fred R. Dallmayr and Tingyang Zhao, eds., *Contemporary Chinese Political Thought: Debates and Perspectives.* Lexington: University Press of Kentucky, 2012.

———. "A Political World Philosophy in Terms of All-Under-Heaven (Tian-Xia)." *Diogenes* 56 (2009): 5–18.

———. "Rethinking Empire from a Chinese Concept 'All-Under-Heaven' (Tian-Xia)." *Social Identities* 12 (2006): 29–41.

Zipp, Samuel. *Manhattan Projects: The Rise and Fall of Urban Renewal in Cold War New York.* New York: Oxford University Press, 2010.

Zuboff, Shoshana. *The Age of Surveillance Capitalism: The Fight for a Human Future at the New Frontier of Power.* New York: PublicAffairs, 2018.

Zubovich, Katherine. *Moscow Monumental: Soviet Skyscrapers and Urban Life in Stalin's Capital.* Princeton, NJ: Princeton University Press, 2021.

Zuckerman, Ethan. "Can Russia Really Disconnect from the Rest of the Digital World?" *Prospect* (May 2, 2021).

Acknowledgments

THIS BOOK WOULD have been impossible without the expertise of, and support from, colleagues across scholarly disciplines and publishing platforms, as well as those in city and national governments, at NGOs, within international organizations, and in the private sector. We are grateful to them all, including: Hannah Abdullah, Penny Abeywardena, Rachel Abrams, Michele Acuto, Rohit Aggarwala, Dan Baer, Jutta Bakonyi, Amir Bazaz, Daniel Levin Becker, Eugenie Birch, Oni Blair, Max David Bouchet, Erin Bromaghim, Christian Bugge, Barry Buzan, Julie Carlson, Alice Charles, Jaya Chatterjee, Xiangming Chen, Matan Chorev, Jennifer Cizner, Elizabeth Cobbett, Michael Cohen, Eric Corijn, Mariano-Florentino Cuéllar, Meghann Curtis, Ivo Daalder, Pietro d'Arcano, David Dudley, Amanda Eichel, Foroogh Farhang, Evan Feigenbaum, Andrea Fernandez, Alan Finlayson, Sheila Foster, Katie Frost, Salin Geevarghese, Amanda Gerstenfeld, Lorenzo Kihlgren Grandi, Florita Gunasekara, Brian Hanson, Mallory Herbert, Alex Hitch, Emily Hruban, Toni Irving, Lee Jarvis, LaShawn Jefferson, Marissa Jordan, Jacint Jordana, Kristin Ljungkvist, Agustí Fernández de Losada, Hussein Kassim, Kristina Kearns, Michael Kelley, Rainer Kern, Juliana Kerr, Robert Kissack, Sam Kling, Peter Kurz, Debra Lam, Amy Leitch, Miriam Magdieli, Alison Markovitz, Lee Marsden, Ra Mason, Maximilian Mayer, Andrew McCracken, Julie Miao, David Milne, Scott Moore, Rob Muggah, Omar Nagati, Kevin Nelson, Fatahi Osman, Mary Pasti, Jocelyn Perry, Emma Pinault, Tony Pipa, Andrea Pollio, Prathijna Poonacha, Raghuveer Ramkumar, Alison Rausch, Luis Renta, Francisco Resnicoff, Aromar Revi, Kim Ridealgh, Debra Roberts,

Mauricio Rodas, Ana Rold, Caroline Schep, Seth Schultz, Adriana Sinclair, Russ Singer, Chandni Singh, Eva Skewes, Nancy Stetson, Beth Stryker, Kirsti Stuvøy, Beth Andrew Tucker, Vanessa Vardon, Roger Walker, William Burke-White, Tommy Wide, and Andrew Wylie.

Jon and Jennie; your silk road took you from East London to China and back.

Bjarne Mork-Eidem; never forgotten.

Elisabeth, Alice, Finn.

Patricia and Robin, Tom and Mary Anne.

Laurie, Louisa, Rem.

Index

Italic page numbers indicate maps.